GREECE

AND THE

AEGEAN

GREECE
AND THE
AEGEAN

WILLIAM O. KELLOGG

St. Paul's School
Concord, N. H.

Longman
New York & London

The photographs on pages 33, 90, 132, 160, 170 and 227 are reproduced through the courtesy of The Museum of Fine Arts, Boston, Massachusetts

The photographs on pages 66, 67, 68, 70, 71, 72, 73, and 80 are reproduced through the courtesy of the photographer Alison Frantz, American School of Classical Studies, Athens, Greece.

The photographs on pages 39, 42, 79 and 83 are reproduced with the permission of the photographer, W. O. Kellogg.

The photograph on page 69 is reproduced with the permission of the photographer, Nick Stournaras, Athens, Greece.

The maps were produced by The Independent School Press in collaboration with the author.

Longman Inc., 95 Church Street, White Plains, N.Y. 10601

Associated companies:
Longman Group Ltd., London
Longman Cheshire Pty., Melbourne
Longman Paul Pty., Auckland
Copp Clark Pitman, Toronto
Pitman Publishing Inc., New York

0-88334-066-6   87
                                                    7890123

For
Julie, Elli and Rico

CONTENTS

MAPS

PREFACE

Greece and the Aegean presents a chronological history of ancient Greece from the period of the Greek "Dark Ages" until Greece became a province of the Roman Empire. The book, following the approach developed in *Out of the Past,* involves the reader in the development of this chronological history by a series of questions and exercises which cast the reader in the role of the historian. Few of the questions have clear-cut answers. Instead, they involve the evaluation of evidence and call for the reader to reach conclusions based on personal interpretation of material. To help in this process concepts and material from subjects other than history have been introduced. Therefore, the reader will find art, literature, biography, sociology, and gaming techniques used within the chronological history to provide a better understanding of the ancient Greeks.

This book has evolved from an interdepartmental course combining history, English, and religion taught at St. Paul's School. The course, titled Origins of the West, has as its focus the Hebraic and Greek roots of our civilization. *Greece and the Aegean* incorporates many of the ideas used in the course to introduce the Greek origins of western civilization.

The Independent School Press has published as part of their history series two other books incorporating material used in this course. *Out of the Past* presents the larger historical perspective of Near Eastern history to c. 800 B.C. into which much of the Hebraic origins of western civilization fit. *Legend, Myth and History in the Old Testament* presents commentary on both ethical and historical Biblical material. In addition to these three works, *Roman Rulers and Rebels* and *Milestones of the Middle Ages* bring the history of western man up to the Renaissance, and thus these five works can provide the basic core of an ancient and medieval history course. It should be emphasized, however, that each book may be used independently in a term course or to support a study of ancient language or ethics. *Greece and the Aegean* was designed to be flexible; to be useful in many situations.

It is customary in a preface to extend thanks to those who have helped in the writing of a book. So many individuals have supported me in the preparation of this book that it is impossible to name them. My students deserve great thanks as do my colleagues at St. Paul's School and my teachers and colleagues at the American School of Classical Studies in Athens. Without their questioning and inspiration this work would have been impossible.

W.O. Kellogg

St. Paul's School
Concord, New Hampshire
September, 1974

GREECE
AND THE
AEGEAN

CHAPTER I

THE AEGEAN AREA:
MINOAN AND MYCENAEAN BACKGROUND

Section I—*Introduction*

The focus of this text is the history of the Greek mainland and the area of the Aegean Sea during the period of Hellenic and Hellenistic civilizations. This period of time includes the "Golden Age of Greece" and the conquests of Alexander the Great. It is part of ancient history and may seem long ago and irrelevant in this age of space exploration and atomic power.

It is the thesis of this text, however, that this time is not irrelevant for many reasons. The most important reasons are first, human beings very much like us lived and acted out their lives in that age. We will ask you to consider this often in the text and we expect you will realize how similar many activities were.

A second reason is that one of the two major roots of western civilization starts in this area. We refer to it as the Graeco (Greek)-Roman root. The other major root begins in the Near East and is called the Hebraic (Hebrew)-Christian root. In order to understand who we are we must understand our roots and what traditions and inherited attitudes are held by our civilization. These attitudes continually narrow our choices of action so it is important we know where our basic attitudes and values were formed and what they are. We may not agree with Greek values that affect us and we may wish to emphasize other roots of our civilization such as Slavic or African, but the basic point cannot be escaped—the Graeco-Roman tradition provides a crucial basis for western civilization. The mere mention of such an important word for the west as democracy (Greek—rule by the people or demos) illustrates this as do these other words with Greek origins—philosophy, politics, tragedy, aesthetic, ethical. Can you add words to the list to illustrate other aspects of our lives that had their origins in Greece? We will return to this question at the end of the book.

A third major reason for studying the Greeks and the Aegean area is simply that the history is interesting and varied. Besides the political and military events in the area great art was produced both in literature and the fine arts. We will use examples from each in our study.

A fourth reason is that this area clearly illustrates an important concept—the interdependence of peoples and regions. The Greeks and the Aegean area did not develop in a vacuum. There were many influences on them from other peoples and areas. These will be illustrated in the text.

A fifth reason and the last we will mention is that the history of the region is not definitive. There is room for interpretation and re-interpretation as new evidence is found especially by archaeologists. This provides us the opportunity to be historians and to develop our own theories and interpretations of many events. This text is designed to bring the reader into the role of historian as you will be asked to interpret events and to develop theories. On many occasions you will not be told what happened but instead you will be asked to decide which of several possible interpretations is most likely and why. This is what the historian is continually doing.

The first thing an historian must do is consider the period of time and the geographic area to be investigated. Our study will focus on the area of the Aegean Sea in the period of time after 1000 B.C. until the death of Alexander the Great in 323 B.C. But first let us consider under what conditions people were living about 1000 B.C. and where civilization was developed.

Everyone today has seen photographs of the earth taken from the moon. It looks like a small ball floating in great, dark space. We have all seen on T.V., via satellite, activities going on in all parts of the world. Instant communication, jet travel, and military involvements around the globe have made us all citizens of the world. We are aware that what happens in China or South Africa affects us. What was man's relation to the entire world about 1000 B.C.?

The usual concept presented of the world about 3000 B.C. is of the Eastern Hemisphere—Europe, Asia and Africa—with four "cradles of civilization". Usually, no mention is made of the Western Hemisphere. The four "cradles of civilization" are portrayed as being in the Yellow River Valley of China, the Indus River valley of Pakistan, the Tigris-Euphrates River valley of Iraq and the Nile River valley of Egypt. By 1000 B.C. it is usually indicated these civilizations had developed and the latter two had interacted to provide a basis for civilization for the entire Eastern end of the Mediterranean basin.

There had been some contact between all four areas, although the other two "cradles of civilization" were confined to their narrow valleys. Usually no mention is made of developments in Central Africa or in the Americas. The focus of attention is on the Mediterranean area. The justification for this focus is that western civilization has its deepest roots in the Mediterranean basin. This book, being a history of the Greeks, has this same focus but we wish the readers to be aware of some contemporary developments in other regions of the world. Students are encouraged to pursue the study of developments outside the area of Greece and the Aegean.

There is little specific evidence of the interrelationships between areas of civilization such as Egypt and the Americas in 1000 B.C. There was no T.V. and no easy means of travel. There is, however, growing agreement based on some evidence of exchange of goods, such as amber[1], and Atlantic Ocean crossings[2] that there was cross fertilization between areas of civilization. There is overwhelming evidence of the interchange of ideas and artifacts within large areas such as Europe or around the Mediterranean basin as early as 3000 B.C. These exchanges have continued throughout man's history and have greatly influenced the development of various cultures. As we begin our study of the Hellenic or Classical Greek Civilization, it is important to realize that it did not develop in a vacuum on the Greek peninsula uninfluenced by other peoples. Men traveled in, traded with, fought over, and studied at many different places. Our world today seems very small and influences spread rapidly but the present speed of communication should not lead us to the error that man 3000 years ago did not communicate also. Before we focus our attention on classical Greek civilization let us look at conditions in other regions of the world. In 1000 B.C. the Greek peninsula was experiencing what has been called a "Dark Age." What was happening elsewhere?

Section II—*China, The Americas and Southern Africa*

Evidence for contact between China and the Mediterranean basin is lacking in the period around 1000 B.C. There is evidence, however, that China at the time had a flourishing culture. Recent

[1] See G. Bibby, *4,000 Years Ago.*
[2] See the many reports of the crossing of the Atlantic Ocean by Thor Heyerdahl in his papyrus reed ship, Ra. The ship was modeled after ancient Egyptian ships portrayed in tomb paintings. *N. Y. Times*, July 1970.

archaeological excavations at An-Yang indicate that this city on the Huan river in north China was the capital of a Chinese nation by 1300 B.C. Bronze was cast and writing was fully developed. About 1100 B.C. warfare broke out in the area between various nobles. Finally, one noble, the Duke of China[3], gained authority over an area that stretched to the China Sea. The dynasty he supported fought off attacks by nomadic horsemen from the Asian plains, rebuilt towns and encouraged the development of military skills. Ancestor worship was followed.

Many questions need to be answered about China in this age but one thing is clear—China was a nation with a distinct cultural development. Many scholars believe the Chinese developed their skills without contact with other civilized regions, but others affirm that there was interaction between cultural areas. What are your ideas on this matter? What information can you find in your library on this question?

The question of contact between the Americas and the civilized areas of the Old World was raised above. We know that there were agricultural communities in Mexico and Peru by 1000 B.C. Pottery of this era has been found in Mexico. Did the Mexicans discover pottery making by themselves or did they learn from somewhere?

A recent book indicates there were many contacts between central and south America and other parts of the world before Columbus.[4] Just how early these contacts occurred is not certain. The evidence is found in terra cotta (clay) figurines found in many locations, especially Mexico. Many figures represent distinctly Negroid and Mongoloid types that bear no resemblance to the native Americans. Either the many artists created these types purely by imagination or they were acquainted with individuals from Africa and Asia. The latter seems more logical. The Ra expeditions mentioned in footnote #2 indicate voyages between America and Egypt were possible as early as the Old Kingdom circa 2700 B.C. Just when these voyages took place and how often is not certain.

In 1000 B.C. throughout most of North and South America the inhabitants were nomadic. Civilization, the settling of peoples in cities, had just begun. For a young person interested in seeking

[3]It is not known what his real Title was so he has been referred to by a western Title of nobility, Duke. For more information see H. G. Creel, *The Birth of China.*

[4]See Alexander Von Wuthenau, *Art of Terracotta Pottery in Pre-Columbian Central and South America.*

the past and interested in archaeology, the Americas provide fertile ground for new discoveries.

Evidence for civilized areas in Africa south of the Sahara Desert in 1000 B.C. is scarce. We know that there was a flourishing trade between Egypt under Queen Hatshepsut c. 1480 B.C. and the land of Punt (modern Ethiopia according to most scholars).

Many scholars believe the Queen of Sheba, whose visit to King Solomon in Jerusalem is recorded in the Bible (*I Kings* 10: 1-13), ruled an African kingdom. So little archaeological work has been done south of the Sahara that we can provide little specific evidence of the level of civilization in the area in 1000 B.C. There is, however, clear evidence from tomb paintings that Blacks were well known in the Mediterranean region at the time.

As we narrow our vision and focus in on Greece, don't forget that there were developments taking place in the peripheral parts of the world. These developments may not have affected the ancient Greeks and they may not have affected the developments of western European history very much but they did affect the history of many peoples living in the world today. Chinese writing and religious concepts, Mexican pottery, African trade and the glory of the Queen of Sheba provide the foundations of other nations' histories. As we begin to concentrate on the historic foundations of Western civilization, let us not become so provincial or narrow that we lose sight of other nations. The world today is interdependent yet made up of independent nations. What each nation does affects all others, unlike the situation in 1000 B.C. Yet today each nation is unique, as in 1000 B.C., and only by understanding the uniqueness and its historic origins can we act interdependently. If we judge all nations from our unique, Western, Greek-based viewpoint, the world will face disaster.

Section III—*Geography of the Aegean, The Mediterranean Basin and The Near East*[5]

The Aegean Sea is the focus point of Greek civilization and not the Greek peninsula. It was by their use of the sea that the Greeks learned of other peoples and in turn spread their ideas.

[5] In this book as in *Out of the Past* we will divide the eastern Mediterranean into four areas. The first is the Greek peninsula, the Aegean and Crete. The second is Anatolia or modern Turkey. The third is the Near East which includes the region from the Persian Gulf through the Tigris-Euphrates valleys. The fourth is Egypt.

6 Greece and the Aegean

It is wise to orient oneself to the geographic names and features of a region or area before studying the history or culture, just as it is wise to identify a person by name and physical appearance before you try to understand the person. A person's name and physique gives one a basic identity, and the geographic features and place names do the same for an area. Can you sketch a rough map of the Aegean Sea? Try on a piece of paper and then check back to the map on page 28. How well did you do? If you simplify the land masses into rectangles, squares and circles, can you produce a simplified pattern that you can reproduce easily? Such a pattern is a schematic map and one can make them for all parts of the earth. They provide a handy hook on which to hang place names and physical features. Make such a schematic map for the Aegean area and as places are mentioned in the chapter locate them on your map.[6]

If you consider the Aegean and the surrounding lands as a target, the center of the target's bull's eye would be the island of Delos. Delos at the center of a group of islands, the Cyclades (wheel), was throughout their history one of the chief religious sites of the Greeks and in later Greek history it became an international trading center as well. Delos symbolized the internationalism of the Greeks in the way the great shrine at Olympia, site of the original Olympic games, symbolized the unity of the Greek world and the shrine at Delphi symbolized the dominance of Greek ideas in the eastern Mediterranean. These three religious shrines were of great significance throughout Greek history.

Moving east of Delos entering what would be the first ring outside the bull's eye one comes to the coast of Asia Minor and the city of Miletus. This coastal region known as Ionia played a crucial role in the development of classical Greek intellectual and political history.

Returning to Delos and moving west again to the first ring of the target, one comes to the coast of the Peloponnesus. This large area of land is linked to mainland Greece by a narrow isthmus at the southern end of which is Corinth and just east of the northern end of which is Athens. Still in the first ring of the target just south of Corinth and dominating a large plain is Mycenae.

Now moving directly south from Delos in the first ring one finds the island of Crete and the famous city of Knossos. Using

---

[6] One possible schematic map of the Aegean area is found on page 10. There are maps included in the Text on which you can locate all the places named in the Text or you can use an atlas.

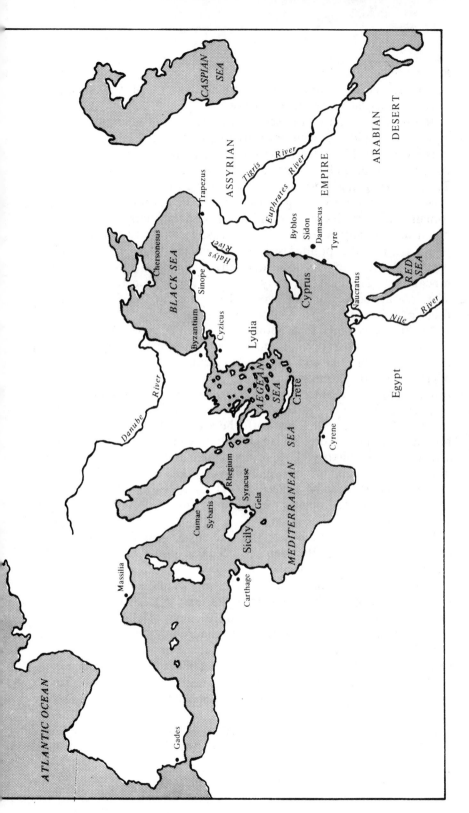

The Mediterranean Basin and the Near East
in the Age of Colonization

the target concept one should gain a concept of the distance between the places mentioned above.

If one moved on to the second ring from the bull's eye, going east one would be well into Anatolia, modern Turkey; going north one would be touching the Hellespont, the water route to the Black Sea, and the city of Troy, famous as the site of the Trojan War; going west one would come to Olympia, mentioned above, Pylos on the west coast of the Peloponnesus, and the Ionian Sea. This should give one an idea of how narrow the Greek peninsula actually is—60 miles from east to west at the narrowest point of the Peloponnesus and 180 miles at its widest above Athens. Moving south the second ring includes only the Mediterranean Sea. The coast of Libya west of Egypt is in the distance. The area included in these two circles forms the chief geographic focus of this book.

Nothing has been said about the physical geography of the Aegean area. Most texts emphasize the mountainous quality of the Greek peninsula and there is no doubt about the ruggedness of much of the country and coast. Most city states were surrounded by mountains. The sea, however, is more important to emphasize. Why do you think this is so? Try to locate some pictures of Greece which show both the sea and the mountains. On the basis of the pictures try to decide how each feature may have affected Greek history. Use any experiences you have had with mountains or water or information you have of other places or nations. As you study Greece and the Aegean area see if your speculations on the impact of physical geography on Greek history are confirmed.

Before you continue be certain you can draw a schematic map of the Aegean area. Be prepared to locate on it all the places mentioned in this section so far.

Now let us add several more circles to the bull's eye to include regions in Europe, Africa and Asia. A third circle at a distance of 1000 miles from Delos would include to the east all of Anatolia, the eastern Mediterranean coast where the Hebrews had established the Kingdom of Israel by 1000 B.C., and the important Nile delta of Egypt. In the west this circle would include the site of Carthage on the north African coast and the Etruscan lands of the Italian peninsula. To the north the Balkans, southwestern Russia, and the Black Sea would be included.

A fourth circle at 1500 miles from Delos would include all of the Tigris-Euphrates Valley, Egypt and the Sudan, the Spanish

Mediterranean coast and most of Western Europe. Thus one sees that the entire homeland of early civilization in the Near East and in North Africa were within 1500 miles of the Aegean and most of modern Europe was included within this distance. These were the regions with which contacts would be easiest for the people living on the Greek peninsula.

You should study the maps as they are included within the text and be certain you are able to locate places mentioned in the text. At this time you should be able to draw a schematic map of the Aegean area and include those places found in the first two circles of our target. You should also be able to locate on a map those places mentioned as being within the third and fourth circles of the target. At the end of this chapter in the chapter review section, you will find a list of places you should be able to locate in this way. You may wish to refer to this section before you read further. Each chapter in the book includes a review section at the end along with a bibliography.

Section IV—*Europe and the Mediterranean Basin c. 1000 B.C.*

In 1000 B.C. there were agricultural communities throughout Europe. Trade between modern Sweden and the Near East was common using the great rivers (Duna, Dniester and Dnieper) of western Russia as easy trade routes. Nomadic tribes were wandering in the forests of Germany. In England Stonehenge had already been built and there was trade, especially in tin, between southern England and the Mediterranean. The Celts, originating apparently in western France, were sailing the Atlantic settling in Ireland and elsewhere. As far as we know, however, nowhere in continental Europe was there a flourishing urban civilization at this time.

In the coastal areas of the western Mediterranean the situation was different. The Phoenicians sailing from their home cities along the eastern Mediterranean coast after 1200 B.C. began establishing colonies along the northwestern coasts of Africa (the most important one, Carthage founded in the 9th century B.C., later rivaled Rome for control of the western Mediterranean), in Spain and in Sicily. The Etruscans were laying the foundations of their unusual civilization north of the Tiber River in Italy. By 1000 B.C. the Etruscans had established several towns which were centers of political activity. Their religious beliefs were similar to

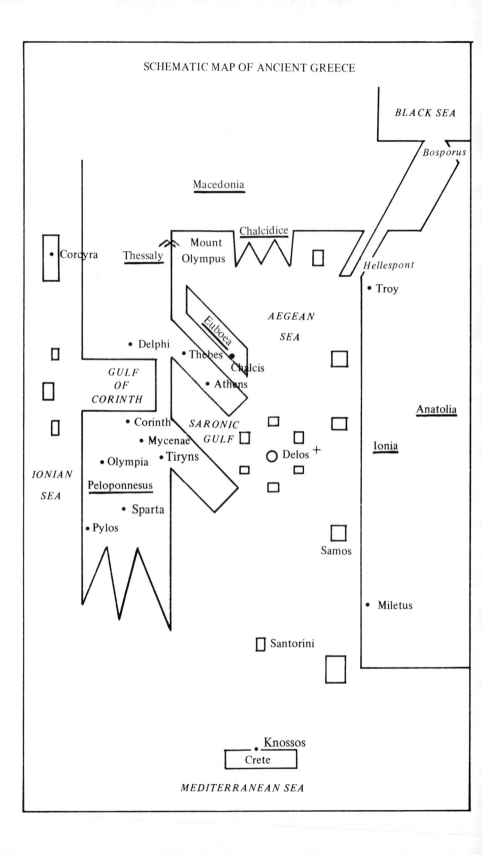

SCHEMATIC MAP OF ANCIENT GREECE

BLACK SEA

Bosporus

Macedonia

Chalcidice

Thessaly

Mount
Olympus

Corcyra

Hellespont

Troy

AEGEAN
SEA

Euboea

Delphi

Thebes

Chalcis

GULF
OF
CORINTH

Athens

Anatolia

SARONIC
GULF

Corinth

Mycenae

Ionia

Tiryns

Delos

IONIAN
SEA

Olympia

Peloponnesus

Sparta

Pylos

Samos

Miletus

Santorini

Knossos

Crete

MEDITERRANEAN SEA

the Greeks' as were their political organizations. The Etruscans later became the great rivals of the Romans for domination of northern Italy. Usually, as in this book, the Etruscans are barely mentioned in ancient history books. They are a fascinating people and you may wish to study them in a special project.[7]

It was not clear about 1000 B.C. what peoples would emerge to dominate and control the future of the Western Mediterranean. One point, however, is certain; it was a dynamic age with great opportunities for those who would seize them. It was not a quiet and stagnant era. It was an age for new ideas. Potential power centers existed in the Etruscan towns. Goods were shipped between small ports. There were potential markets for manufactured goods and great sources of raw materials just inland from the coastal cities.

The eastern end of the Mediterranean was also in the throes of dynamic change about 1000 B.C. This area where the early civilizations of Egypt and the Tigris-Euphrates Valley (Sumer) had developed was experiencing one of those periodic readjustments of political power. Egypt after the Battle of Kadash, 1288 B.C. had declined in power. The later invasions of the "sea peoples" had weakened the land of the pharaohs and in 1000 B.C. she was weaker and less politically and militarily powerful than she had been for 2000 years.[8]

The Hittites in Anatolia by 1000 B.C. had been overwhelmed by Indo-European invaders and internal dissensions. The Hittite empire had collapsed leaving small pockets of power scattered

[7]For information on the Etruscans see A. Bloch, *The Etruscans.* There are many theories as to the origins of the Etruscans. The most interesting is that they escaped from Troy when that city was destroyed by the Greeks in the Trojan War (see Homer, *The Iliad* and Virgil, *The Aneid*). The Etruscans were later conquered by the Romans and their culture was absorbed. As in so many cases of conquest, the victorious Romans then wrote the history of the Etruscans and presented them in a very bad light or ignored them. You might be interested in trying to find out about other nations that were treated in the same way by the conquerors.

[8]For an account of this battle and of the conditions of Egypt see Kellogg, *Out of the Past* pp. 175-182. There is a chronology in Appendix I which will help put people and events mentioned in this chapter in order.

The origin of the "sea peoples" is one of the mysteries of the ancient world. They attacked the eastern shores of the Mediterranean between 1200 and 1000 B.C. One group, the Philistines, settled in Palestine. Some scholars suggest the "sea peoples" came from Norway as the Vikings were to come later; most scholars believe they were from the Italian or Greek peninsula.

about in Anatolia and what is now Syria but there was no strong empire in the area.[9]

The Assyrians living along the upper reaches of the Tigris River had been important as a power several hundred years before 1000 B.C. and they would emerge as a great nation again. At the moment, however, there was no great power in the area. The conditions recall those of the Near East at the time of Abraham about 1800 B.C.[10]

The collapse of the great empires of the Egyptians and the Hittites, the invasion of "sea peoples" along the Mediterranean coasts, the invasions of Indo-Europeans into Anatolia and the northern region of the Near East, and the raids into the area of modern Iran by the Scythians created conditions of confusion but of opportunity. We will note similar conditions on the Greek peninsula. As always in these circumstances, one group of peoples capitalized on these conditions. In the Near East it was the Arameans from the desert of Arabia. These peoples founded the trading cities of Phoenicia along the north half of the eastern Mediterranean coast and sailed out to found colonies. It was they who kept trade moving over the caravan routes. And it was their relatives, the Hebrews of Palestine, who established the most significant nation of the age—the Kingdom of Israel. David, the Hebrew ideal of a king, was establishing his power at Jersulaem c. 1000 B.C. His son, Solomon, was to rule over the most important nation in the Mediterranean area during the 10th century B.C.[11]

Section V—*The Aegean Area about 1,000 B.C.*

The point to note about 1000 B.C. in the Aegean is that its civilization, as measured by archaeological evidence, was at a lower level than in the preceding 500 years. The Aegean was experiencing what has been labeled a "Dark Age", a period of time between two great civilizations. About 1400 B.C. a civilization which we call Mycenaean, after the town of Mycenae where evidence of the civilization was first found, flourished on the Greek peninsula and dominated the Aegean. It had been preceded and heavily influenced by another great Aegean area civiliza-

[9] See Kellogg, *Out of the Past,* Chap. 16 and 17.

[10] See Kellogg, *Out of the Past,* Chap. X for information on the political conditions at the time of Abraham.

[11] See *Samuel* and *I Kings* in the *Bible.*

tion called the Minoan after King Minos in Greek myth. Minoan civilization reached its peak of development on the island of Crete about 1600 B.C. Apparently the Mycenaeans of the mainland overcame the Minoans and absorbed many of their ideas, especially their alphabet. Several hundred years later Mycenaean civilization had almost disappeared. Historians are not certain why Mycenaean civilization declined, but there is clear archeological evidence that by 1200 B.C. the Mycenaeans had declined in artistic ability, in trade, and in military influence. The Aegean area slowly slipped into the "Dark Ages" during which the great palaces and towns connected with the height of Mycenaean civilization became small houses and villages and many skills, including the art of writing, were forgotten.

A thorough study of the Minoan and Mycenaean civilizations can be very rewarding. Nothing was known about these civilizations until a hundred years ago. The German archaeologist, Heinrich Schliemann, inspired by the ancient Greek poet Homer's work *The Iliad* (an account of the Trojan war between the people of Troy and the Greeks from the mainland under command of Agamemnon, King of Mycenae) discovered both the site of Troy in Asia Minor and the site of Mycenae in the Peloponnesus. Schliemann's digging at both Troy and Mycenae gave the modern world its first information on the Mycenaean civilization. Later archaeologists have proven that many of the places mentioned in *The Iliad* did exist, and therefore that work was not just fiction but includes a good deal of historic information. Many Mycenaean palaces and towns such as Pylos, Tiryns, Athens, and Thebes, have been discovered on the mainland of Greece. They are strongly fortified, which suggests the inhabitants were a war-like people.

In the early 1950's, less than 25 years ago, Michael Ventris deciphered the writing on Mycenaean clay tablets. The tablets have given us a great deal of information about the Mycenaean way of life. We now know that the language used by the Mycenaeans was similar to the Greek spoken in the Aegean in later times. Therefore, there is a close connection between the peoples who developed the Mycenaean civilization and those who developed the more familiar classical Greek civilization which is the main subject of this book. The tablets also indicate the Mycenaeans worshipped many of the same gods as did the later Greeks. We have clear evidence, thanks to Henrich Schliemann and his archaeological followers, that classical Greek or Hellenic civilization did not develop on the mainland in a vacuum.

We also now know that the Mycenaean civilization of the period 1600-1200 B.C. did not develop in the Aegean uninfluenced. Again, however, until the end of the last century, nothing was known of the great civilization that so strongly affected the Mycenaeans and thus indirectly the Greeks. In the 1890's Sir Arthur Evans began excavating a mound at the little town of Knossos on Crete. He discovered a magnificent palace. A number of factors led Evans to decide the civilization discovered was not the same as the Mycenaean. He named it Minoan. Among the factors which distinguish the two civilizations are their art styles, their languages (the Minoan script has yet to be deciphered), their manner of palace construction, and their use of walls for defense. Both civilizations carried on extensive trade, and we can trace both Minoan and Mycenaean trade contacts all over the eastern Mediterranean through the distinct pottery of the two civilizations. The amount of pottery and the style of the pottery in the various locations gives us invaluable information. Part of our knowledge of the decline of these two civilizations comes from this pottery.[1,2]

Since Evans first found evidence for the Minoan civilization at Knossos, many other sites have been found. Three other great palaces have been found on Crete and recent discoveries on the island of Santorini (Thera), north of Crete in the Aegean, indicate Minoan civilization flourished on that island. New discoveries about both Minoan and Mycenaean civilization are continually coming to light. The more that is discovered, the more we realize how great were the developments of these two Aegean area peoples before 1000 B.C.

The relationships between these two civilizations and the reasons for their collapse are not known. There are many theories. On the matter of the collapse of the Mycenaean civilization, one scholar has suggested an ecological cause and several scholars have suggested overpopulation. Both these reasons seem like very modern problems. The traditional reason for the collapse of the Mycenaean civilization was invasion. The theory held that a different Greek-speaking people, the Dorians, invaded the area at

---

[1,2] Pottery is one of the most helpful artifacts (an object modified or made by man) an archaeologist can find. Civilizations not only make their own distinctive pottery but man continually changes its style and decoration. A skillfully trained person can recognize and date tiny pieces of pottery or sherds. This identification provides invaluable chronological information and data as to where people lived and travelled.

about 1200 B.C. This theory ties in neatly with the idea of the unrest and invasions in the Near East at about the same time. Several scholars, however, reject this idea today. They believe that the evidence for invasion, burned palaces and towns, is not sufficient. The dates do not agree as they should if there was a consistent pattern of invasion. These scholars suggest that the palaces were burned either by accident or by internal rebellions.[13]

We will probably never know the real reason why these civilizations collapsed. It is important to know that civilizations do collapse. The Minoan and Mycenaean civilizations faded away so completely they were unknown a century ago. What other civilizations do you know of that have collapsed and faded from record until rediscovered by archaeologists? Do you think our civilization will ever collapse and fade away? With the decline of the level of civilization in the Aegean about 1200 B.C., the area slowly entered what historians have called the "Dark Ages."

In many ways, "Dark Ages" is an unfortunate term because no age is "dark" when you live in it. There is trade, there are people living the normal human existence—songs are sung, planting is done, thoughts are developed, plans are made in every age. The degree of sophistication of thought and the variety of material objects produced may not be as high as at other times in human history but they are always present. In the specific case of the "Dark Age" of Greek history it is true we know less about it and have less archaeological evidence from this time period than from the ages that preceded and followed but that may be due to our failure and not to their lack of development. Maybe we have not found the right archaeological sites to give us full information on the "Dark Age". In spite of these qualifications, the term "Dark Age" does convey the point that from our limited perspective the time around 1000 B.C. in Greece does not seem as exciting and as advanced as other eras.

In 1000 B.C. on the Greek mainland and around the Aegean there were small villages. Settlements existed at the great Mycenaean centers—Mycenae, Pylos, Athens, Thebes—but they were small villages with little wealth or power compared to 1350 B.C. How these conditions in the Aegean area slowly changed and how the foundations of classical Greek civilization were laid in the period after 1000 B.C. is the subject of the next chapter. What conditions and factors do you think may have led to the emergence from the "Dark Ages"?

[13] See the books listed in the bibliography for further information. Rhys Carpenter in *Discontinuity in Greek Civilization* offers the ecological theory.

Section VI—Summary

In 1000 B.C. there were many areas of advanced civilization scattered about the world. Some people lived in highly developed cities while others lived nomadic lives not far away. Whether in cities in China or the Near East or in the fields of Europe or Mexico human beings lived with all the concerns, worries, hopes, and dreams that have made up human history. The human species has evolved very little physically since then. We humans have changed our environment and we are closely interconnected by the rapidity of communication but even 3000 years ago man exchanged ideas and attitudes. It is hard for us to present specific evidence as to how these exchanges affected different civilizations but art provides us some evidence and we can trace contacts of peoples through trade.

As we focus our attention on the development and flowering of Greek civilization in the period 1000-300 B.C., don't forget that the Greeks lived in an interconnected world. They did not develop in a vacuum any more than we do. The fact that their level of material civilization was low about 1000 B.C. may have been the result of influences from other areas. Their later rise to great intellectual, artistic, and political heights was in part stimulated by others.

Yet even with the apparently low level of development in 1000 B.C., the Greeks were human. Try to think of them in these terms as you read along. How would you feel living as they did? How would you react to events described? As a human what might you learn from other humans who have lived full, sometimes exciting, often dull, lives?

Section VII—*Chapter Review and Bibliography*

At the end of each chapter in this book is a review section followed by a bibliography. You may find that you prefer to look at this section before you begin the chapter so you have some sense of what information you should retain from your reading. The chapter reviews will usually include a list of places and events that are of particular importance and a series of questions. These questions may be answered in essays or they may be used as a starting point for discussion. Also at the end of many chapters will be several suggested projects. These projects may be assigned by your teacher or they may be something you would like to undertake on your own. In many cases these projects will require additional research but sometimes they will simply require your thinking on an issue.

There were two main emphases in this chapter. First, there was an emphasis upon geography and, second, an emphasis upon the situation in the world about 1000 B.C. Section II dealt largely with geography. You should be certain you can draw a schematic map of the Aegean area and locate the following places on it before you go further.

Delos	Peleponnesus	Anatolia
Cyclades	Corinth	Hellespont
Olympia	Athens	Black Sea
Delphi	Mycenae	Troy
Miletus	Crete	Pylos
Ionia	Knossos	Ionian Sea
		Mount Olympus

In addition to the immediate area of the Aegean the chapter discussed the geography of the Mediterranean Basin and the Near East. To illustrate your understanding of this region you should be able to locate the following places on a map.

Israel	Black Sea	Tigris River
Carthage	Spain	Euphrates River
Etruscan lands	Russia	Nile River
Hittite Empire	Egypt	

Finally, mention was made of civilizations in other parts of the world. You should be able to state where those civilizations were located. For instance, you should be able to locate both the Yellow River and the Indus River.

In order to indicate a knowledge of the factual information in this chapter you should be able to identify the following terms or people. You may have read about some of these people before. If you have, you may like to make reports about them to the class.

"Dark Age" of Greece	Queen of Sheba
"sea peoples"	King David of Israel
Homer	King Solomon of Israel
Sir Arthur Evans	Hellenic Civilization
Heinrich Schliemann	King Agamemnon
The Iliad	

There are many questions which one might ask concerning information in this chapter. Among these questions are the following.

1. What contacts were there between the Mediterranean area and China about 1000 B.C.?
2. What was the origin of the Etruscans?
3. What contacts were there between Egypt and the Americas before 1000 B.C.?
4. What danger is there in viewing the world from a provincial or narrow perspective?
5. Why is the fact that the Mycenaeans spoke Greek important?

There are other questions which might require additional research in order to supply a sufficient answer. You may wish to pursue any of these or your teacher might assign several to the class. You can make up your own questions but among those suggested by the content of the chapter are the following.

1. How have conquerers portrayed or written the history of peoples they have conquered? (For instance, what had the white man written about the American Indian or Native American in history books up to 1960?)
2. Why did the mainland of Greece probably emerge from the period of time referred to as the "Dark Ages"?
3. Why did the Mycenaean civilization collapse? Write a paper in which you present your own theory after doing research on the topic.
4. Why is geography important in the history of nations?

The following bibliographical suggestions will provide a starting place for further investigation of material presented in this chapter. You will find a bibliography of this type at the end of most chapters.

Bibby, G. *Four Thousand Years Ago.* N.Y., Knopf, 1961.

Block, Raymond. *The Etruscans.* N.Y., Praeger, 1958.

Carpenter, Rhys. *Discontinuity in Greek Civilization.* N.Y., W.W. Norton Co., 1968.

Chadwick, John. *The Decipherment of Linear B.* Cambridge, Eng., University Press, 1958.

Chapin, Henry. *The Search for Atlantis.* N.Y., Crowell-Collier Press, 1968.

Cottrell, Leonard. *The Bull of Minos.* London, Evans Brothers.

Creel, H. G. *The Birth of China.* N.Y., Frederick Ungar, 1954.

Grant, Michael. *The Ancient Mediterranean.* N.Y., Charles Scribner's Sons, 1969.

Gordon, C. H. *Ugarit and Minoan Crete.* N.Y., W.W. Norton & Co., Inc.

Gordon, C. H. *The Near East.* N.Y., W.W. Norton & Co., Inc.

Heurga, Jacques. *Daily Life of the Etruscans.* N.Y., Macmillan Co., 1964.

Hill, D. *Abraham: His Heritage and Ours.* Boston, Beacon Press, 1957.

Marinatos, Spyridon and Hirmer, Max. *Crete and Mycenae.* N.Y., H. N. Abrams, 1960.

Palmer, L. R. *Mycenaeans and Minoans.* London, Faber & Faber, 1961.

Taylour, L.W. *The Myceanaeans.* London, Thames and Hudson, 1964.

Schliemann, Henrich. *Mycenae.* N.Y., C. Scribner's Sons, 1880.

Ventris, Michael and Chadwick, John. *Documents in Mycenaean Greek.* Cambridge, Eng., University Press, 1956.

Vermeule, Emily. *Greece in the Bronze Age.* Chicago, University of Chicago Press, 1964.

Von Wuthenau, Alexander. *Art of Terracotta Pottery in Pre-Columbian Central and South America.* N.Y., Crown Publishers, 1969.

Ward, A. G. *The Quest for Theseus.* N.Y., Praeger Publishers, 1970.

Willetts, R. F. *Everyday Life in Ancient Crete.* N.Y., G. P. Putnam's Sons, 1969.

CHAPTER II

THE CHANGING MEDITERRANEAN WORLD
—900-600 B.C.

Section I—*Introduction*

In the last chapter we considered the Aegean world of 1000 B.C. and the period of the "Dark Ages." The "Dark Ages" slowly ended. It is impossible to date this ending specifically since one era merged with the next. The historian, after the facts, imposes on an age a structure which the age did not have. We must deal, therefore, in general patterns of time and not in specifics. The time line given in Section II will provide a guide to some of the key events that led the Greeks from the "Dark Ages" to a new and important approach to this world and the conditions in it.

Archaeologists have found very limited evidence of living styles in the "Dark Ages". Reasons for this have been suggested such as the fact many dwellings were of wood and writing as a skill was lost to the Greeks after the fall of the Mycenaean civilization so we have no written descriptions of the period.

Archaeological evidence suggests that about 1,000 B.C. a number of Greeks from the area around Athens left their homes for the Aegean Islands and the coastal areas of Anatolia. These so-called Ionian Greeks may have left because of population pressures or because of continuing disturbances created by moving tribes in the peninsula. They established towns, for example, Miletus, on the Anatolian coast, and had important settlements on Aegean islands such as Samos. These Greeks had a common spoken language and religious ideas. Poseidon, worshipped as the God of the Sea in classical Greece, was an important diety worshipped at a common festival held near Miletus. Also, on the island of Delos there was another common shrine for the Ionian Greeks of the islands and the two coasts.

Contemporary with this Ionian movement was the establishment of the Kingdom of Israel by Saul and David and the emergence of the Aramaic and Phoenician City States at the eastern end of the Mediterranean. The Aramaic Kingdoms were established by peoples who moved out of the Arabian desert and who had common ties in their trading interests and their Semitic language. They were related to the Hebrews and Phoenicians. They established several small kingdoms. The most important was Damascus. The Phoenicians established great trading cities, Tyre, Sidon and Byblos, along the coast. We find similar movements of people in the Near East and the Aegean area—a phenomenon that has occurred many times in history.

In the mainland regions of the Greek peninsula about 1,000 B.C. most inhabitants lived in small farming villages. One might find several such villages scattered over a small plain cut off from neighboring plains by mountains. There was no one dominant village or city in these plains as there had been in Mycenaean times. Family connections were important. Several related families formed a clan and the whole valley might be inhabited by related and intermarried clans which formed a tribe. Homer in *The Iliad* and *Odyssey* describes the social organization of the Greeks and what he presents is similar to what we've described here. In fact, Homer's *Iliad* and *Odyssey* written about 800 B.C. are considered by many scholars our best source of information about the period of the "Dark Ages."

In each small village there would be a leader and he would get advice from elders in the village. Perhaps there was a person who, for religious or military reasons, was important for the entire valley and was the overlord. Farming was the main sustenance for these people. Villages were not built on the coast because of the fear of pirates and there was probably very limited trade between one valley and another unlike in the Mycenaean age when there had been extensive contacts. This was the general economic and political situation of the "Dark Ages" as pieced together by historians. The revival of trade suggested in Homer, the growing political unity of valleys suggested in several legends,[1] and the immigration of the Ionians were events that led to changes. What precipitated these events? It is almost impossible to be certain but it seems obvious that many factors, some emerging from within the local populations and some introduced by outside sources, were responsible. Let us consider some of these factors.

[1] The Athenians ascribed the unifying of the several villages in the plain of Attica to Theseus who, according to legend, achieved the union after his return from Crete where he killed the Minotaur.

Section II—*The Development of the Near East and its Influence
on Greece*

Date B.C.	*Greece and Aegean*
1000	Ionian migrations to Anatolian coast and Aegean islands.
900	Delos becomes important central shrine for Ionian Greeks.
850	Phoenicians trading with Ionians; Geometric pottery.
800	Homer; Miletus builds thick walls; First Olympic Games; Writing found on Athenian pottery; Dipylon Vases; Hesoid.
750	Hoplite military tactics introduced; Sparta conquers Messenia; Bireme invented.
700	Corinthian "orientalizing style" pottery.
650	Tyrtaes writes in Sparta; Laws of Draco in Athens; Reforms of "Lycurgus" at Sparta.
600	Periander—Tyrant of Corinth; Free standing statues created; Solon at Athens reforms government.

Near East and Anatolia	*Western Mediterranean*
Kingdom of Israel—King David; Phoenician cities along coast— Hiram King of Tyre and Sidon; Arameans rule Damascus; Phrygians dominate Anatolia; Urartians control eastern Anatolia and Syria.	
Re-emergence of Assyrian power— Damascus conquered.	
Al-Mina on Phoenician coast is international trade center; Greeks from Chalcis very important at Al-Mina.	Phoenicians establish first trade contacts with Greeks—Carthage founded.
Jeroboam II of Israel—Prophets Amos and Hosea; Assyria conquers Tyre, Sidon, Damascus, and Israel; Phrygia destroyed.	Cumae—first Greek colony in the West. Syracuse founded.
Lydia dominates western Anatolia— money invented; King Psammeticus restores Egypt—throws out Assyrians.	Naval victory of Corinth over Corcyra—Corinth controls trade route to Italy.
Trading center of Naucratus founded in Egypt; Neo-Babylonians (Chaldeans) and Medes conquer Nineveh and destroy Assyrian Empire.	Byzantium founded; Syracuse establishes colonies in Sicily; Carthage establishes control in Spain and western Sicily; Etruscans control northern Italy.
Neo-Babylonians conquer Judah— end of Hebrew Kingdom.	Sinope founded.

This comparative time chart indicating developments in the Aegean area, Anatolia, and the Near East summarizes the history of the period 1,000 to 600 B.C. in a brief way. The important item to note and to follow in the reading is the manner in which events interrelate. Again we see that the history of one area affects the history of another. It makes no sense to study the history of a nation or area in isolation from that of their contemporaries. The map of the Mediterranean area in this chapter will allow you to locate and identify places that are unfamiliar to you. Be certain you can locate places mentioned in the text.

By 900 B.C. the Greeks were established on the Aegean islands and Anatolian coast and the Phoenicians, whose chief cities were Tyre, Sidon and Byblos, had established thriving kingdoms along the eastern end of the Mediterranean. The stage was set for the redevelopment of trade and contacts between these areas. With apparently little knowledge of the Mycenaean age and little contact with more civilized regions the Greeks were slow to start trading. The Phoenicians, however, had the opposite situation. They were at the cross roads of the great early civilizations. Inland from the coast new nations were emerging that blocked their inland trade since the Phoenicians were too small a group to contend with the larger forces of Urartu and Assyria. These emerging powers did have items to trade and needed supplies that the Phoenician ships could bring from trading stations established in the Aegean islands and around the Mediterranean shores. The Urartians dominated eastern Anatolia and what is now Syria for well over a century. They are a little known people but apparently spoke a Caucasian related language, *used the horse*, and became very skilled at metal work especially in iron.[2] We can trace by archaeological remains the widespread distribution of Urartian metal cauldrons and other metal items. There is clear evidence of their influence in the art work of the Greeks. The Urartian domination of the inland area pushed the Phoenicians to the sea and blocked the expansion of the inland nation of Assyria for several generations.

Assyria had a long history going back before 1700 B.C. Her location in the upper reaches of the Tigris and Euphrates rivers opened her to many invasions of tribes from the Anatolian and

[2] Several nations that are rarely mentioned and about which little is known will be included in this chapter. You may want to learn more about these countries. In Kellogg, *Out of the Past,* Chapter XVII, a technique for investigating a new nation is presented and you may wish to look at it.

Caucasus mountains, and the Iranian plateau. Her development
was first blocked by the Hittites. After Egypt and the Hittites
fought to a draw in 1288 B.C., Assyria under Tiglath-Pileser I had
a brief moment of power before being blocked by the Phrygians
and the Uratians. Finally, about 850 B.C. several powerful kings
pushed the borders of Assyria southward reducing the power of
Urartu and making Damascus, the Aramean Kingdom closely connected with the history of the Hebrews, a tribute territory. The
areas inland from the coast were dominated by this nation noted
for its cruelty in warfare and for its introduction of new military
and political techniques for keeping an empire together. The
Assyrian king was supreme and the effectiveness of the nation
depended upon his intelligence. Under him were vassal kings conquered in war. If they were suspected of disloyalty, governors
were appointed in their place. The Assyrians practiced deportation
of conquered people and were the first to establish colonies of
their own in conquered lands, a technique used effectively by both
Alexander the Great and the Romans. A vast system of road com-
munications was established that the Persians later expanded. In
military activity the Assyrians were noted for cruelty killing all
the women and children in towns that resisted conquest and often
flaying alive the men and nailing their skins to the wall of the
town. Their siege equipment was the highlight of their great
engineering ability. They developed an efficient espionage system
to aid them in their conquests. The symbol of the nation was
Assur, God of War. With such a power inland, no wonder the sea
appeared attractive to the coastal dwellers.

A series of incompetent rules and palace intrigues (a matter of
great concern and potential disastrous results for any nation
resting full authority in one person) hit Assyria in the years between 830 and 750 B.C. She was not the threat to the Near East
she had been. This allowed the Hebrews in Israel to have a re-
surgence of importance under Jeroboam II. He established trade
and brought wealth to many in Israel. His actions were criticised
by the first of the great Hebrew prophets, Amos and Hosea. They
criticised the wealth accumulated by the Hebrew king and his
abandoning of the true religion of Yahweh. Their message was one
of concern for the poor and the widows and an interest in justice
as the goal of the society. Amos reported these thoughts of
Yahweh's,

"I hate, I despise your feasts and I take no delight in your solemn
    assemblies . . . .
Take away from me the noise of your songs; to the melody of your
    harps I will not listen.
But let justice roll down like waters, and rightousness like an ever-
    flowing stream."[3]

We will note later a Greek contemporary of these prophets, Hesiod,
who was commenting on the conditions of life in Greece at this
same time. The parallels are most interesting.

During the period 830-750 the Phoenician cities of Tyre, Sidon,
and Byblos were heavily engaged in maritime trade. Several colonies
were founded. The most important were Gades in Spain on the
Atlantic coast and Carthage on the coast of Tunisia opposite
Sicily. The latter became more important in history than the
founding city of Tyre. It was Carthage which fought Rome for
control of the western Mediterranean in the Punic Wars.[4] Carthage
provided a good mid-point on the trade route from the Atlantic
to the home ports. What were the items traded by these Near
Eastern cities?

For us, the most important item was the alphabet. The increasing
trade required records. Hieroglyphics and cuneiform were too
cumbersome and slow for rapid record keeping and so there was a
need for a simpler syllabary or set of characters for writing words.
Several were developed in the early iron age period of the Near
East but that used by the Phoenicians, whose roots can be traced
to the workers in the Egyptian mines on the Sinai Peninsula, took
hold. There were 22 symbols and their etymology is very interesting showing how the symbols evolved from drawings of common
objects. For instance, alpha was originally aleph written ⊿ and
it meant ox. It looks like the sketch of an animal head. The Greeks
stood the letter up and we see our A. Beth was originally a drawing
of the floor plan of a house and was written ⊔ . When reversed
it became B. Dealt, originally daleth drawn as a ◁ represented
a tent door in the original Phoenician. Turned sideways one sees it
as D.

The first writing found among the Greeks after the Mycenaean
age dates from c. 800 B.C. and appears on pottery. The letters
employed are the Phoenician ones. The Greeks eventually added

[3] Amos 5:21-24. For more information on Amos, Hosea and the events in
Hebrew history of this era, see Jackson, *Legend, Myth and History in the Old
Testament,* Chapters XV-XVII.
[4] See Stillman, *Roman Rulers and Rebels,* Chapter I.

the vowels to create an efficient and very quick method of writing the many words of their language. They used Phoenician symbols for the vowels, using Phoenician consonants for which there was no equivalent sound in Greek. They also added 4 new consonants for sounds unique to Greek. Writing at first was done either right to left, vertically or alternately right to left and left to right. The left to right form developed slowly into the standard method of writing. At first different areas had variations in the alphabet but the Ionian form used in Athens became standard in the 5th century. Romans learned from the Etruscans a variation of the Phoenician alphabet developed in the Greek town of Chalchis which Chalchis used in her colonies in Italy. The re-introduction of writing into the Greek world was one of the great events of this age and clearly indicates the interdependence of the Mediterranean peoples.

Material items exported from Tyre and Sidon consisted of dyed cloth, carved ivories, and metal work. The name Phoenician is derived from the Greek word phoinikes meaning red or purple men. The Phoenicians developed the finest dye of the ancient world from the tiny murex, a rock-whelk caught off their coasts. Each murex secreted two drops of a yellowish liquid from which colors ranging from rose to violet could be extracted. These colors were permanent. They did not run like vegetable dyes and gave the Phoenicians a great product for trade. They could dye materials woven elsewhere or they could import raw wool and weave and dye material in the port cities.

The Phoenicians were not very original artists but they synthesized Egyptian, Canaanite, and Aramean styles to produce gold, silver, and bronze pieces for export. Many designs later appearing in Greek art work first came to Greece in the holds of Phoenician ships. The Phoenicians also learned to make glass from the Egyptians and for centuries this area produced the finest glass of the ancient world. To supply their factories the Phoenicians imported raw materials from all over the Mediterranean and even went to England to get tin.

An example of exchange of artistic symbols can be seen in the sphinx—a part human, part animal figure. In use from at least 2700 B.C. the Egyptian sphinx, originally a symbol of the power of the pharaoh, showed the human part as male. The Arameans of Damascus used it in art work and changed the human part into a female figure. The Phoenicians adopted the Damascus version on some of their metal work and exported it to Greece. In Greece

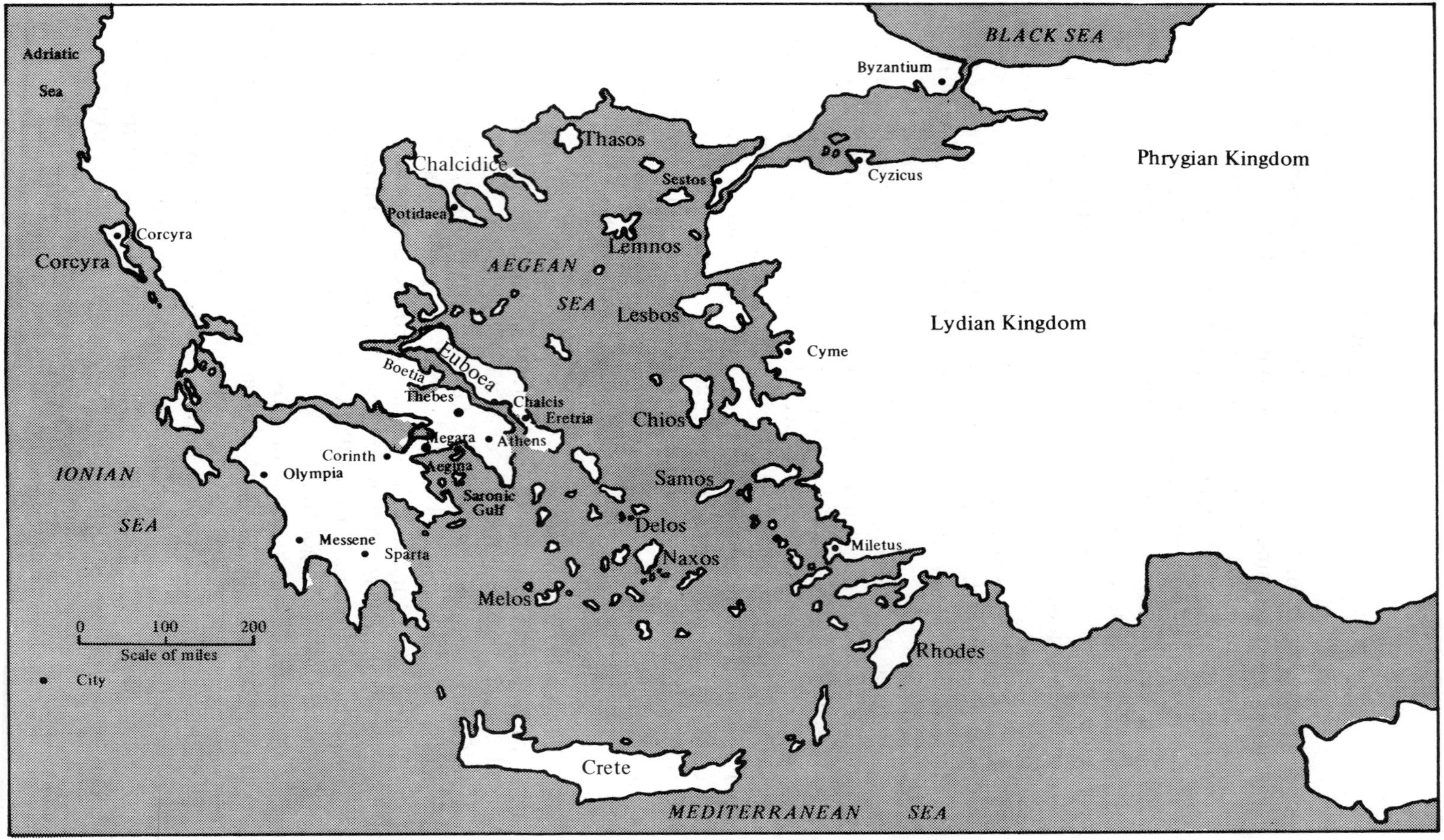
BLACK SEA
Adriatic
Sea
Byzantium
Thasos
Chalcidice
Sestos
Cyzicus
Phrygian Kingdom
Potidaea
Corcyra
Corcyra
Lemnos
AEGEAN
SEA
Lesbos
Lydian Kingdom
Cyme
Boetia
Euboea
Thebes
Chalcis
Eretria
Chios
Megara
Athens
Corinth
Aegina
IONIAN
Olympia
Samos
Saronic
Gulf
SEA
Delos
Messene
Sparta
Miletus
Naxos
Melos
0
100
200
Scale of miles
Rhodes
City
Crete
MEDITERRANEAN
SEA

the female version of the sphinx became an important decoration on Corinthian pottery and an object for funereal sculpture after 600 B.C.

As Phoenician trade expanded in the Mediterranean and Aegean, the Greeks began to participate in the commercial development. During the Mycenaean age the city of Ugarit (Ras Shamra) on the eastern Mediterranean coast had been a great trading center for Mycenaean goods. In this age of revived trade after 900 B.C., the town of Al Mina (Posidium) took its place and became a great shipping center for goods from Greece. More products from the island of Euboea and especially the town of Chalcis, which means place of bronze, have been found there than from any other Greek city.

Why this town should take the lead in the revival of Greek trading is open to speculation but there are several possibilities. Its location on an island gave it some protection from wandering tribes of raiders on the mainland. Chalcis's location at the narrowest point between the island and the mainland may have allowed it to extract tolls from passing ships, perhaps Phoenician or other Greek ones, which supplied wealth. A small interior plain provided good soil for growing food and some land for raising sheep but not enough to allow it to be fully self-sufficient. Being on an island it had to master the sea in order to supply its increasing needs. Its protected location away from the strong prevailing winds made it possible to develop shipping skills in a protected area. It had access to the wool produced in Boetia and this provided her an important raw material needed in Phoenicia. Finally, there was copper in the interior areas of the island. With this raw material at hand, the way was open for Chalcis to develop its own metal working industry following Near Eastern models. This is what happened after 800 B.C. when Chalcis became noted for its excellent iron swords and its fine bronze armor modeled on the new styles developed in the Near East. Thus we find trade and industry developing at Chalcis on Euboea. Later this led to the establishment of overseas bases by Chalcis to support its trade.

At about the time Chalcis was developing her trade contacts, across the Euboic Gulf in Boetia the poet Hesoid was writing the first poetry clearly identified with an individual and his personal life. Hesiod is usually considered to have lived about 750 B.C., a contemporary of Amos and Hosea, and at the time that Al Mina was flourishing as a trading center for the Greeks. His works, *The Theogony* and *Works and Days*,[5] show definite links with literary

[5] See Kellogg, *Out of the Past*, Chapters VI and VII for more information on Hesiod and for several extracts from these two works.

works of the Near East. The *Theogony* is a hymn of priase to Zeus but it has close connections with the stories in the Babylonian *Enuma Elish.* This myth was recited and acted at the Babylonian New Year Festival. It conveys a sense of praise and glory for the god Marduk who brings order out of the chaos of the world as does Zeus in the *Theogony.* Hesiod combined in the *Theogony* many stories of the gods told by the Greeks in his day. Many stories had roots in the Near East and some were Greek variations on a Near Eastern theme. For instance, Typhaeus, the serpent that Zeus destroys, appears in contemporary or earlier tales from the southern coast of Anatolia.

The *Works and Days* recounts the story of how Hesiod's brother cheated him out of land inherited from their father. The judge helped in the cheating. It is an anti-establishment story. This is the theme of the story but Hesiod goes on to present a full agricultural almanac. We have similar works from the wisdom literature of Egypt and a farming calendar has been found in Israel dating from c. 900 B.C. that is quite similar. We do not wish to negate the achievement of this great Greek poet but it is crucial to a true understanding of man's past that we realize how influences were being spread throughout the Mediterranean area by 750 B.C.

Another aspect of Greek history of this age is reflected in the *Works and Days.* Hesiod claims to have visited the island of Euboea across a narrow strait from his home and also to have won a prize at a poetry competition at Chalcis held in conjunction with funeral games. The travel and funeral celebration recall parts of the *Iliad.* Also, the argument between Hesoid and his brother reflects the changing economic and political life of the Greek peninsula.

It was stated above that the Greeks during the "Dark Ages" lived in small villages scattered about the plains of Greece. As prosperity slowly returned and as the population grew, more land had to be cultivated. The first logical step was to organize the plains into a consolidated unit and secondly to develop the hillsides. The villages were usually inhabited by families related in clans. These clans together formed the tribes of the plain. The consolidation could be effected via family or tribal leadership. Legends, such as that of Theseus in Athens, developed around the historical events of these consolidations. As consolidation took place, problems arose of ownership. The village land had been owned by the whole community. As families died out and others grew or moved in, confusion as to rightful shares developed. Out of this confusion, the need of a central organization that controlled the whole valley and decided on matters of land emerged. Thus, central government developed for the area of each plain or large part of a plain. Also, as the land on the hills was developed, this land became the property of those who developed it and not of the whole village. Thus, extensive private ownership emerged in Greece in this period after the "Dark Ages" stimulated by the exploitation of new lands and the consolidation of village lands in the hands of a few of the more important and powerful individual families. Those who got control of the land became the powerful people in the area. Because their power gave them certain advantages, they were viewed as better than others in the community. The term, aristocracy, from the Greek for best, was later applied to this group of people.

Soon the consolidation led to what is the characteristic political organization of Greek civilization—the polis, translated as city-state. We will consider the phenomenon of the polis at greater length in Chapter 4 but around 800 B.C. what began to emerge for each valley or plain was a chief town centered around an easily defendable location such as the Athenian acropolis. Walls were built to protect the homes and especially the temples which became the unifying feature of the polis or city-state. Often the inhabitants of each plain worshipped the same god. If they did not, one god emerged as supreme in the polis as in the case of Athens. This is reflected in the story of the contest between Posiedon and Athena to determine who would be the patron of the newly centralized Attic plain. In the myth Athena won because of her gift of the olive tree to the people of Athens—an item of great importance in the future economic development of Attica.

Hesiod reflected these changing economic conditions in his *Works and Days*. He said the good old days were better and that in this "age of Iron" the lot of man was to struggle. He encouraged the farmers to work hard and not to try the easy way to riches. He indicated sailing was dangerous and not for him. His brother was obviously of the new type getting rich by trade and using the new political institutions. Hesiod's tone is that of a farmer who has worked hard and likes the traditional ways who is unhappy with the new developments of his society. This is a viewpoint often found in history in times of change. Can you think of examples from other ages where the traditional ways are supported by vocal groups who do not want change to take place? Unfortunately for Hesiod, the new ways could not be stopped. A growing population, economic prosperity, and trade contacts with the

Near East were changing the old ways. The rapid changes of this age laid the foundations for the later rise of tyrants and ultimately the greatness of 5th century Greece.

With the growing unity of each plain and the cultivation of the hillsides between the plains the situation became ripe for one of the great characteristics of the Greeks to emerge—conflict and rivalry between the poleis (city states). Although there were many factors holding the Greeks together—religion and language being most important—they still became extremely committed to their own territory and values so that warfare between poleis was common. In fact, one of the first events recorded by the Greeks themselves after the Mycenaean age was the struggle of two towns on the Island of Euboea, Eretria and Chalcis, over a tiny strip of plain that separated them by only ten miles. The struggle occurred about 700 B.C. a little after our date for Hesiod but the war suggests the Greeks were already living up to one of Hesiod's comments that "Strife is wholesome to men" and to his suggestion that war was a natural source of income in which poleis could procure wealth from enemies. As many people consider Greek civilization a major root of our own, it is interesting to note this recording of military activity at the very root of western civilization, an activity that provides a recurrent theme in the history of western man.[6]

Not only was warfare widespread but this age of colonization saw the introduction of a new method of warfare which relied on the common foot soldier or hoplite rather than on cavalry and chariots. It is probable that this method of warfare was introduced from the Near East where Assyria pioneered new military tactics. The aristocracy, who could afford horses, had supplied the cavalry. They welcomed the new tactics which removed from them the full burden of military activity. Little did they realize how the new tactics would undercut their authority when they no longer were the defenders of the poleis but rather the defense rested on the common soldier.

The hoplite was heavily armored and Chalcis was an important producer of this bronze armor. It is possible that both the impetus for colonization by Chalcidians and the wealth of Chalcis were based on her manufacture of weapons for war.

In considering hoplite armor it is interesting to note the origin

---

[6] Consider also the Hebrew's approach to warfare recorded in the Biblical books of Judges and Joshua as another source of the western man's approach to military activity.

of the horse hair plume found on helmets designed for the hoplites. It is first seen in tomb paintings of New Kingdom Egypt. It is next found in the Near East. There it was no doubt copied by the metal workers of the bronze city, Chalcis, from armor they saw displayed in the port of Al Mina or brought to Euboea by Phoenician sailors. Therefore, this distinctive characteristic of early Greek hoplite armor had an Egyptian origin just as the tactics for employing massed foot soldiers originated in the Near East.

All the developments of the eighth century B.C. did not divide the Greeks. In fact, one of the great symbols of Greek unity—the Olympic Games—began according to tradition at the very start of the age in 776 B.C. and were apparently held every four years from then on. Later the Greeks dated their history from this event using four year olympiads as their dating system. In the *Iliad* Homer describes the athletic events used to celebrate the funeral of a hero, Patroclus. The same events were celebrated at the Olympic Games and by reading Homer or studying the paintings on later Greek vases we can get an excellent idea of what the events at the Olympic Games were like. The Games brought all Greeks together every four years for a week of praise to the father of the gods, Zeus. A truce in all warfare lasted during the games and they were held in a neutral area in the Peloponnesus where all Greeks could gather.

Courtesy, Museum of Fine Arts, Boston

Another unifying factor in the Greek world about 776 B.C. was the style of pottery. It is called geometric and a view of any vase produced in this style clearly tells you how it was named. Perhaps the most famous geometric vases were produced in Athens and were found near the Dipylon Gate. These so-called Dipylon vases were funeral urns and stand several feet high. Almost the entire vase was banded in circles and hatch marks. On some vases at the upper levels scenes of mourning women and corpses stretched out on wagons were portrayed. These are the first representation of the human figure in Greek pottery decoration. Athenians in the classical age were noted for their portrayal of human figures on vases. Potters, as mentioned above, began to write on their vases and this archaeological evidence allows us to be certain that the Phoenician script as adapted to Greek use was known and utilized by 750 B.C.

As trading increased, the Phoenicians founded colonies such as Carthage. The Greeks, perhaps inspired by this Phoenician activity, began a new era of extensive colonization. The many reasons for this and its development will be traced in Section III below. Eventually many poleis participated in this Age of Colonization. Here it is important to note that the first colony established by the Greeks in the west was at Ischia, (Pithicusae) an island just north of the bay of Naples. The founding was a cooperative effort. Already mentioned Chalcis was joined by its neighbor Eretria (before they went to war) and the town of Cyme on the Anatolian coast. This threesome is interesting. We already know that Chalcis was deeply involved in trade. She may have needed the raw materials the Etruscans of the northern part of the Italian peninsula could supply for her bronze making industry. Eretria may have been involved for the same reasons but we are not sure. Asian Cyme brings us back to the Ionian towns of the Anatolian coast that were mentioned at the start of the chapter. These towns were rapidly developing during this period. Miletus as early as 800 B.C. built great 13 foot walls for defense. It was an exchange station for Phrygian products from inland Anatolia which came to the coast over land and the products of the Near East and Greece that came by sea. The greatest days of Miletus were in the next century but these coastal cities were as involved in the trade development and colonization as were the cities of Euboea and mainland Greece. The colony on Ischia was soon moved to the mainland due to earthquakes and volcanic activity on the island. The new settlement was on a high hill, an acropolis, dominating a

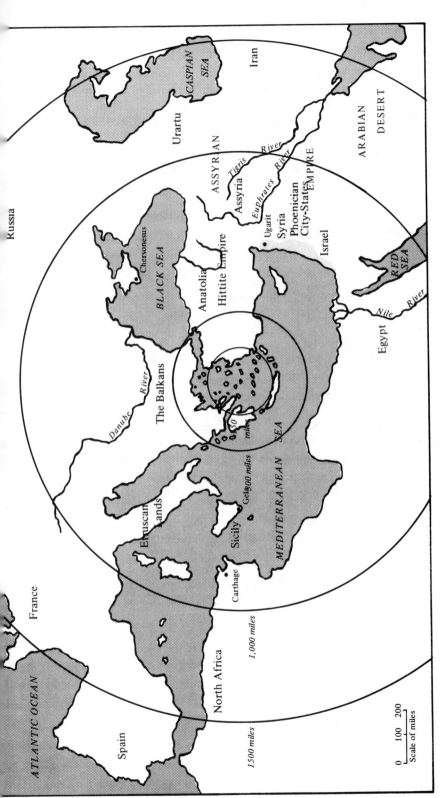

The Mediterranean Basin and the Near East
A Target Centered on the Island of Delos

peninsula (the northern arm of the Bay of Naples) backed by an inland plain where food was grown. There was a good beach where the ships could be drawn up easily. Asian Cyme, which we know in its Italian form, Cumae, gave her name to the colony. Cumae was the first permanent Greek colony in the west.

The traditional founding date was 753 B.C. The colony was just south of the land controlled by the Etruscans.[7] It was from here that extensive exchanges between Greeks and Etruscans took place including the introduction of the alphabet. We may never know how important these exchanges were for bringing civilized ideas to the inland tribes of Italy from whence came the later power of Rome. Today some of the finest examples of Greek pottery, which was found in Etruscan tombs,[8] can be seen in museums in Italy, especially in Rome (Villa Julia) and in Florence.

A Near Eastern event contemporary with the founding of Cumae is the revival of Assyrian power. The impact of this event on the history of the era was great although it is seldom linked to events in other areas of the Mediterranean. Establishing himself with full authority at home, Tiglath Pileser III (745-727 B.C.) embarked on a series of conquests that rapidly brought the Phoenician cities of Tyre and Sidon under his control with Assyrian governors set up in each city by 740 B.C. The trade of these cities was now under Assyrian control and those who did not wish to trade on Assyrian terms had to seek other ports. In 733 Damascus fell followed in 721/2 by the conquest of Israel by Tiglath-Pileser's successor Sargon II. Sargon II spread Assyria's power from the border of Egypt to Cyprus and the Halys River in Anatolia. It was he who began the policy of establishing Assyrian colonies in conquered areas and he established Assyrian border posts throughout his empire. He reflects another side of Assyrian rule in addition to the cruel, militaristic conqueror. Assyrian rulers supported the arts and encouraged the development of intellectual concerns. For the first time one empire controlled the entire Near East and Anatolia making it easier to exchange ideas and goods than ever before in history. The Assyrian kings were great city builders in their homeland and, although there were already three capital cities including famous Nineveh, Sargon II determined to build his own new capital at Dur-Sharrukin (Sargontown). It was a fortified palace with high castellated walls, a technique the Assyrians had

---

[7] See the end of Chapter I for suggested books on the Etruscans.

[8] The Metropolitan Museum in New York acquired a superb Greek vase in 1973. Apparently it came from an Etruscan Tomb. The museum paid over a million dollars for the vase.

developed for fortifying places lacking natural defenses. There were extensive halls and courts where the semicircular arch was used, an architectural innovation and advance associated with the Assyrians. The decorations were of great human headed stone bulls and lions, a device copied by the Greeks in their art. They also copied the Assyrian idea of linking single scene carved reliefs into a continuous frieze depicting a full story. Assyrian artists were very effective in their depicting of animal scenes and royal hunts. There was heavy concentration on surface patterning and the geometric designs thus achieved perhaps inspired Greek pottery designs of the same era.

Assyrian rulers also encouraged work in astronomy, geology, law, religion, medicine and geography. One of the last great kings, Ashurbanipal III (668-633 B.C.), collected an extensive library and it is from the tablets found there by archaeologists that we have learned a great deal about the intellectual developments of the time. These tablets were written in cuneiform and can easily be read by a trained Assyriologist. Many of the ideas found in the tablets formed the basis for the later speculations of the early Greek philosophers of Ionia. For instance, Thales of Miletus was able to predict the eclipse of 585 B.C. using records from the Near East. Perhaps these were collected and saved by one of the conquering Assyrian kings and then passed down to the Neo-Babylonians and Greeks through trade.

Sargon's successor, Sennacherib, tried to consolidate the empire but was blocked by the Hebrew Kingdom of Judah which successfully withstood a seige in 701 B.C. About the turn of the century several events took place that were to change the power structure of the eastern Mediterranean area in the next century. First, the kingdom of Phrygia in Anatolia was destroyed by raiding nomads from the Caucasus region, the Cimmerians. Their place was soon taken by the Lydians who quickly established a strong kingdom that controlled the region just inland from the Greek cities along the Anatolian coast. There will be more said about Lydia later.

The second event was the capture of Egypt by Assyria c. 671 B.C. For the first time the center of one of the earliest civilizations was controlled by a power based in the other center of early Near Eastern civilization. There was the possibility of amalgamation and interchange of concepts unlike any that had taken place before but the conquest was to last only 20 years. About 660 B.C. an Egyptian King, Psammetichus, united the country and with help from Greek mercenaries threw out the Assyrians. Egypt was thus opened to Greek trade at a time that other areas were being closed for in 680 B.C. the Assyrians had destroyed the city of Sidon for its part in an attempted rebellion against Assyria.

Finally, a new force was stirring in the area of ancient Babylon. Chaldean emigrants from the east had settled in the region and were beginning to consolidate their power. By 612 B.C. these peoples joined with the Medes who lived on the Iranian plateau and together they took advantage of the growing weakness of Assyria to capture the capital of Nineveh and destroy it and Assyrian power forever. When this happened, the Medes and their relatives and allies, the Persians, gained control of the northern provinces of Assyria and the Chaldeans took over the "fertile crescent" area and ruled it for three generations as the Neo-Babylonian Empire. Their rule and defeat provides the focus of 6th century history in the Near East, and we will return to them.

What do you think the impact of those events in the Near East would have been on the Greeks? How might the emergence of a great new power dominating the trade centers of the eastern Mediterranean affect Greek trade? What importance might there be in the new relationships established between Egypt and the Greeks? We know some of the history of Greece in this period and we can piece together some possible answers to these questions.

Generally during the 8th century B.C. there was a gradual shift of trade to the western Mediterranean. This shift was intensified in the 7th century and there was intensive colonization by the Greeks in the west and later in the area of the Black Sea. It can be assumed that this shift was due to the closing of markets in the Near East and to the collapse of Phoenician power in the west. The leadership of the western movement passed from Chalcis to Corinth around 700 B.C.

The first recorded naval battle in Greek history took place in 664 B.C. between Corinth and a fleet from the island of Corcyra. Corcyra, a colony founded by Eretria, lost. This gave Corinth control of the island and with it control of the trade route from the Gulf of Corinth to the tip of Italy.

By the time of this battle a new naval vessel had been designed, the bireme. Whether this ship was first designed by the Greeks or the Phoenicians is not clear but it revolutionized sea warfare. The bireme had two banks of oars on each side thus increasing the number of rowers and the speed of the ship as well as the size so more goods could be carried. Also, a bronze point was developed for the prow that allowed for ramming ships just beneath the water line. Although this new development was not inspired by the Assyrian advance, it provided the Greeks with new technology with which to expand their trade.

The emerging economic power of Corinth is reflected in the pottery development of the age. Around 700 B.C. a new style swept Greece and the Corinthians dominated in its production. Corinthian "orientalizing style" pottery is found throughout the Mediterranean world in the next century. This reflects the shifting trade patterns brought on by the upheavals in the Near East. Corinthian "orientalizing" pottery is distinct with a purple color prominent in the decorations that cover the yellowish pots. The decorations show strong Near Eastern influences with their bands of sphinxes, lions, an animal which was no longer found in Greece, and rosettes. A strong desire on the part of the artist to cover all of the pot with designs is another characteristic of these pots. Many pots were small and used for oils or unguents and other luxuries of the day reflecting the increasing wealth of the Greek cities. The Near Eastern designs used on the pottery may reflect a desire to capture markets formerly dominated by Phoenicians.

Typical Corinthian
Orientalizing Pottery

With Sidon destroyed and Assyrian power established along the coast, the Greeks turned to Egypt as a port of call in the eastern Mediterranean. King Psammetichus encouraged this trade and allowed the Greeks to set up a colony in Egypt. The founders were from the island of Aegina just off the coast of Attica but soon the colony of Naucratus became a joint colony of 12 cities where goods from Greece and other places were exchanged for the products and ideas of the Egyptians. It is important to note that it was soon after the founding of Naucratus that we find the first life size free standing statues being created by Greek artists, a form of art with a very long history in Egypt. Thus, by forcing the Greek traders elsewhere, the Assyrian conquests may have had an impact on Greek artistic developments.

While Corinth came to dominate trade with the west, the city of Miletus on the coast of Anatolia emerged as the great colonizer of the Black Sea area. The changing political situation in the Near East, a need for expanded trade, and the pressures of a growing population probably led to this development. Byzantium was founded by 660 B.C. and Sinope in the middle of the southern coast of the Black Sea was established by 600. Trade with the hinterland including the great plains of Russia became very profitable as the Greeks exchanged their manufactured products—textiles, pottery, iron work, leather goods, jewelry, and art objects—for the region's raw materials—wool, timber, hides, metals, salt fish, and dried fish. As in the case of Italy and the Etruscans, the impact of this penetration of the Greeks into Russia can not be underestimated in the development of civilization in this area.

It was the Greeks along the Anatolian coast who first learned of coined money. They learned from the Lydians who by 700 B.C. had replaced Phrygia as the center of culture and wealth in Anatolia. The legend of King Midas (everything he touched turned to gold) had its origins in the actions of a Phrygian king and the wealth suggested in the story passed to the Lydians. For many years gold and silver had been used for exchange in place of simple barter but the weight and purity of the lump of metal had to be established at each transaction, a slow and time consuming process full of possibilities for cheating. The Lydian king developed the idea of weighing and then stamping lumps of gold with his sign as a guarantee of purity. Later he used a mixture of gold and silver called electrum. The efficiency of the method was obvious and soon the Greek cities of Asia were copying the Lydian practice. The advantage to trade of this simple invention was great and the

impact of increased trade and wealth on the political life of Greece
was even greater. By 600 B.C. a new political situation had developed in Greece.

The developments mentioned above are closely interconnected.
They reflect the impact on Greek history of developments in the
Near East although some of these developments have often been
considered strictly Greek. What ones do you believe are most
clearly related to Near Eastern developments? Be prepared to
explain your choices in class.

Before considering in detail the development of Greek colonies,
let us summarize the Mediterranean situation as it has been developed in this section. Look back at the time chart at the introduction to the section and see if you can identify the events in
the three columns and relate them to each other. You should be
prepared to do this in class discussion. You should also study the
map and be able to locate places mentioned in the text.

The "Dark Ages" in Greece lasted from about 1200 to 800 B.C.
However, about 1,000 B.C. changes began to take place in the
area that were to end the "Dark Ages" and to affect the succeeding
centuries of Greek history. The most important of these changes
beginning about 1,000 B.C. was the movement of Ionian Greeks
from mainland Greece to the coasts of Anatolia. Cities slowly developed and as they established contacts with the inland areas,
they emerged as trading cities. Miletus became the most important
city by 800 B.C. Later, as the trade with the Near East was limited
by Assyrian expansion, Miletus took the lead in the establishment
of colonies along the Black Sea. She had a ready market inland in
Lydia and she used the Lydian invention of coinage to help in her
trade.

In the Near East in 1,000 B.C. Phoenician coastal cities were
developing their inland trade but first Urartu and later Assyria
thwarted these efforts. There was, however, a market in these
states for foreign goods. The cities of Tyre and Sidon turned to
trade with the western Mediterranean and by 812 B.C. Tyre established a colony at Carthage. The Greeks were exposed to Phoenician traders and began to develop their own shipping with the Near
East. Chalcis led in this movement perhaps as she needed raw
material for her metal working industry. Chalcis or other Euboean
cities introduced Greece to the Phoenician alphabet, which made
writing possible; to Near Eastern stories, which influenced the development of Greek literature; and to objects of trade, such as
carved ivory and fancy metal products, which influenced Greek art

and industry. Chalcis turned to the Western Mediterranean for trade and colonization when the exchange port of Al Mina came under Assyrian control. At about this time, Chalcis, Eretria, and Asian Cyme established the first permanent Greek colony in the west at Cumae. Access to the raw metals controlled by the Etruscans was one reason for the establishment of these colonies but changing political and economic conditions at home and abroad also helped precipitate colonization.

The city of Corinth took the lead in western trade and colonization after 700 B.C. as Chalcis became involved in local land warfare. Corinth developed a new type ship, the bireme, and an excellent product, Corinthian "orientalizing style" pottery, which was in great demand overseas. By 600 B.C. there were Greek colonies in the Black Sea area and in the western Mediterranean and the Greeks had established a port in Egypt at Naucratus with the permission of King Psammetichus who had thrown out the Assyrian occupation forces.

By 600 B.C. Assyria had been defeated by the Chaldeans and Medes and there were two new kingdoms to contend with in the Near East. These two people would dominate the history of the area in the next century and have a great impact on the Greeks.

The François Vase

Review this summary and be certain you can add detailed information. For example, you should know what objects were traded and what techniques of political control the Assyrians developed. Your facts plus this summary should provide you with the framework of Mediterranean history between 1,000 and 600 B.C. You should have considerable data about the Greeks in this age of colonization. Now let us take a more detailed look at these colonies, their mother countries, and why they were founded.

Section III—*Patterns of Greek Colonization*

In Section II we mentioned the founding of several colonies by the Greeks. Below there is a list of the most important Greek colonies with their traditional dates of founding and the name of the founding city. Analyze the list. What settlement patterns can you establish? You will want to consider location and founding cities carefully. Be prepared in class to discuss the pattern you have established. Be certain you can locate the starred places on a map. Next, using information in Section II, establish some reasons why the various colonies were established. Analyze the chart for your answers and do not read ahead until you have done the work called for here unless your teacher has given you other instructions.

Date (all are approximate)	Colony	Location	Founding City
753	*Cumae	Italy	*Chalcis, Eretria Asian Cyme
730	Rhegium	Italy	Chalcis, Eretria
	Methone	Chalcidice (3 peninsulas in Northern Aegean)	Chalcis, Eretria
721	Sybaris	Italy	Achaea
734	*Syracuse	Sicily	*Corinth
735 (fall to Corinth in 664)	*Corcyra	Corcyra	Chalcis and Eretria
728	Catana	Sicily	Chalcis
715	Messana	Sicily	Chalcis
705	Taras	Italy	*Sparta
688	Gela	Sicily	Rhodes
660	*Byzantium	Black Sea	Megara
667	Chalcedon	Black Sea	Megara
675	Cyzicus	Black Sea	*Miletus
	Trapezus	Black Sea	Miletus

600	*Sinope	Black Sea	Miletus
640	*Naucratus	Egypt	Miletus and others
609	*Potidaea	Chalcidice	Corinth
630	Cyrene	Egypt	Thera
559	Heraclea	Black Sea	Megara

In considering the material in the chart you probably noted the following:

1—The earliest colonies were founded in Italy and Sicily
2—The earliest colonies were founded by Eretria and Chalcis, cities on the island of Euboea. (They had been involved in Near Eastern trade before this time)
3—Sparta, Achaea, and Corinth also became involved in founding colonies in the west. (All three cities are in the Peloponessus and closer to these colonies than Chalcis and Eretria.)
4—The last colony founded in the west was founded by the island of Rhodes. (It was founded just before there was a wave of settlement in the Black Sea area.)
5—The Black Sea colonies were all founded by Megara or Miletus. (Megara thus controlled the entrance to the Black Sea the way Chalcis controlled the straits between Sicily and Italy. Such control means the possibility of taxing shipping.)
6—Chalcis founded colonies in the west and in Chalcidice in the 8th century while Corinth founded colonies in these two areas in the 7th century. Miletus founded colonies in the Black Sea region and in Egypt. These are the only three cities that had colonies in two regions. (It might be assumed that they were therefore the most important commercial cities of the 8th and 7th centuries B.C.)

Looking over the material not in parenthesis, a pattern of settlement seems to emerge. This pattern seems to indicate that the Greek cities established their colonies at different times and in different areas and that they divided the areas to be colonized between them. Does this seem familiar to you from other periods in history? Do you recall ever studying the establishment of colonies in the New World by the Spaniards, Portuguese, French. English, and Dutch? If so, you may remember how Spanish colonization took place after Portuguese exploration and that the English and the Dutch were late arrivals on the colonizing stage. There were good reasons for this pattern in the development of the New World. Now, if you have considered the material in Section II perhaps you have developed some theories as to why the above pattern was followed in the establishment of Greek colonies.[9]

One possible explanation of the different founding dates of the colonies is connected with the amount of contact the founder had with the Near East. This contact would stimulate trade and economic development and Chalcis is an example of this phenomenon.

A second consideration would be the shifting needs and wants of society. As prosperity increased, trade was no longer confined to leather, metal products, and cloth from Greece in exchange for raw materials such as lumber, corn, hides, and raw metal. Luxury items were wanted and colonies around the Black Sea had access to amber, furs, and gold. Thus as tastes changed, the pattern of colonization changed.

A third factor would be the location of the founding city. As trade and colonization developed in the Black Sea area, Miletus emerged as a major city. The little city of Megara between Athens and Corinth capitalized on her location when trade and colonization in the western Mediterranean was important.

An excellent example of the importance of location is Corinth. Her location as a middleman between east and west set the stage for her emergence as a trading and colonizing city. She became the most important Greek city of the 7th century. She had ports on both the Gulf of Corinth to the west and the Saronic Gulf to the east and her great ruler, the tyrant Periander, built a road across the narrow isthmus of Corinth on which boats could be pulled from one gulf to the other. This location made it easy to have colonies in both east and west. In addition to location, Corinth had the advantage of developing a highly popular manufactured product—her very distinctive and often copied pottery in the "orientalizing style." A great market developed for this style pottery and, in theory, colonies protect trade routes and markets.

The role played by Corinth may remind you of the role of Great Britain in the 19th century when, as a trading nation producing distinctive manufactured goods, she established a world

---

[9] Some students may be familiar with the 19th century colonization of Africa and they may be able to make parallels to that.

wide colonial empire. Many of the conditions that led to British domination—location, crowded living conditions, political tensions that led to new institutions, a growth in manufacturing, the rivalry of other colonial powers, and the ability to learn from others and do a better job than they were doing—were present in Corinth.

So far in considering the reasons for this movement towards colonization, we have considered individual city states and the colonies they set up. It was noted that the first colony in the west was a joint effort of Chalcis, Eretria and Asian Cyme. The colony at Cumae flourished under this joint sponsorship but we also noted that the first war recorded in Greek history after the Mycenaean age took place between two of these founding cities, Chalcis and Eretria. They struggled for control of the small plain that separated them because of the need for food and for a sense of control over borders.

As mentioned above this struggle for power or domination of others is a recurrent theme in Greek history. No unified nation appeared on the Greek peninsula until it was forced upon the Greek inhabitants by outsiders. Cooperation between the various city states on joint efforts was apparent several times but no lasting unified approach to political or economic matters emerged among the Greeks. There were many great political ideas developed by different Greek city states but a concept of national unity was not one of them. The Greeks knew they were of the same blood. They spoke the same language and worshipped the same gods. They even stopped war with a truce in order to celebrate games to the gods together but that is as far as the cooperation went. Scholars have seen in the colonization an indication of this rivalry and lack of unity. They have suggested that two groupings, too loose to call alliances, emerged during the colonizing period. Thucydides as early as 400 B.C. indicated that the city states of Greece first took sides at the time of the war between Chalcis and Eretria and this division or some form of it continued with only minor changes within the alliances throughout Greek history. This theory supplies us with a new pattern or explanation of why the colonies were founded. Let us look at it more closely.

The development of this commercial-colonial rivalry reflects the political development of unified city states. In Section II we discussed how the villages united and people occupying a small plain developed the land on the hills. Borders became important as the territory of one polis touched that of another and the need for cultivated land was crucial. Under these conditions the neighboring state became the natural enemy and the rivalry was extended overseas and to the neighbor's friends. Thus, Megara emerges as the natural enemy of her neighbor Corinth, and later of Athens. At first this enmity was directed towards Corinth as Corinth was both a neighbor and an overseas rival. Athens, who until 600 B.C. was not involved in colonization, became an ally of Corinth, the enemy of Megara and so it went. What emerges is a world divided into rival groups engaged in small scale struggles. During the 7th century B.C. Miletus, Eretria, Megara, Aegina, Argos and Messenia emerge as one group opposed to Samos, Chalcis, Corinth, Athens, Sparta, and Elis. You can copy these two lists pairing the poleis off—Miletus vs. Samos, etc.—and then locate them on a map. Do you see the geographic reasons why a rivalry might develop between these paired cities? Do you think this rivalry supplies a good explanation as to when colonies were founded? Do nations who are neighbors have to be rivals? What evidence do you have from other periods of history that help in a discussion of this question? The Greek rivalries led to the growing strength of some city states, for example, Corinth in the west and Miletus in the Black Sea area. Some cities faded in power as the struggles proved too much for their resources and this is apparently what happened to Chalcis and Eretria. By 600 B.C. Corinth and Miletus had emerged as the major cities of Greece. Athens was not yet important. Sparta, the other major city of the 5th century B.C., had founded one colony but she became involved in unusual internal developments in the Peloponnesus and was not an active participant in the colonial development.

Section IV—*Further Reasons for Colonization*

So far we have explored many aspects of colonization. Let us now consider what was happening internally in Sparta. Then we'll see how this compares to the internal developments of the poleis deeply involved in colonization. From this perhaps we can deduce further domestic causes of Greek colonization.

The inhabitants of the plain of Laconia in the south eastern Peloponnesus united and established their central city at Sparta just as other Greek villages were consolidated around a central point during the age of colonization. In this process several important things happened at Sparta. First, a class structure was confirmed. The old aristocracy, the Spartiates, descendants of the Dorian tribes that came into the Peloponnesus after 1200 B.C. and seized control of the land, maintained their supremacy. They, unlike the old aristocracy in many poleis, were able to retain control throughout the age and this control was codified in law by the reforms attributed to Lycurgus. The descendants of the original inhabitants were forced to remain as workers or serfs on the land. They were called Helots. They worked the land for the Spartiates. Between the two classes of Spartiates and Helots a third class emerged, the Periocei. They were the traders and merchants of Sparta. Perhaps they were descendants of the Mycenaean Greeks or of the leading families of some of the villages of the Laconian plain which Sparta absorbed.   The Periocei class was always important but never gained control of the government as the merchants did in many city states. This Spartan class structure was to continue throughout her history.

Second, Sparta conquered her neighbor. Rather than turn overseas for new lands for her growing population and for new sources of wealth, Sparta attacked Messenia, her western neighbor and her "natural enemy" on the other side of the Taygetus Mountains. Sparta conquered Messenia by 720 B.C. Sparta's military advantage was great. She controlled the mountain passes and the only Messenian defensive positions were on the far side of the valley. Even so, the Messenians revolted about 630 B.C. and it took Sparta 20 years to crush the rebellion. Sparta had aid from Athens in doing so which is an interesting point considering the later rivalry of the two cities. The impact of this revolt on Sparta was great.   Sparta became very conservative and turned in on herself to develop protective policies at a time that other Greek city states were turning outward and overseas developing new economic and political ideas.

Third, Sparta remained predominantly agricultural and did not develop extensive trade or industry. With good soil in both the Messenian and Laconian (the land around the city of Sparta) plains, she was quite self sufficient. Whether this was what made it possible for the aristocracy of the Spartiates to remain in power we are not certain but it would seem likely.

Fourth, Sparta which had a brilliant tradition of art and music up to 650 B.C. gave up the arts for concentration on other matters. Early Spartan sculpture was as fine as any contemporary works found in Greece but the tradition was abandoned as Sparta turned conservative and focused her concerns on keeping the Helots under control.

Fifth, Sparta did not build a defensive position on an acropolis. She had a garrison at Sparta but she relied on her soldiers, her own military prowess, to defend the plain.

Finally, Sparta evolved a governmental structure different from most of Greece. Sparta did not abolish the kingship, as did so many poleis, nor did she turn it into a symbolic office. Instead, Sparta established a dual kingship with the idea that one king would always lead the army and the other would remain at home to oversee domestic developments. The Spartan constitution and government structure of 600 B.C. reflected a conservatism that was not found elsewhere in the Greek world at that time. The Spartan way was admired by many Greeks who did not wish to follow it themselves.

The reason usually given for the uniqueness of the Spartans is the fact they conquered Greek lands rather than colonized distant areas. What do you think of that as an explanation for uniqueness? The Spartans did not become deeply involved in founding colonies founding only the one at Taras. Perhaps the need to control the Messenians took all their energy and the territory of Messenia provided the land needed for growth. Sparta remained a conservative center in a rapidly changing world.

If Sparta was unique, what was the usual pattern of domestic evolution and how did it relate to colonization?

In 750 B.C. it would have been difficult to set Sparta apart from the other Greek poleis as unique. In most poleis the old aristocracy was well established, the position of king or overlord dating from Mycenaean times was weakened and a class structure was clearly present. The consolidation of small towns of a plain into a centralized poleis as described above was well advanced if not completed. Unlike at Sparta, the new political center would have a natural acropolis for defense. The need to consolidate about an easily defensible position such as the Athenian acropolis was perhaps first precipitated by the danger from wandering tribes. As suggested above another reason for the movement towards consolidated political authority may have been the pressure of a growing population or of struggles within the clans that made up the tribe of each inhabited valley. What ever the causes for this change, by 750 B.C. the aristocrats, which in Greek means the "good or best," in many areas of Greece controlled consolidated poleis each of which dominated a valley.

Some scholars suggest that the poor quality of Greek soil and its rapid exhaustion by poor farming methods forced poleis to trade and colonize. Combined with this was limited technical knowledge which produced only a very light and simple plow which could not turn the soil over deeply. These factors led to pressures for more land which was satisfied by either going to the hills or to new colonies. The aristocracy encouraged the latter because they thought they could control the polis if the more daring and radical citizens were sent away to new colonies but this backfired.

The basis of aristocratic wealth and authority was their control of large amounts of land and with this control a new element was introduced into Greek society—people without land. Thus, the class structure of 750 B.C. begins to emerge. All societies have a class structure and the structure of Mycenaean Greece is clearly reflected in the Linear "B" tablets from Pylos. This structure, in which the king or wanax always held "land for the people", had been destroyed and a landless or "mean" class now existed with three options open to them. One group hired themselves out as farm laborers, a situation of serfdom not far removed from slavery and similar to the serfs of Sparta. A second group either were able to hold on to small private holdings or went to unclaimed land in the hills and staked out claims and were able to make a living on their own land in this way. They formed a class of independent or yeoman farmers—citizens of the polis but with little or no power in 750 B.C.

As the city grew, economic activity increased and became more specialized. A third option emerged for the "mean". They could become craftsmen. These people produced the products that supported the growing level of culture and civilized life. These early craftsmen had no protection from the city or the aristocrats who controlled the political power. In each city state there was also a slave class originally formed from captives in war but as the complexity and luxury of life increased slave trade developed to supply the house servants and farm hands needed. The extent of slavery in the age of colonization varied from city to city. There is some thought that the lot of the slave was much better than that of the hired farm hand or the city craftsman. Slaves were property and as such were valuable to the owner who would treat them well enough to keep them alive. There was no such concern for the local free man in the Greek world of 750 B.C. This then was the social structure of Greece in 750 B.C.

The aristocracy based their power on land. The land gave them the wealth to supply themselves the weapons required for military action and they owned the horses upon which much of the military activity of that age depended. The new hoplite military techniques of the Near East mentioned above had not yet been introduced into Greece. The small landowners, the hired hands, the craftsmen, and the slaves all making up the "mean" elements of society had little to offer politically or socially yet their economic contributions would destroy this world in the next 200 years as trade and colonization developed and as a whole new view of the universe and of the role of man in it emerged. Sparta, however, would not change. Her class structure remained as described above.

The aristocracies of many city states viewed colonization as a great help to them in controlling the city. They could sponsor colonies and encourage all the dissident elements of the city to go away. It also relieved the population pressure on the city and created new wealth. Raw material shipped back for processing by the city craftsmen created new products that could bring wealth to the poleis and particularly the aristocrats who controlled the trade. Thus, the aristocratic governments encouraged colonization and even Sparta sent out one colony, but unlike other poleis, Sparta did not pursue this policy.

The actual planting of a colony was a private enterprise in the Greek world. The oecist or founder gathered together the new colonists. They often came from more than one city although one city or polis was considered the mother city and it was from here that the oecist took a brand from the sacred fire to kindle the holy flame in the colony. The speech or dialect of the new city was that of the mother city as were the religion and customs. The oecist was later viewed as the founder of the city and the lawgiver. Each colony was unique and, unlike colonies founded by European nations since the 15th century A.D., it was a new polis—a fully independent state. The only *official* tie to the mother colony was one of sentiment. There was no political connection although it was traditional that if the colony wished to plant a new colony of its own, it would turn to the mother city to supply an oecist. Also, since the mother city supplied ships and helped to fight off encroachments from other cities, she had a clear influence in the new polis. The economic relationship was only that which benefitted both the colony and the mother city.[10]

[10] Although as noted above there was extensive competition present in the founding of the colonies and the rivalries of the city states led to military

There were many advantages in this relationship but there was also potential danger to the established political authorities of the Greek mainland—the aristocracies. New ideas developed among the new cities; ideas of the value of each person in the society and the potential contribution of each person to the society; ideas that wealth was not to be measured only in land but also in material goods and money as well as individual ability; ideas that traditions did not have to be followed but that new views and interpretations might better meet new situations; ideas of art styles and new intellectual stimulation. These ideas were brought back to the mainland and destroyed the established patterns of life and class structure that existed at the start of the age of colonization. By the end of the age of colonization an entirely new political and economic situation existed in the Aegean area.

skirmishes, there was a degree of orderliness in the colonization process. This was the contribution of the priests of the religious shrine at Delphi. The original oracular shrine of greatest importance for the Greeks was the shrine at Dodona in the northwestern mountains of Epirus. Here priests of Zeus handed down advice to the Greek people but the location was inconvenient as the center of population shifted towards Athens and the Peloponnesus. At Delphi there had been a Mycenaean shrine and perhaps a Minoan one according to archaeological evidence. By 700 B.C. this shrine with its priests of Apollo had become the most important place in the disunified Greek world. The highly organized arrangements allowed anyone seeking advice to come and contact the priests. The god, Apollo, gave advice through a priestess who went into a trance and spoke words that only the priests could interpret. For a fee all kinds of advice could be had and, for the oecist planning a new city, the advice could be invaluable. Delphi became a great clearning house of knowledge about the developments throughout the Mediterranean and the priests could arrange the words of the priestess to convey the latest information to the men seeking to found new cities. In addition one could find in the restaurants, rooming places, and bars of the neighboring village people from all over the world with knowledge of the best sea routes, harbors, friendly natives who would welcome a Greek settlement as a source of new products, and location of other new colonies that had met with either success or trouble. In return for its role as a clearning house for crucial information, Delphi grew to be the richest and most important shrine and the symbolic center of the unity the Greeks never achieved in actuality.

It must have been an exciting place in the 7th century B.C. and the fact that a foreign ruler such as Midas of Phrygia consulted the priestess and donated a gold throne to the god attests to the worldwide importance of the shrine as well as to its wealth. The Delphic oracle continued to be important until closed by the Christian emperor Theodosius after 500 A.D. but it lost much of its prestige and power as the "foreign office" of the Greek world when the priests supported the losing side in the Persian War of the early 5th century B.C. Before that, however, with the help and advice of the Delphic oracle many oecists set out from the mainland to found successful and ultimately extremely wealthy colonies which sent rich gifts back to Delphi.

The frontier of the Greek world, a frontier that was scattered about the entire Mediterranean and Black Sea basins had an impact on Greek life as great as the impact the frontier has had on the development of American life and institutions according to the celebrated thesis of Frederick Jackson Turner.[11]

The impact of these ideas were gradual but by the middle of the 7th century B.C. a new form of political organization appeared in the more important trading cities. The old aristocracy was being overthrown in these cities and in their place the political power was being taken by tyrants. The Greek meaning of the word tyrant does not have the negative connotations associated with the word in English. The Greek tyrants often worked for the benefit of the "mean" elements in the society aiding the craftsmen, the small farmers, and the struggling tradesmen. They gained support from these groups and seized the government. Then they ruled almost as a dictator to benefit those groups involved in the new economic activity. Sparta by-passed this stage of development and remained under the control of the old aristocracy—the Spartiates. We will investigate further the role and impact of the tyrants on Greek history in Chapter IV where 6th and early 5th century history will be considered. This period is often referred to as "The Age of the Tyrants" just as 7th and 8th century Greek history is often considered "The Age of Colonization."

Sparta shared two problems of the age but again she found different solutions. The first was a growing population that put pressure on the area controlled by each poleis. Many scholars suggest that population pressure was the primary reason for colonization but that appears a very modern concern. It is true, however, that the population of Greece increased during the age of colonization and this certainly created problems as it does today. Sparta conquered Messenia to gain new land while most poleis sent their surplus population to colonies.

A second problem that affected the entire Aegean area was a growing inflation. This forced farmers and craftsmen to borrow at high interest rates in order to buy seeds and raw materials. Eventually many were forced into debt and came under the control of the richer members of society. The more daring no doubt became

[11]See Turner "The Significance of the Frontier in American History." A particularly good presentation is found in the D.C. Heath Problems in American Civilization series where the pros and cons of the thesis are discussed in the pamphlet *The Turner Thesis* ed. G. R. Taylor.

the settlers of colonies but many stayed in the poleis where the gap between the new rich and the poor widened. The introduction of money speeded the process and this split in wealth provided one foundation for the age of tyrants who championed the poor. Sparta attempted to control inflation by outlawing gold coinage and using iron instead and requiring that no Spartiate participate in trade. This conservative decision further widened the gap between Sparta and the other poleis.

We have seen how most of Greece differed from the Spartans in their evolving governmental structure and their committment to trade and colonization. All Greece had been much alike in government and class structure about 750 B.C. Except in Sparta colonization, trade, and increasing wealth precip itated changes in these institutions. Sparta, with large areas for farming, remained agricultural while many areas of Greece turned to industry and trade.

Section V—*The End of Colonization*

As is evident from the list of colonies given in Section III, there were few colonies founded after 600 B.C. Many of the internal conditions that had led to colonization had changed by this time but there were still people who would have left for new cities if it had been possible. Wealth was not evenly distributed and although the political forms had changed there was oppression of some groups and classes. There was still not enough land for everyone and the living conditions for many of the craftsmen had not improved much but the age of colonization slowly came to an end during the first half of the 6th century. What were the reasons?

As we did in looking at the start of colonization, the place to look is away from the Aegean area. By 550 B.C. several events of major significance had occurred. In the western Mediterranean there had been extensive colonization and several of the colonies in Sicily, such as Gela, were founding colonies of their own along the southern coast of Sicily at such places as Acragas. This meant that many of the best locations had already been taken.

Another factor was the growing strength of the Old Phoenician colony of Carthage. Carthage had extended her control along the north coast of Africa and had colonies of her own in Spain. She had converted Phoenician trading bases in western Sicily into colonies. Within two generations these colonies and Carthage would engage the Greek settlements of Sicily in a major war that ended any hope for Greek expansion in that area in the 5th century.

At the same time the Etruscans in northern Italy were blocking any expansion in that area and about 507 B.C. a new power began to emerge in central Italy which would eventually take over and impose political unity on the Greek world while absorbing much of her culture. The new power was Rome. The city threw out her kings in 507 B.C. as many Greek cities had done about 200 years earlier. Rome established an aristocratic government which later was transformed into the Roman republic.

While colonization was thus being checked in the west, developments in the Near East and Egypt made expansion in that direction impossible. The Medes who with the Chaldeans had defeated the empire of Assyria in 612 B.C. united with the Persians and they gained control of Anatolia. By 545 B.C. the new Persian Empire had defeated the Kingdom of Lydia and had become the neighbor of the coastal Greek cities of Anatolia. The happy position of Miletus as a middleman between the interior of Anatolia and the Near East and Black Sea regions disappeared as a Near Eastern power was now encamped on the borders of the Ionian cities. The Persians under Darius I in 512 B.C. mounted a campaign that crossed the Bosporus and reached the Danube blocking any further Greek expansion in that direction. This clearly indicated the expansionist quality of the Persian Empire and provided a foretaste of the events on the Greek mainland in the early 5th century.

Earlier the Chaldeans or Neo-Babylonians mentioned above in Section II spread their power southward wiping out the Hebrew Kingdom of Judah in 586 B.C. This marked the end of an independent Hebrew nation as the leaders were all taken to Babylon as captives—an event of major importance in Biblical history but one that is hardly mentioned in a general history involving the changing empires of the Near East.

The Neo-Babylonian control was short lived as their former allies, the Medes now absorbed in the Persian Empire, turned on them. The city of Babylon was captured in 538 B.C. and so another empire ended. Persia went on to conquer Egypt in 525 B.C. Persia thus became the greatest empire the Near East had known controlling Anatolia, Egypt, and all the Near East from the Mediterranean to the edges of modern Pakistan. With the choice sites for colonies taken, with Persia in control of the Near East and Anatolia, with Carthage blocking the western Mediterranean, and with emerging Rome and the Etruscans stopping expansion to the north the age of Greek colonization came to an end in the early years of the 6th century. Internal forces might have kept it going for longer but the external situation of the Mediterranean world stopped it. The Greeks in the 6th century were forced to develop their own civilization based upon the world they had settled in the previous two centuries. During this century and the all important 5th century of Greek history, the Greeks had to reckon with the power of Persia and Carthage. We will return to these foreign struggles, but before we do we will consider in Chapter III the evolution of Greek art and how it reflected developments in Greece.

Section VI—*Review*

There has been a great deal of information presented in this chapter and much of it may seem unrelated. There are beneath the details patterns that can be imposed upon the material. We attempted one such pattern in the exercise of dating the colonies. Another pattern that was mentioned briefly is that of a parallel to the colonization of the new world in the history of western civilization. The emergence of patterns does *not* mean that history repeats itself but it may indicate that when certain conditions of human existence are present, people with certain attitudes and values about life will react in *similar* ways.

There are three methods of review suggested for this chapter. If your teacher has not given you specific directions, you should decide which method is most meaningful to you and follow it.

Review Number 1: Go back to the time chart at the start of Section II and add to it the colonies listed at the start of Section III. Be prepared to relate the events in the time chart to the founding of the colonies. Of course, you should be able to locate all the places mentioned.

Review Number 2: Be prepared to do the following—some of the questions appeared in the text of this chapter.

1. Locate on a blank map the most important places included in this chapter. (Below is a list of places mentioned in the chapter.) Write at least one sentence indicating something significant about *each* place in the "Age of Colonization."
2. What did the Greeks gain from their contacts with Phoenicians?
3. What united the Greeks during the "Age of Colonization"?

4. What impact did the conquests of Assyria have on the Greek world?
5. Describe the relation between a Greek colony and the mother country.
6. Why did Corinth emerge as such an important city in the "Age of Colonization"?
7. Describe the political and economic situation in Sparta in the "Age of Colonization".
8. What was the class structure of Greek poleis about 750 B.C.?
9. What events brought about the end of the "Age of Colonization"?

Review Number 3: Compare the Greek "Age of Colonization" with the period of the Renaissance and colonization of the New World. You may desire to do additional research on this matter or you may find there is enough information given here to establish a basic comparison. Another pattern to help explain colonization should evolve from this exercise.

When western man embarked on new world colonization, he was experiencing what has been called the Renaissance. The Renaissance has been defined as a rebirth of Greek and Roman ideas put together in a new form by the people of the Italian peninsula and later by all of Europe. It was not a repetition of the history of Greece and Rome because a new and important element had been added—Christianity and its 1400 year history—but there were many conditions that parallel and recall Greek history of the "Age of Colonization". Some of these conditions were:

1. The emergence of city states in Italy controlled by powerful aristocracies some based on wealth (ex. Venice) but more often based on the strength of individuals who could deal with changing conditions. These individuals were called condottiere (ex. Francesco Sforza in Milan.)
2. Developing trade with the Far and Near East (ex. Portugal, Venice.)
3. Renewed interest in art, and other creative work that can only be accomplished after the basic necessities of life are filled (ex. Leonardo da Vinci, Florence in the age of the Medici.)
4. The development of new political concepts which in the west of Europe led to the concept of a unified national state (ex. Tudor England under Henry VIII and Elizabeth.)
5. New technical developments that allowed for more extensive voyages at sea (ex. compass.)

6. New thoughts about the universe and man's place in it (ex. Galileo, Copernicus.)
7. Emerging alliances between states to suppress the power of a neighbor (ex. alliances formed by Italian city states to oppose the invasion of Italy by Charles VIII of France in 1494.)
8. The previous period of history appeared less advanced and of less interest (ex. the period before the Renaissance is called the "Dark Ages".)
9. Government support for overseas expansion and colonization (ex. Prince Henry the Navigator of Portugal, Henry VII of England's support of the voyages of Cabot.)
10. Development of warfare between rival colonizers (ex. the attack of the Spanish Armada on England in 1588, English conquest of the Dutch in New York.)

Look at the above list of events in Renaissance Europe and find a parallel to each in the history of Greek colonization. As a special project, some class member or members might be interested in seeking evidence from other civilizations of periods of colonization. Is this a phenomenon confined to Greek and Western civilization? Or does this reaching out and establishing control over other lands reflect an aspect of human nature? This is certainly a complicated but important question that you may find interesting to investigate.

In addition to the methods for review suggested above there are many places mentioned in the chapter that you should be able to locate on a map. The following places have been mentioned. Those with stars are particularly important.

Samos	Urartu	*Byzantium
*Miletus	Gades	*Sinope
Damascus	*Carthage	*Syracuse
Israel	Ugarit (Ras Shamra)	*Corcyra
Tyre	Al Mina (Posidium)	*Naucratus
Sidon	*Chalcis	*Potidaea
Byblos	*Cumae	*Sparta
Assyria	Halys River	*Corinth
Chalcidice	Gulf of Corinth	Saronic Gulf

In the chapter a number of words with special meanings for Greek history were introduced. You should know the definition given in the text for each of the following words.

clan	bireme	Periocei
tribe	olympiad	"yeoman farmer"
polis, poleis	electrum	the "mean"
aristocracy	Spartiates	oecist
hoplite	Helot	tyrant

The following books are suggested if you wish to do further research on the Greek "Age of Colonization". You should consult your library's card catalogue or your librarian for suggestions of books on the Renaissance and the period of western colonization that followed if you plan to do Review Number 3.

Burn, A. R. *The Lyric Age of Greece*. N.Y., St. Martin's Press, 1960.

Bury, J. B. *History of Greece*. London, Macmillan, 1963.

Gordon, C. H. *The Ancient Near East*. N.Y., W. W. Norton & Co., 1953

Grant, Michael. *The Ancient Mediterranean*. N.Y. Charles Scribners and Sons, 1969.

. . . *Horizon Book of Lost Worlds*. ed. Horizon Editors, N.Y., American Heritage Publishing Co., 1962.

Rice, T. T. *The Scythians*. N.Y., Frederick A. Praeger, 1957.

Vermeule, Emily. *Greece in the Bronze Age*. Chicago, University of Chicago Press, 1964.

Warmington, B. H. *Carthage*. N.Y., Frederick A. Praeger, 1960.

Woodhead, A. G. *The Greeks in the West*. London, Thames & Hudson 1962.

CHAPTER III

ART AND THE GREEKS

Section I–*Introduction*

We have considered the history of the Aegean area during the "Dark Ages" and the "Age of Colonization." It should be clear that the history of this period was complex and the area and the people in it underwent many changes. In the period between 600 and 323 B.C. ancient Greek or Hellenic civilization reached its peak and during those 277 years—a hundred years less time than the history of English speaking settlements in the Americas—many changes in attitudes and values took place among the Greeks. Probably more changes occurred than occurred in the Aegean in the previous 1,000 years. What were some of these changes? Most of this book will focus on the chronological political and military changes of these 277 years but before we do that, we will take a look at the overall development of that time span as seen in the art of the period.

Mycenaean frescos and pottery styles attest to an ability and interest in art. The palaces of Pylos, Mycenae, and Tiryns indicate an interest in architecture. Thus the Greeks by 600 B.C. had a long history of artistic expression. Many consider the culmination of this long development, the sculpture, architecture, pottery, and literature of the 5th century produced throughout the Hellenic world but especially in Athens, the finest artistic production of mankind. What were some of these works? What do they indicate about the Greeks who produced them? Why are they considered so fine?

We will explore these questions in this chapter but first let us see how the art of a period already studied might indicate or reflect what was happening at the time of its creation. In the last chapter we mentioned Corinthian "orientalizing style" pottery. Do you recall what was said? Check back and see what you can find in the last chapter that might relate the development of the age to this pottery style.

Obviously, the name of the style is a give away. Orientalizing (orient meaning the east) indicates there was an inspiration of some form from the Near East. The decorations on the pots were full of rosettes and sphinxes and other designs inspired by eastern art.

The extensive trade of the age and the place of Corinth as the leader in this trade is reflected in the quantity of pottery produced in Corinth and found around the Mediterranean from Egypt to Etruria.

We can discover, when we can recognize the pottery of an age, many economic factors about the age just as we can learn a great deal from any economic production. Pottery and art can reveal many other factors. With study, careful analysis, and sophistication one can develop an ability to relate artistic expression to the mood of the people. For example, Corinthian vases were covered with patterns and the colors were purples and reds on a tan color background. The colors are exciting and the patterns are intricate. The entire vase is covered with designs. Study the picture of the Corinthian vase on page 39. What would lead a people to express themselves in this way? Does it seem to you that the bright colors and the desire to cover the pot with designs would express sadness, depression or exuberance—a desire to show the world what the artist could do? This latter is what many people believe. They sense that the artists working in the Corinthian style were proud of what they could produce; they wanted to express their new sense of power and economic prosperity to the world. Thus, the conclusion is that in looking at designs and artistic expression, one can learn what the mood and feelings of a people were when they produced such works. This viewpoint is not agreed to by all scholars and you may wish to debate it in class.

There is a corollary to this idea of art indicating the mood of a people which is often debated and should be considered by you before going on with this chapter. The corollary is that art *reflects* the age in which it is produced.

There is strong opinion among other scholars that art does not reflect an age but *leads* it. Their point is that the great artists of any culture are sensitive and feeling individuals and they do not relate to the common mass of a society. Their art reflects what they personally feel and think and not what the masses feel or want. They are really not of their age but are leaders of it expressing what will often not be accepted or if accepted, will not be profitable or accepted by many until after they are dead. Artists themselves often express this sentimental feeling that they are not accepted in their own age. However, many people feel rejected and alienated from the society in which they live and are still very much a part of that society. An alienated artist may be very much a part of an age. Therefore, in my opinion this argument can be used to support the original contention that artists, including the true individual artist, do reflect the age, moods, and attitudes of the people living in their time. An artist may not be accepted but he produces works that reflect the basic viewpoints of the people living as his contemporaries.

Let us illustrate this with modern examples. The "pop" art of Andy Warhol and the abstract work of a Jackson Pollock reflect certain basic attitudes of mid-twentieth century America. Add the work of Andrew Wyeth, who paints very realistic, almost photographic, scenes far different from the other two painters, to the group. What do you have? How can such different artists reflect the society? The answer seems to me to be that we are a greatly torn and diversified society and our artists reflect it very well in their paintings. "Pop" art's tomato soup cans, Pollock's drippings of paint on canvas which convey to me a totally disintregated concept of the world, and Wyeth's painfully realistic pictures of individuals and farm scenes represent extremes of art style. What could be more reflective of the United States today than such diversity? Do these artists seem to be leading our society? It is hard for me as an historian to accept this viewpoint. Perhaps this is the root of the disagreement as to whether artists lead or reflect a society. The artists see their roles as leaders and the historian looking back at events use the artists as reflectors of their society and the conditions in it. What do you think? You may wish to consider several artists of the Italian Renaissance, artists such as Michelangelo, Leonardo Da Vinci or Raphael and relate their artistic expressions to their age. This would follow naturally on the Renaissance exercise at the end of the last chapter. Whether you pursue this discussion further with research or simply go on with our discussion of Greek art, be certain to consider the two sides of the argument before class and be prepared to express your opinion on the matter. You should have clearly in your own mind what you believe before going on with the assignments in Section II. Which side you take is not going to affect the exercise but you should know upon what assumptions you are operating before you try analysing Greek sculpture.

What we will do in the next three sections is discuss and take a look at some Greek art of the period between c. 650 and c. 325 B.C. We are doing this at this point in the text to provide us with an overview of the development of the Greeks. We are assuming that you can learn from their artistic expression a great deal about them as a people and as a civilization. Once this overview has been established, we will go back and fill in some of the details.

We are introducing another medium, another discipline—art criticism—that the historian can use in gaining a sense of the past. At some time you have probably used literature to learn about the past either with historical novels, biographies, or perhaps poetry and essays. What can you learn from art? One warning, you do not have to be an artist to appreciate and see what is in a work of art. All you need are good eyes, sensitivity to what is presented, and a willingness to explore all possibilities and speculate.[1]

Section II—*Greek Sculpture*

Very little large scale sculpture from the Aegean area has been found that dates before 650 B.C. Perhaps large stone statues were made and later destroyed since it is difficult to hide life size statuary whereas small six to twenty inch statues are easily buried. We may find some large statues but, with the exception of a few highly stylized, marble statues representing female goddesses found on the Cyclades islands and dating from c. 2500 B.C. we have no marble statues over four feet high from the Minoan or Mycenaean periods or from the "Dark Ages". The Greeks began to carve six to nine foot high marble statues of humans during the latter part of the "Age of Colonization." In the chapter you will find pictures of six such statues with closeups of the heads of three of them. These statues represent changing styles in Greek art during a 250 year period. Statues of males were chosen for two reasons. First, there are more of them which perhaps reflects the male dominance in Greek life. Second, females in Greek sculpture until the 4th century B.C. were usually portrayed clothed whereas males usually were shown nude. It is easier for an amateur

[1] There are many excellent art books which provide illustrations for what is discussed here. There are slides available from museums and filmstrips from several manufacturers. If you have access to any of these or if you can visit a museum with a collection of classical Greek art, do so, preferably after you have completed this chapter. Several well illustrated, inexpensive art books are suggested at the end of the chapter. The *Life* magazine reprints on Greece and the *Life* filmstrip on Athens and the "History Through Art" filmstrip series produced by Warren Schloat are helpful. Many school libraries now have filmstrips in their collections. Be sure to check your school library for such items.

to analyze and understand the changes in the presentation of physique than to analyze the changing dress styles which were peculiar to Greek civilization. Standing male statues of the archaic or early period of Greek art are referred to as Kouroi (singular—Kouros). You may wish to use the term in the following assignment.

Assignment: Look at the nine pictures of statues. Then read the following questions and write a paper answering the questions. Depending on the instructions from your teacher, you may answer each question separately or write one essay incorporating your answers to all nine questions so that you do not need to repeat ideas. Each picture is numbered. Refer to the numbers in identifying the works in your paper. Most students can do an excellent analysis in under three pages, but ask your teacher about paper length. Do *not* seek additional information or read Appendix B until after you have completed your paper. This is an exercise of your powers of observation and analysis. It is not an exercise in library research. When you have handed in the paper, you may wish to check your ideas in other sources.

Questions:
1. What is the order (time sequence) in which the statues were created? Explain your reasons for placing them in this order.
2. What change or development in style and presentation do you see?
3. What evidence is there in the statues that might indicate an influence from other peoples and/or areas?
4. What do you see in the statues that might make them distinctly Greek? Use any information you already have to answer this question—ideas from this text, information from myths you have read, from other books or courses, from a study of art, from movies you have seen, etc. Treat the statues individually and/or as a group.
5. Explain who or what you think these statues represent. Again use all the evidence you have without research.
6. What can you deduce about Greek thought, life, and attitudes from these statues? Speculate and use specific evidence from the statues and from every source you already have to support your hypotheses. Be certain to trace changes or developments that you see reflected and do not treat the statues as a group but as individual works created in the progression you established for question #1.

7. What changes in Greek thought, life, and attitudes do you see reflected in these statues?
8. Which statue(s) do you like the most? Why?
9. Would statues of this type be created in America today? Why? Explain.

You should come to class prepared to discuss your paper and your ideas. If you have any questions about the exercise, be certain to raise them in the class discussion. We will not indicate any answers to the questions here but in the chapter some points may become obvious. Your teacher may make a special assignment concerning material in Appendix B which you should not read until assigned.

Fig. 1

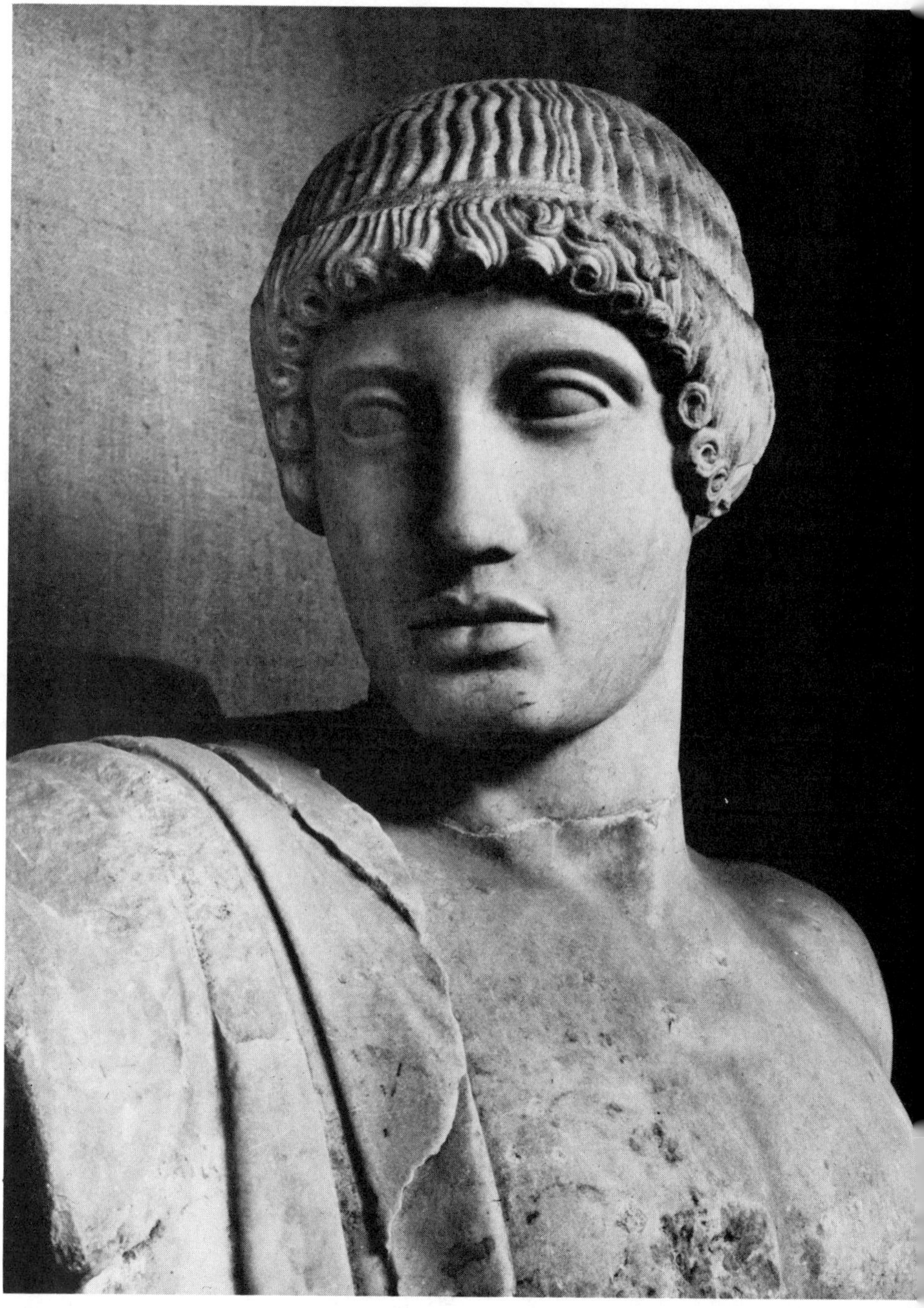

Fig. 2

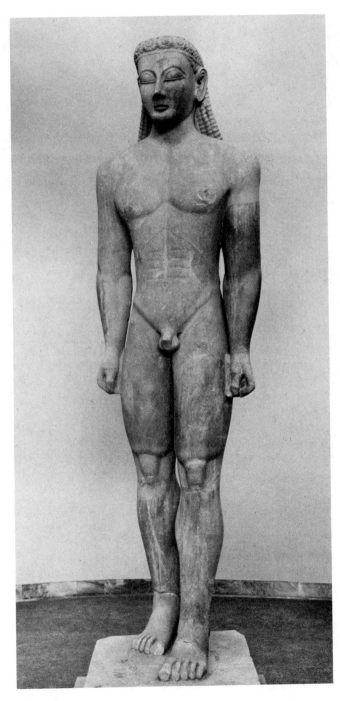

Fig. 3

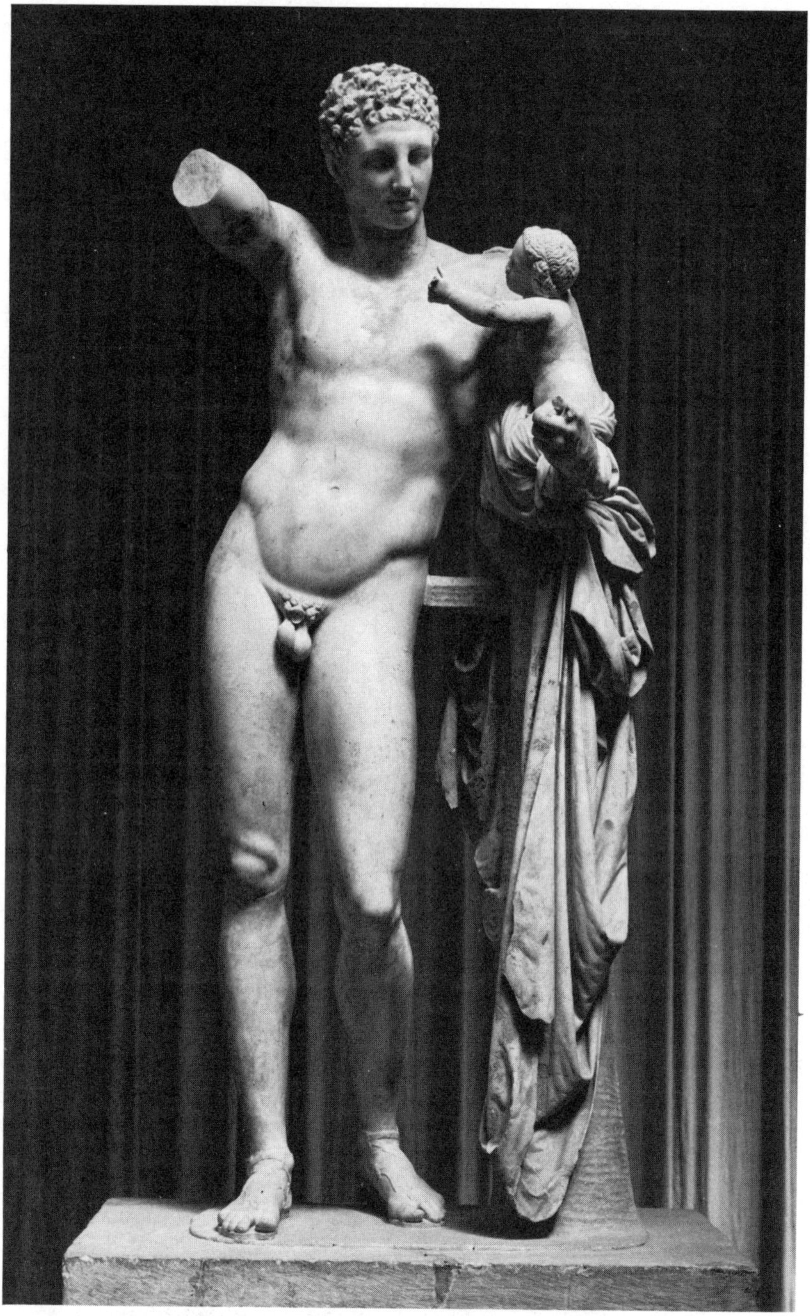

Fig. 4

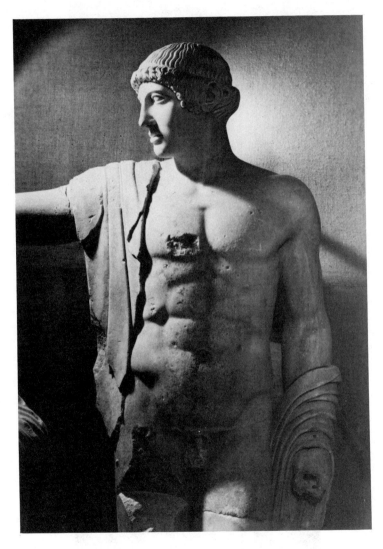

Fig. 5

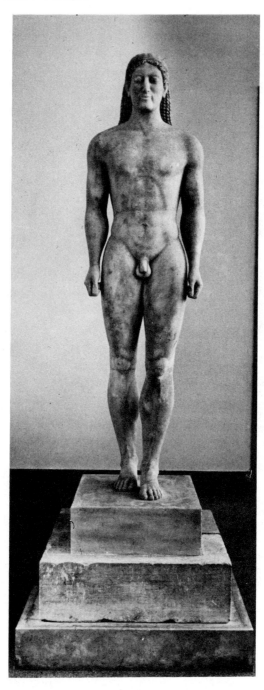

Fig. 6

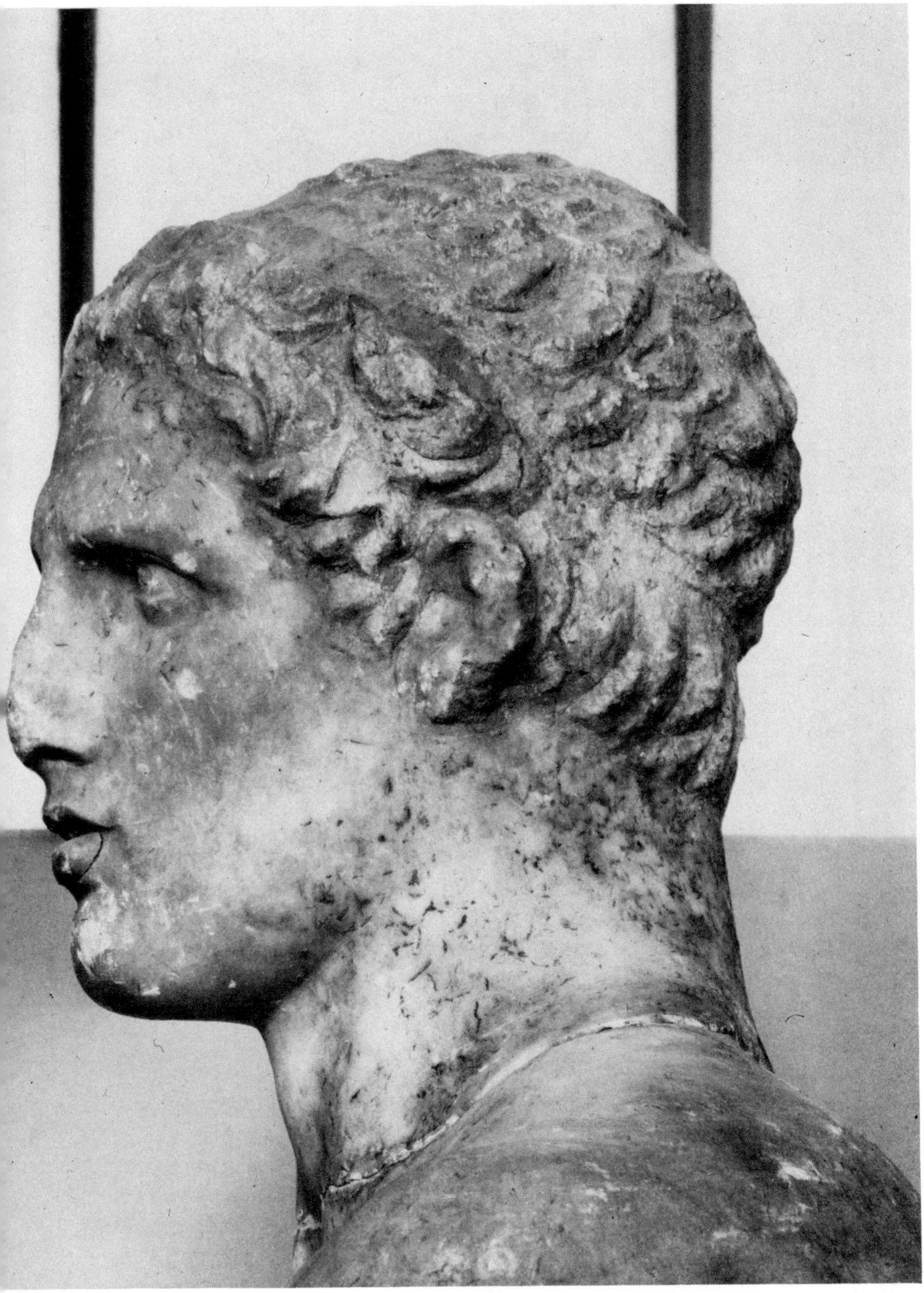

Fig. 7

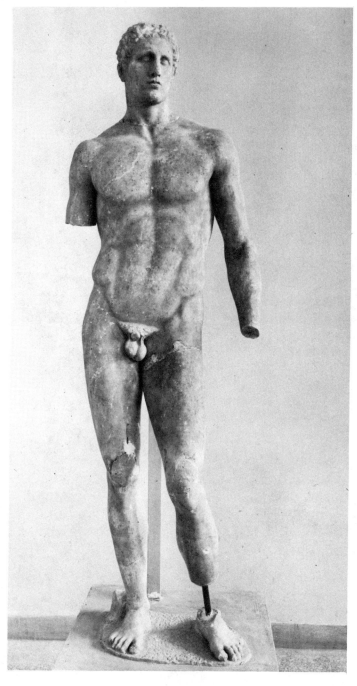

Fig. 8

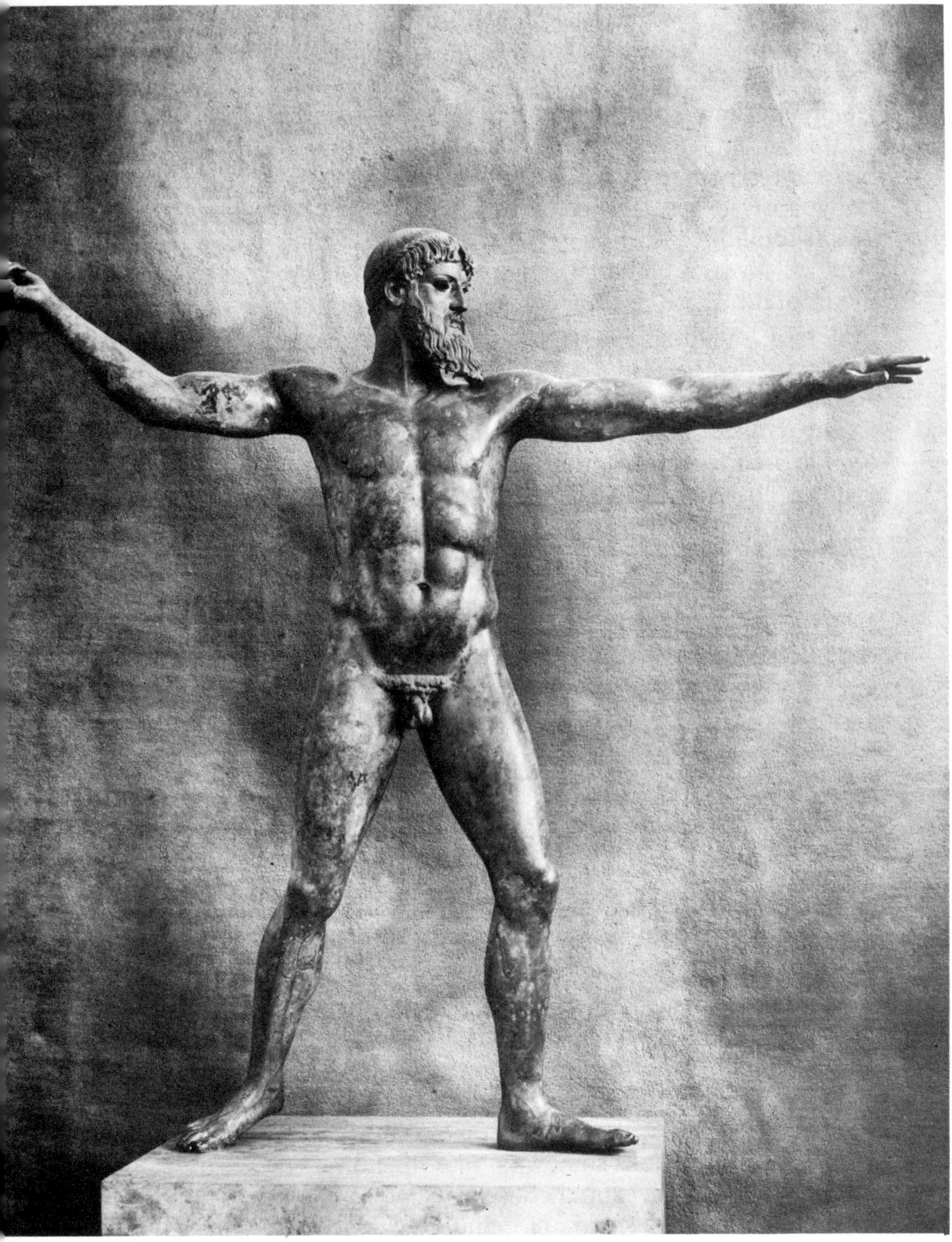

Fig. 9

Section III—*Greek Architecture*

As with any subject, architecture has its own vocabulary. In order to understand what is meant one must master certain terms before plunging in to a study of the subject. In order to understand Greek temple architecture and the differences between the styles, to understand the progession of building style and the different viewpoints the Greeks were trying to express, one should know basic terms. A sketch is included which identifies the parts of the building. As you look at these sketches and the pictures, you will no doubt be able to recall buildings you have seen that incorporate these elements. We are surrounded in the United States by buildings incorporating ideas and architectural features developed by the Greeks. This should make it easier for you to visualize and appreciate Greek architecture.

The Greeks invented three distinct styles or orders for their temple architecture, Doric, Ionic, and Corinthian. Each order has distinct characteristics. You can see this in the pictures and they are described below. The following terms are important in Greek temple architecture. The terms are listed starting at ground level and working up to the peak of the roof.

Stereobate—The substructure of the temple which is often partly underground.

Stylobate—The top three steps of the sterobate. The columns rest on the top step.

Column and Drum—The vertical post that supports the horizontal lintel above. It is often made of several parts—drums—placed one on another. In the Ionic style the bottom drum is carved into a base.

Entablature—The area, from the capital of the column to the cornice, which gives the distinctive quality to each architectural order. It is the "signature" of the building and the key area for analysis in determining the date of the building. It includes the following:

Capital—The top drum(s) carved into special patterns that identify the architectural order. The Corinthian capital is ornate and looks somewhat like leaves. The Ionic capital looks somewhat like the horns of a sheep.
The Doric capital consists of two parts:
Abacus—The square piece upon which the freize rests.
Echinus—The slanting piece below the abacus at the top of

the column. The relationship between the size of the echinus and abacus and the degree of slant of the echinus dates Doric buildings. The relationship changes the effectiveness of the overall style. (See Parthenon)

Architrave—The horizontal beam or lintel that rests on the capital.

Freize—The second horizontal line where the ends of the beams running the length of the building are supported. In the Doric Order the freize consists of alternating tryglyphs and Metopes. In the Ionic Order it is either blank or contains a continuous carved freize.

Tryglyph—Three short vertical pieces which were originally the ends of three beams running the length of the building. These were incorporated in the stone buildings as carry overs from the days of wooden temple construction.

Guttae—In the Doric Order little pegs that stick down from under the tryglyphs. Originally they were wooden pegs which held the long beams in place. The guttae are another reminder of the former wooden construction.

Metope—The spaces between tryglyphs. The space was often filled with sculpture and in that case the sculpture is referred to as a metope.

Cornice—The roof overhang above the freize.

Pediment—The triangular area created by the pitch of the roof and cornice.

Akroteria—Carvings that were placed where the roof and the cornice meet and at the top of the pediment. They were often statues or faces of mythological creatures.

Three other terms are significant in architecture.

Entasis—The swelling of a column that the architect employs to create the optical illusion of a straight column. This reflects a great scientific knowledge of optics. To illustrate draw two parallel lines on a page and stare at the center of the lines. They should appear to bend towards the center and this is what happens architecturally when you look at a building using truly straight columns. To compensate for the tendency of the eyes to pull the lines together, the Greek architects developed entasis. The effectiveness of the entasis helps to date temples. The Parthenon is perfect and the illusion is of straight columns although in actuality they swell out.

Necking—The fluting carved on the columns.

Carved Freize—In the Ionic Order instead of Tryglyphs and Metopes there is often a series of figures carved in relief. They present a continuous scene usually mythological. (See Temple of Nike.)

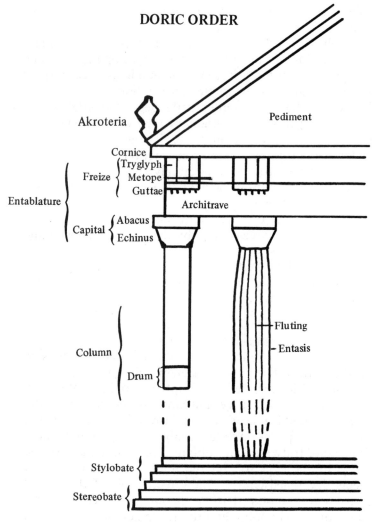

DORIC ORDER

Drawn by W. O. Kellogg

The Greek temple was usually rectangular. It was surrounded by columns on the outside called a colonnade. The number of columns on the short side of the rectangle had a mathematical relationship to the number on the long side (6 in front—13 on the side or double the number plus one for the side). Some temples such as the Temple of Nike had columns only in front and back.

Your teacher may ask you to do an exercise or to memorize these terms. They are given here for reference. Let us now consider Greek architecture, especially temple architecture of the period c. 600 to c. 350 B.C. If you were given a series of photographs of Greek buildings of the same period as the sculpture, you could with careful analysis put them into an order that would reflect the same changes and shifts in attitudes and values established by the statues. The wooden houses of the "Dark Ages" were built with thatch roofs with a high pitch to them. According to archaeological evidence, they were rectangular or square. We have several replicas of 8th century shrines made of pottery and we should start looking at Hellenic architecture by studying one of these. The pottery shrines show columns holding up a porch. This recalls the Mycenaean megaron and indicates the early origin of the tradition of the post and lintel building pattern in Greek history. The column is the post and the horizontal beam that rests on the column is the lintel. This pattern is rectangular. We are familiar with it as most of our buildings are rectangular and, of course, we use the post and lintel pattern in all our doorways.

As trade with the Near East and particularly with Egypt developed after establishment of the trading center at Naucratus, strong influence came to Greece from Egypt. Egyptian architecture always used columns and the post and lintel design. Egyptian columns were first of papyrus reed, then of wood, and finally of stone. Egyptian architects were inspired by nature and the capitals and shapes of the columns in the multi-columned halls of Egyptian temples reflected this. The Greeks saw these Egyptian temples and they reinforced their own ideas. The Greeks too adapted natural forms into their architecture and they used columns and rectangular floor plans in their temples. Because of the climate of Egypt, it was more pleasant for worship to have high rooms closed off from the heat than to worship in open areas. The climate of Greece was such that one could enjoy the outdoors during most of the year. Therefore, columns could be on the outside of the buildings giving covered areas for shade and protection from the rain and allowing the architect to develop a contrast between the bright

Aegean sun hitting marble columns and the shadowy open areas between.

The Greeks used the post and lintel construction throughout their history. They did not use the arch and vault that was known and used widely in the Near East at this time. The Romans later made effective use of the arch but we do not find it as an element in Hellenic architecture.

Climate, tradition, and invention confirmed that the pitch roof seen in the pottery shrines would become a regular part of the Greek temple. The pitch and overhang allowed the rain to run off. The development in Corinth of heavy terracotta (pottery) tiles for roofing in the early 7th century forced the Greek architect to deal with two engineering problems which, when solved, gave the emerging Doric order distinctive characteristics. The weight of the tiles required heavy interior walls if the roof was to hold up. It required the columns to be spaced close together or else to have some manner of carrying the weight from the lintel to the post. A capital for each column was developed to carry some of the weight off the lintel and the development of this capital (see the photograph of the columns of the Basilica at Paestum) is the most obvious clue to the development of the Doric style and its growing refinement.

The Doric Order of style dominated in the Peloponnesus and spread throughout the Greek world from there. The first temples in the style are heavy and crude and date from c. 600 contemporary with the first of the statues. By the time the style was used for the Parthenon in Athens (447 B.C.) it had been so refined and developed that many people believe the building to be the most beautiful ever built. It is considered the architectural culmination of the Age of Pericles, the so-called Golden Age of Hellenic Greek civilization. The building expresses architecturally what the Poseidon (statue number nine) does sculpturally.

Look at the two pictures of Doric temples included in the chapter. The earlier of the two, The Basilica or Temple of Hera at Paestum just south of Naples on the Italian coast, is one of the earliest Doric temples that stands today and it is almost contemporary with statue number 3. Do you see a similarity? There is great entasis or swelling in the columns, so much so that they are often referred to as cigars. The distinctive Doric capital is crude. The echinus is big and flat and this column drum looks like a large cushion while the abacus on top of each column is very heavy and they almost touch. The abacus supported the lintel and helped

carry the weight to the columns. The sterobate is entirely underground. The overall impression is of a heavy, squat building.
Inside the roof support consists of short Doric columns on top of a
row of fatter, taller columns running down the center of the building. As you can see, it is not a very attractive building.

Doric Columns
The Basilica, Paestum, Italy

The second Doric Temple pictured is the Parthenon at Athens.
The Parthenon, dedicated to Athena Pronaos (the maiden), is one
of the most remarkable buildings conceived by the human mind.
There is not a straight line in the building. The architect, Ictinus,
understood optics and the need to curve all lines to counteract the
effect of the eye on parallel lines. The entasis of the columns is
perfect so they appear straight to the human eye. The balance of
the building is most pleasing. The mathematical relationships
worked out between the various parts of the building is remarkable.
It recalls the philosophy of Pythagoras mentioned below. Although
the Greeks never established a standard set of proportions for
buildings as Polycleitus, the contemporary sculptor, did for ideal
human bodies, Ictinus must have had such a scheme for the Parthenon. For instance, the space between columns is equal to half
of each column's height. The mathematical relationship between

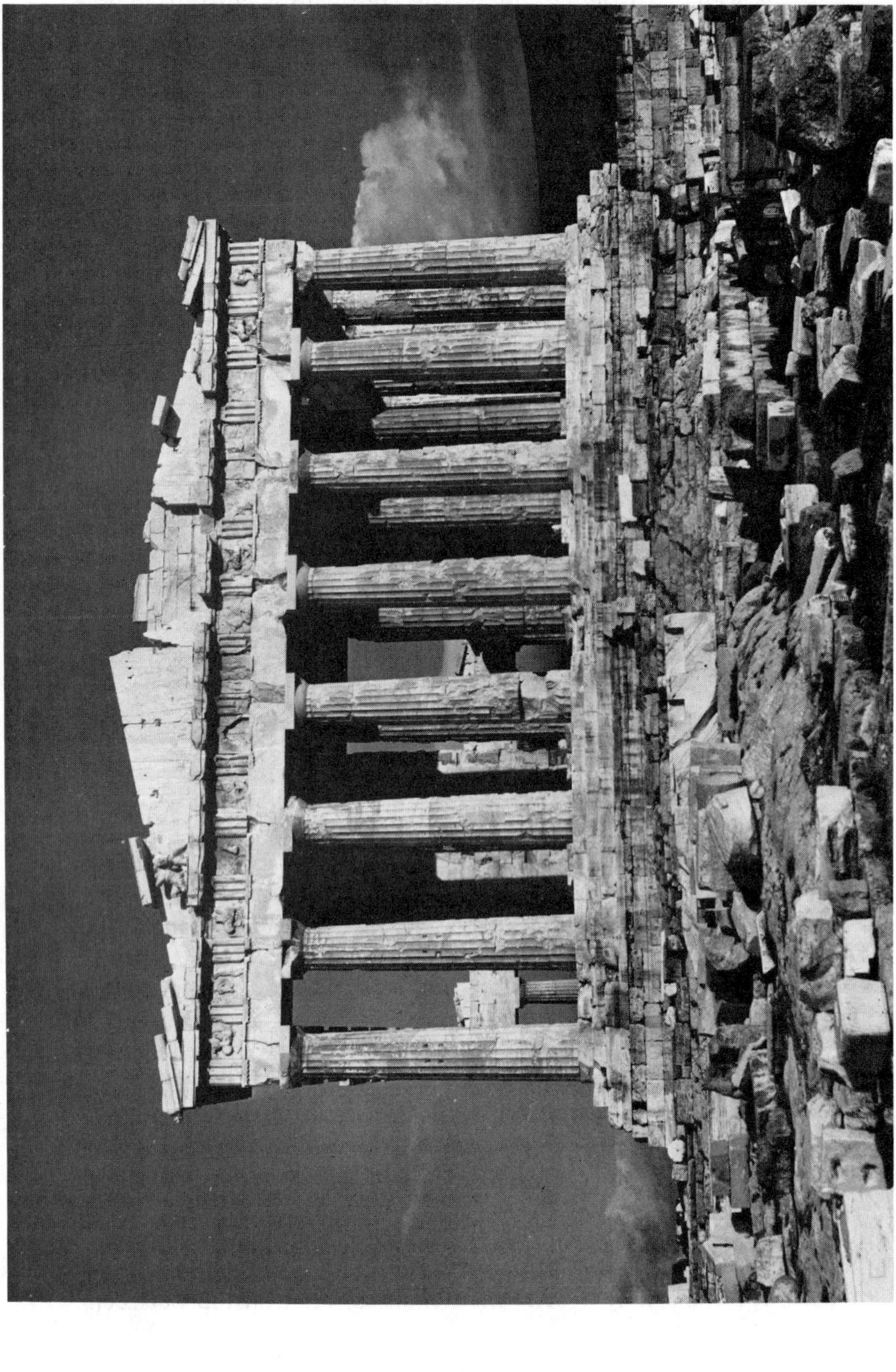

The Parthenon

the number of columns in front and on the side has been mentioned. The capitals are beautifully proportioned. Ictinus could calculate the weight of the architrave and roof and was able to design capitals that carried the weight and yet blended easily onto the columns. The pediment has a pitch that rises gracefully to a peak over the eight columns on the short ends and it provides a well defined area for the sculpture created by Phidias, the great 5th century sculptor, and his workmen. The metopes were filled with sculpture also. Several are still in place and give a slight sense of the balance and effective use of size and proportion—more so than one gets when viewing the many pieces that are in the British Museum, the so-called Elgin marbles.[2] Inside the temple was a huge statue of Athena the work of Phidias himself. The statue was said to have cost the equivalent of $10,000,000 in today's money. It was of gold and ivory and including the 12 foot pedestal stood 37 feet high.[3]

Around the top of the wall inside the colonnade Phidias designed a great freize that showed the procession of the people of Athens up the acropolis to the Parthenon to present the goddess with her newly woven garment. This procession was the highlight of the Panathenaic games.[4]

[2] The Parthenon stood almost complete until 1687. It was blown up then in a war between the Turks and Venetians when a shell fired accidentally by a French lieutenant on the Venetian side struck it. The Turks had stored powder in the building. It remained largely a ruin until archaeologists began partial restoration in the last century. Early in the last century, the British Ambassador to Turkey, Lord Elgin, collected the pieces of sculpture that were lying about the acropolis and sent them to England. They are now beautifully displayed in the British Museum but many people believe they were stolen and should go back to Athens. This is an endless argument and there is justice on both sides. We do have the marbles in a fairly good state of repair thanks to Lord Elgin rescuing them 150 years ago. It would be good to have the marbles at their original location but perhaps preservation is more important.

[3] We will consider later the history of this period. The money to construct these buildings and statues came from the members of the Delian League, a protective league headed by Athens. Many members of the league objected to the beautification of Athens with league money but were powerless to do anything about it. There is considerable reason to believe that Pericles undertook the construction of the new temples and the beautification of the city to supply work for many unemployed Athenians. This does not detract from the beauty of the buildings but it may make one wonder about how government funds are spent to provide relief and employment. These seem to be recurring problems in society and are handled in many different ways by different cultures.

[4] Major Panathenaic Games were held every four years to honor Athena, patron goddess of Athens. There were athletic contests, music, poetry,

Presently, the Parthenon stands alone on the south side of the acropolis. The modern visitor sees the impressive setting, the golden marble, the balance and symmetry in a way the ancient Athenian did not. In 430 B.C. the acropolis was crowded with other shrines and statues. A wall surrounded the Parthenon and the statues and temples were painted in bright colors, a fact often overlooked by students and scholars alike in describing the balance and calmness of Greek art. The Parthenon stood out as a building but there was a great confusion of objects around it. The approach to the Parthenon through the marketplace or agora up the steep, winding path and through the great gateway or Propylea, also built in the Age of Pericles but never completed because of war, set a contrast to the harmony and proportion that Ictinus achieved within the building itself. It sets the Parthenon off more effectively than would a more planned and structured approach. It also reflects clearly the two aspects of the Greek personality—the sense of order and symmetry also seen in the great statues of the 5th century and the sense of freedom of spirit and vitality reflected in the growing political democracy of Periclean Athens.

The second great architectural order developed by the Greeks, the Ionic Order, was begun in Ionia and spread to the entire Greek world. Miletus may have been its home. The strong influence of Egypt is seen in the colorfully painted, superficial patterns of decoration which recalled Egyptian patterns of palms and lotus. The famous egg and dart pattern used in Greek Ionic architecture is an adaptation of an Egyptian pattern in which lotus flowers alternated with lotus buds. The Ionic Order columns are taller, thinner and more graceful than Doric columns. The voluted capitals, that some suggest were inspired by the horns of the ram, recall the strong influence of nature on developing Hellenic art. These developments can be linked with the increasing trade with the eastern Mediterranean and the Greek's interest in the world around them.

Ionic temples were built in many places. The style became very popular. Perhaps the finest example extant is the little Temple of Nike on the Athenian acropolis seen in the photograph.

While Athens was building the great temples on the acropolis, in an isolated valley in the Peloponnesus another great 5th century temple, the Temple to Apollo at Bassae was being built. It is a

drama contests, and the procession at the end of which the peplos or garment to cover the old wooden statue of Athena was presented to the Temple. This procession was portrayed in the freize.

Temple of Nike, Athens

notable temple for several reasons. First, it is well preserved and
was unknown to the modern world until 1795. Second, it reflects
the same sense of perfection seen in the Parthenon. Third, it
shows that although the Greek architects adhered to many strict
concepts of design and construction many dating back to the
beginning of temple architecture in wood they were still able to
·experiment and try new things within the established pattern.
At Bassae the architect used both the Doric and Ionian Order in
one temple and introduced a new order, the Corinthian. Its name
indicates its connection with the city of Corinth in the Peloponnesus. In form it was inspired by the acanthus plant and the story
is told that its originator saw a basket of acanthus plants growing
on the top of a marble funeral drum and was inspired by this natural
sight to create the most ornate and latest to be developed of the
Greek architectural orders. The greater ornateness and the complexity of the Corinthian Order reflects the changing attitudes of
the Greeks. This change is also seen in 4th century sculpture.
In sculpture at that time more attention was paid to the individual.
Emotion shown in the face and the movement in the body became a part of the sculptor's presentation (statue number four)
and the Corinthian Order too appeals to the emotion and indicates
a greater complexity of style and greater ability with tools. The
Corinthian Order originating in the 5th century was popular

in the 4th century and became widely used in the Roman Empire. We use all three Greek Orders in America today.

We have mentioned balance, proportion, and perfection several times in this section. These are terms often linked to the Greeks of the 5th century B.C. In connection with these terms, we must mention one of the earliest Greek and therefore European philosophers and scientists, Pythagoras. He lived in Italy at Croton but was born on the Aegean island of Samos and traveled widely. Around 530 B.C. he made the first experiment recorded in Europe; an experiment that identified the musical notes made by different length strings with mathematical relationships. This led him to develop a whole philosophical system based on proportions and relationships. His concept of harmonia—being in tune—affected much Greek thought and has an impact on our lives today. Pythagoras felt that there was a harmony in the world that man could achieve in which reason, instinct, and feeling would all be in balance, thus creating a perfect form which would function ideally. At the heart of Pythagorean philosophy was number and proportion. True proportion led to true grace and beauty and it was this approach to life that led one sculptor, Polycleitus, to set up a code of proportions for sculpting the human body. This seeking of a relation between form and function following logical rules of mathematics (geometry) greatly affected 5th century Greek thought and can be seen in the sculpture and architecture of the age. It has led many scholars to extol the rationalism of the Greek mind; to glorify the Greek reason and its understanding of symmetry, harmony, and proportion. This was an important element in Greek thought and the precept inscribed at Apollo's shrine at Delphi, "Nothing in Excess", reflects this side of Greek thought. The Greek worship of Apollo is linked to this rationalism as are the teachings of the great philosophers.

This rationalism is an important side of Greek thought and should never be neglected. There is, however, another side that is just as important. That is the aspect of freedom and vitality, of emotionalism and excess, which is often connected with the Greek worship of Dionysus. No great philosopher extolled this side of man's nature as it does not have the appeal to the rational and enquiring mind that proportion and order has. The Greeks understood this side of life fully and it is apparent in literature.[5] It

---

[5] For a full discussion of this aspect of Greek thought see Dodds *The Greeks and the Irrational.* The plays of Euripides particularly the *Bacchae* present this side of human life. The Greek play follows a formal structure and presents the emotional material within it showing how these two forces can be combined.

can also be seen clearly in some scenes painted on vases between 600 and 350 B.C. The later sculpture you have studied has some touches of emotionalism and in many small clay figurines erotic and emotional poses are presented indicating a willingness to express this aspect of life in such works.

In architecture one of the three great buildings on the Acropolis, the Erechtheum, clearly indicates that one can not make a blanket rule for symmetry and proportion even in architecture. This building, built at the same time as the Parthenon, combined shrines to three different gods. There were three porches or entrances facing three directions. The north porch is a beautiful example of Ionic style but the south porch is held up by six caryatids, columns carved in the shape of young maidens. The porches are at different levels and although the building is a tribute to the architect who had a difficult commission to execute, it clearly indicates all 5th century temple building did not follow the proportional and balanced scheme that one might think if Doric temples alone were considered.

Certainly, the superb settings of most Doric temples, the exciting play of strong Mediterranean sunlight and dark shadows on the buildings, the severe lines yet lightness achieved by the proportions used in the greatest 5th century temples, the simple plan often set off by complex surroundings, make of the Doric temples a great example of the harmony and proportion so often considered to be the essence of the Greek mind. It is the same harmony and proportion seen in the idealized statues of Poseidon and Apollo (photographs number 2, 5, and 9.) Perhaps they represent the ideal of 5th century Athenian society but that society was well aware of the other aspect of man's nature.

The Greeks not only built rectangular temples. They also by the end of the 5th century perfected a circular temple, the tholos. Public buildings existed from the earliest times. The stoa, a long, roofed gallery, was popular. These were columned on one side, usually the south side to get the most from the winter sun, and walled on the other with small shops and offices. The American School in Athens has helped to rebuild the 4th century Stoa of Atticus in the Athenian agora. It gives one an excellent idea of what such buildings were like when they served as the meeting place for business men and philosophers. Gymnasia and palestras or outdoor exercise areas surrounded by walls were also popular. Other buildings functioned as law courts and warehouses but we have only the ruins and the reconstructed drawings of archaeologists to indicate what these were like.

The Hellenic Greeks, unlike their Mycenaean predecessors did not build palaces, or if they did, we have found no remains. There were some large houses for the wealthy. They were built around an open courtyard with a door and small windows on the street. For the most part, housing arrangements were simple as so much of the life of the Greeks, certainly for males, was lived outside in the agora or market-place. We have the remains of some fine 4th century houses on the island of Delos but all the evidence we now have indicates that in the 5th century houses were small, mere hovels with few windows and flat roofs for the poorer city dwellers. They were often built of wood or mud brick and could be easily broken into by thieves. Sanitary arrangements were largely non-existent and water was brought from the city wells and chamber pots supplied the bathroom facilities. In 5th century Athens public baths were built and in the 4th century these facilities were wide-spread. Fountains were often donated to the city by wealthy benefactors.

In summary, the Greeks created three architectural styles that can be seen in use today, Doric, Ionian, and Corinthian. In tracing their development we see they combined foreign elements with native Greek ideas and their evolution from the rather crude, unpleasing Temple of Hera at Paestum through the Parthenon to the more emotionally appealing Corinthian Order parallels the evolution of Greek sculpture. Both arts reflect the Greek sense of order and proportion seen so clearly in the philosophy of Pythagoras but the Dionysian side of Greek attitudes can also be seen in these two art forms. Greeks also built many large public buildings besides temples but until the 4th century, homes were rather small.

Section III—*Greek Pottery*

Pottery provides one of the great keys to understanding the ancient world and its inhabitants. Greek pottery can be traced in an unbroken line from the Mycenaean age to the end of Greek history. In the period 650-323 B.C. the changing styles and decorations can be clearly followed and any museum with a Greek collection will provide an opportunity for one to follow the development and test his skill in identifying the changing styles. The skill can be highly developed so that one can identify the style of many individual artists or may be only rudimentary enabling one to trace the major style changes only. Whatever the degree of skill, a museum visit clearly shows that pottery style changes. These changes can be identified and related to changing attitudes and conditions perhaps even more easily than changing styles in sculpture or architecture. The chart below sets forth in a comparative summary the major pottery and sculptural styles.[6]

AEGEAN AREA—FIRST MILLENIUM B.C.

Sculpture Styles	Date B.C. at which period begins	Pottery Styles
	1100	Sub-Mycenaean
	1050	Protogeometric
	950	Geometric
Archaic	800	
	700	Orientalizing Corinthian
	600	Black Figure Attic
Transitional	500	Red Figure Attic
Classical	479	
Late Classical	404	
Hellenistic	338	Hellenistic Styles

The Sub-Mycenaean style, the style of the late Mycenaean age noted for its crudity, was followed by Protogeometric or first geometric. Produced mainly in Athens, Protogeometric was a style in which strictly geometric patterns were alternated with areas of no design. Normally, the neck of the vases and the belly or fattest part of the vase were decorated with circles and wavy lines—the chief characteristics of this style. The makers were not afraid to leave areas undecorated. This style was soon replaced by the Geometric Style in which the entire surface of the vase was covered with spirals, concentric circles, swastikas, zigzags, and lines.

The vases made in Attica (the territory around Athens) were the finest examples of geometric pottery. The vase color was buff and the patterns done in dark red and black. As the style

[6] In Appendix B these sculpture styles are discussed briefly.

was developed, the lines on the vases were more delicately drawn. By 800 B.C. human and animal figures were introduced. The Dipylon Vases, from the Dipylon cemetery in Athens, portray scenes of lamentation and burial using highly stylized human figures. Humans and animals soon became a regular part of the decoration of Geometric pottery.

With the growing influence of the Near East, rosettes, palmettes, sphinxes, griffens, and other strange beasts together with human figures were used in bands as decoration and a new style, called Orientalizing, became popular. The style was produced in many areas but Corinth capitalized on it more than other places. She dominated the trade routes with small vases that were designed after Egyptian and Cretan prototypes. They were used for exporting the perfumed oil for which Corinth became noted. At first these vases had isolated figures as decoration but by the mid 7th century the decoration covered the vases in bands of different designs. The colors were usually a very light buff, almost white, background with maroon, red, white, and black decorations. The artists cut into the clay through the colors to allow the natural clay to show through and this incising allowed them to add details such as eyes, muscles, hair, and even expressions on the figures.

There seems to be a connection between the geometric patterning of eyes, ears, and muscles on the Archaic Kouroi statues, (see statue number three) and both the Geometric and Orientalizing pottery styles. The placement of design in Orientalizing pottery was done quite geometrically in rows and patterns. Both pottery styles were strongly influenced by the trade with the Near East and Egypt just as the archaic statues indicate Egyptian influence.

Finally, the black figures became dominant on the pots and this technique was taken up by Athens and highly developed. With the development of Black Figure pottery Athens came to dominate the Greek pottery industry for two centuries. While Corinth concentrated on Oriental ware, the Athenians had worked for a century developing the stylized figures of the Dipylon vases into more naturalistic presentations. By 600 B.C. the technique had achieved some success and Black Figure vases developed along with the archaic style in sculpture until a more realistic portrayal of the human figure was possible. It was the Athenians' skill in pottery making that laid the economic foundation for Athens' emergence as the most important polis in Greece.

In Black Figure pottery the natural color of the clay is

covered with slip or a thin layer of black colored clay except in the panel or area on the side of the vase where the design appears. This is left the natural reddish color of the clay and the figures are painted there in the black slip. The design was usually confined to a panel on the side of the vase and the evolution of the placement and the pattern of the design within the panel reflects the growing interest in Pythagorean ideas of order, balance, and symmetry. The artist incised or cut the features onto the figures drawn on the vase in black slip. There is a limit to the sublety of expression that can be achieved by cutting which was more like scratching into the clay.

About 540 B.C. the colors began to be reversed and by 500 B.C. Red Figure pottery became dominant except for certain traditional uses such as for the prize vases given at the Panathenaic Games. In Red Figure pottery the background is covered in black leaving the figures and other decoration the natural red clay color. The artist then painted on the red clay with black slip. Sometimes the artist added white or even gold leaf to create delicate expressions and fine details. We'll describe the subject matter of Red Figure pottery below. On the finest early 5th century vases the scenes were beautifully and delicately handled. The beauty of the works recall the Parthenon and the 5th century sculpture (statues number five and nine).

Around 540 B.C. vase painters began signing their works. Sometimes there are two names, one for the potter and one for the artist, but often the same individual did each. These individually signed vases are significantly Athenian and indicate the growing importance of the individual in Athenian and all Greek society of the late 6th and 5th centuries B.C. Democratic ideas about the importance of the individual were growing in Athens as we will see in the next chapter. The sculptors of the age were striving towards an idealized individual in their work and vase painters were producing beautifully executed scenes of daily living. Athenian Red Figure pottery dominated the potter's market of the 5th century. The finest work was done early in the century.

Immediately after 404 B.C. little pottery was produced in Athens, probably as a result of losing the overseas markets in the Peloponnesian War. Later in the 4th century Athens again made some pottery but by then other cities were producing large quantities of vases. In fact, the Greek cities of southern Italy dominated the pottery trade in the early part of the 4th century. Red Figure pottery remained the dominant style but the quality of the painting on the vases declined. The types of scenes por-

Attic Red Figured Kylix

Courtesy, Museum of Fine Arts, Boston

trayed changed greatly as the artists concentrated on appealing to the emotions of the individual viewer. Erotic Dionysian scenes are often portrayed as well as emotional scenes of war time— departures or death—or bedroom scenes of ladies dressing. They are much more intimate and personal than the scenes of the 6th and 5th centuries. There appears a direct correlation between these scenes and the work of the 4th century sculptors where the emphasis was on the individual and the emotional quality of life rather than on the idealized, well proportioned work of the 5th century.

Hellenistic art, the art of the period after the conquests of Alexander the Great, is noted for its individualized, emotional quality. This was true in all Hellenistic art forms as is seen in Hellenistic pottery where 4th century Red Figure styles are continued with even more emphasis on emotional, individualized, exaggerated, and sometimes cute scenes.

The Greeks developed several shapes for their pottery that they used over and over throughout their history. Each shape evolved for a special use and the shape was apparently very effective for the designated use. It is reminiscent of the basic structure used for temples where the form varied little from 700 to 323 B.C. Within this given framework the architect exercised creativity and so did the potter creating scenes which fit the given space and shape in a balanced and effective manner. In each case the structure was imposed from the outside by tradition and the society—a conservative element in the Greek approach to life. Given the structure, the artist then could create.

The scenes portrayed on the Black and Red Figure pottery present a full history of changing views and attitudes, values and life style, and reflect the same changes we have seen in sculpture and architecture. The scenes on the vases give us a quantity of information on the daily life of the Greeks—just as do the works of Homer for an earlier period of Greek history. The Geometric pottery which had the first human figures give us confirmation of ideas presented in Homer about funerals. The early Black Figure vases give us indications of what the Greeks were thinking and doing towards the end of the "Age of Colonization." For instance, the decoration on the "Francois Vase" named after the finder and signed by the artist and potter in 575 B.C. consists of scenes from Greek mythology and the vase has been called a "sort of Bible" showing what the Greek myths were at the time. Theseus's landing at Delos, a battle between the cranes and the pygmies, the murder of Troilus by Achilles are portrayed. All of these characters are identified by names written on the vase beside the figures. Studying the vase in the museum in Florence, Italy, can be a day's occupation as each time one looks at the vase, another detail emerges.

Around 550 B.C. at the time the Archaic sculpture was becoming more realistic, the scenes on the vases were reflecting a new love of luxury. In Athens, this was encouraged by the ruler Peisistratus. The arrival of Ionian refugees fleeing from the power of Persia which was pressing on the Anatolian coastal cities influenced Athenian development at this time. Scenes of Oriental goddesses protecting wild animals alternate with scenes of licentious revelry as satyrs chase maidens about in celebration of the rites of Dionysus. Other scenes portray very human figures who are identified by writing on the vases as gods or heros, Castor, Ajax, the Dioscuri, or Herakles. A scene of Dionysian revelry shows Dionysus on a couch drinking from a cup in the typical dining manner of the age. The patterns on the dress and the wreaths on the heads as well as the couch give us details about Greek living. Another scene shows three women filling pitchers at a fountain, a scene that was common in every Greek city of the age.

With the development of Red Figure pottery after 540 B.C. scenes change somewhat and reflect the growing importance of Athens as a young and autocratic political power in the Greek world full of youthful ambitions. The growing interest in athletics and in what has been termed the "cult of the nude" is indicated as many scenes portrayed are of athletic events—young men training to box, jump or throw. the javelin. On some drinking cups individuals are shown playing musical instruments. One can learn a great deal about the athletic and musical life of the age by studying the vases. Red figure allowed for much more detailed work on the anatomy and clothing and slowly the artists mastered the details of human anatomy as did the sculptors of the period before the Persian Wars of 490-479 B.C. Many details of hoplite armor are indicated and battle scenes are presented. The first nude females were shown on some vases in scenes of girls bathing. Scenes of revelry continued. (See the photographs of Greek vases.)

After the Persian Wars as democracy became more important than the life of aristocratic youths, family and love scenes on vases reflect this. By 450 B.C. war is more likely portrayed by a soldier saying farewell to his family than by a battle scene.

Domestic life scenes of dressing, bathing, or the work of the crafts-men, the potter and sculptor are often portrayed. Scenes of drunken revelry and athletes practicing are replaced by scenes of the rape of mortals by the gods and young women adorning themselves in front of mirrors. One of the most popular scenes of this era is that of the Judgment of Paris, the mythical event in which Paris decided who was the most beautiful of the Olympian goddesses. The dresses on the women indicate highly decorated fabrics—inspired by oriental luxury.

As mentioned above during the 4th century the quality of vase painting declined considerably and emotional and erotic subjects became very popular. Many scenes indicate an interest in mysticism—a desire perhaps to escape from the troubles of the age also reflected in the new philosophies of Stoicism and Epicureanism. Many vases have scenes relating to the dead and to events portrayed in plays. A great many portrayals of Aphrodite indicate the popularity of this goddess of love which is also re-flected in 4th century sculpture in which female nudity appears. The concern for the individual, emotionalism, and the declining artistic ability all reflect the attitudes and life style of this century as we will see when we consider the political history of the age. Again art closely relates to changing attitudes, values, and life styles.

Section IV—*Literature*

A quantity of Greek literature has survived. It can be divided into works of poetry both epic and lyric, works of the philosophers from the pre-Socratics of Ionia, such as Thales, to Plato about whom it has been said that all philosophy is simply a footnote to his works, works of drama, works of history, and speeches. The Greeks did not develop short stories and novels. These literary works can be analysed with great effect giving the reader know-ledge of the individual writers and information of the age.

For instance, reading the historians Herodotus or Thucydides will give you a sense of how the Greeks viewed their own past. Herodotus writing about the Persian War tells stories and collects as much information as he can. He indicates his own opinions on matters but presents conflicting views. He is extremely pro-Greek and particularly pro-Athens in his account of the Persian War and this bias is not hidden at all. Thucydides tries to be more objective using careful analysis to try to find the true causes of events but he blatantly recreates speeches to convey his sense of what happened in the Peloponnesian War, putting words into people's mouths in a manner we might consider unhistorical. Parts of Herodotus' *Persian War* and Thucydides' *Peloponnesian War* should be read by all historians and by all Greek students. The difference of approach in the two men, the exuberance of Herodotus extolling the youthful vigor of Athens, and the sober analysis of Thucydides (which makes him less interesting to read) writing after the glory of the Age of Pericles has ended reflects the shift in attitude that came in the 5th century. The growing concern with self analysis, with causes, and with rudimentary science, together with the pessimism of the end of the century compared with the enthusiasm, with the self confidence, and with the vitality of the start of the century after the defeat of the Persians is clearly seen in a comparison of these two works. The 5th century B.C. was full of excitement and rapidly changing conditions in Greece and especially in Athens very much as the 20th century has been for the United States. The attitude of America before World War I and her attitude today towards world affairs is reminiscent of the great shift of attitude in Athens in the 5th century B.C. The historians of Greece show this as do American historians.[7]

Any literature can be used to learn about the age which produced it. Poetry has an advantage this way since it is often short so more can be read. The ancient Greeks wrote notable poetry. Greek poetry can be classified under four types. Epic poetry such as the *Iliad* was the earliest form. It had roots in the Mycenaean age. Epics were chanted perhaps with accompaniment and had a distinctive measure or beat, the hexameter. A second and very popular type developed early in Greek history is called lyric poetry. In fact, 6th century B.C. has been called the Lyric Age in Greece. Lyric poetry is composed in stanzas. It was originally intended to be sung while accompanied on the lyre, a guitar-like instrument. It is called lyric for this reason. Lyric poetry was written by many people in different parts of the Greek world. Lyric poetry is personal. It deals with many subjects from a personal point of view.

The third type, elegiac poetry, was first written before the 6th century and many different ideas were expressed in elegiacs. Epigrams, war songs, and laments are most often thought of as elegiacs but poets used the distinctive elegiac meter for love songs and to express political thoughts. It is believed elegiac poetry was origin-

[7] See Kellogg *Out of the Past* Chapter XIII for excerpts from Herodotus.

ally written to be accompanied by the lute. The elegiac meter, just as lyric and epic meter, did not reflect the normal patterns of speech. The elegiac meter is often referred to as pentameter (penta = five) but technically this is not correct. The fourth type of poetry is classified as chorales or choral lyrics and were written to be sung by a chorus. Chorales also have a distinctive meter and usually have a chorus.

It is hoped everyone at some time will read the great Greek epics, the *Iliad* and the *Odyssey*. We have chosen several examples of lyric and elegiac poetry to illustrate the variety of style and theme found in Greek poetry. All poetry suffers in translation especially when the translator ignores the true meter of the original, but these should give the reader some ideas of how people in different city states thought as seen in the writings of several sensitive individuals.

Archilochus from the island of Paros was the illegitimate son of a noble father and a slave girl. Much of his verse written in the early 7th century B.C. reflects a bitterness. One of his most famous passages tells of a Thracian who is now carrying Archilochus' shield which he had left behind when he ran from the battle field. He concludes that at least he got home living. What impression of the writer and perhaps of the Greeks of the Aegean islands of this age do you get from this poem?[8]

TO HIS SOUL

Tossed on a sea of troubles, Soul, my Soul,
    Thyself do thou control;
And to the weapons of advancing foes
    A stubborn breast oppose;
Undaunted 'mid the hostile might
Of squadrons burning for the fight.

Thine be no boasting when the victor's crown
    Wins thee deserved renown;
Thine no dejected sorrow, when defeat
    Would urge a base retreat:

Rejoice in joyous things—nor overmuch
    Let grief thy bosom touch
Midst evil, and still bear in mind
How changeful are the ways of humankind.

Translated by William Hay.

[8] Unless otherwise noted all the selections of poetry in this section are taken from *Masterpieces of Greek Literature* ed. J. H. Wright 48-81.

Tyrtaeus fought for the Spartans in the Second Messenian War in the later 7th century (c. 630 B.C.) and although it is believed he was not born in Sparta, he wrote poetry that for many generations inspired the Spartans in war and peace. His verses were sung around the Spartan camp fires by Spartan soldiers and you can see why. What do these lines indicate about the values and attitudes of the Spartans?

MARTIAL ELEGY

How glorious fall the valiant, sword in hand,
In front of battle for their native land!
But oh! what ills await the wretch that yields,
A deserter outcast from his country's fields!
The mother whom he loves shall quit her home,
An aged father at his side shall roam;
His little ones shall weeping with him go,
And a young wife participate his woe;
While scorned and scowled upon by every face,
They pine for food, and beg from place to place.

Stain of his breed! dishonoring manhood's form,
All ills shall cleave to him: affiliction's storm
Shall blind him wandering in the vale of years,
Till, lost to all but ignominious fears,
He shall not blush to leave a deserter's name,
And children, like himself, inured to shame.
But we will combat for our fathers' land,
And we will drain the life-blood where we stand,
To save our children.—Fight ye side by side,
And crowded close, ye men of youthful pride,
Disdaining fear, and deeming light the cost
Of life itself in glorious battle lost.

Let not our fathers to stem the unequal fight,
Whose limbs are nerved no more with buoyant might;
Nor, lagging backward, let the younger breast
Permit the man of age (a sight unblest)
To welter in the combat's foremost thrust,
His whitened head dishevelled in the dust,
And venerable bosom bleeding bare.
But youth's fair form, though fallen, is ever fair,
And beautiful in death the boy appears,

The hero boy, that dies in blooming years:
In man's regret he lives, and woman's tears;
More sacred than in life, and lovelier far,
For having perished in the front of war.

Translated by Thomas Campbell.

Sappho from the island of Lesbos was born c. 610 B.C. at a time of changing political conditions. She was of noble birth and forced into exile yet her poetry reflects none of this but rather it is devoted to one subject, love. She is a rarity in Greek history— a noted woman—one of the very few whose contributions have been recorded for us by the male dominated Greek world. Her verses inspired many Greek poets and others through the ages. Her often expressed love for girls has led to great speculation about her own life. Greek ethics and morality were very different from ours. All indications are that Sappho was married and had a daughter, Kleis. How expressive are these poems to you? All Greek poetry suffers in translation but do these verses suggest love to you? How do they compare to the poetry of Tyrtaeus? Do they have points in common?

TO A LOVED ONE

Blest as the immortal gods is he,
The youth who fondly sits by thee,
And hears and sees thee all the while
Softly speak and sweetly smile.

'T was this deprived my soul of rest,
And raised such tumults in my breast;
For while I gazed, in transport tost,
My breath was gone, my voice was lost:

My bosom glowed; the subtle flame
Ran quick through all my vital frame;
O'er my dim eyes a darkness hung;
My ears with hollow murmurs rung.

In dewy damps my limbs were chilled;
My blood with gentle horror thrilled;
My feeble pulse forgot to play;
I fainted, sank, and died away.

Translated by Ambrose Phillips.

A PRIZE

Like the sweet apple
   turning red on the branch top
On the tip of the
   highest branch —
   unnoticed by the gatherers;
Rather, noticed
They could not reach to the prize.

Translated by William Kellogg

Anacreon c. 570-485 B.C. was born on the island of Teos. He lived through the Persian Wars and saw many changes in the Greek world of his day. His early works include a poem about losing his shield. He obviously had been a warrior but his later work turned to love and humour. He lived in Athens and his style greatly influenced the playwright Aeschylus. What feeling of the Greeks do you get from this verse? Do you know anybody who feels this way about age?

THE WISER PART. ODE VIII

I care not for the idle state
Of Persia's king, the rich, the great:
I envy not the monarch's throne
Nor wish the treasur'd gold my own.
But oh! be mine the rosy wreath,
Its freshness o'er my brow to breathe;
Be mine the rich perfumes that flow,
To cool and scent my locks of snow.
To-day I'll haste to down my wine,
As if to-morrow ne'er would shine;
But if to-morrow comes, why then—
I'll haste to drink my wine again.
And thus while all our days are bright,
Nor time has dimmed their bloomy light,
Let us the festal hours beguile
With drinking cup and cordial smile;
And shed from each new bowl of wine
The richest drop on Bacchus' shrine.
For Death may come, with brow unpleasant,
May come, when least we wish him present,
And beckon to the blackened shore,
And grimly bid us—drink no more!

Translated by Thomas More

Theognis of Megara lived during the time that democracy was established in that city. He was opposed to this development and much of his poetry is bitter as he was dispossessed of his inherited aristocratic position by this action. These two verses date from 540 B.C. What is Theognis' view of the common man? Do his complaints of the change in events as the formerly dispossessed take over and rule have parallels at other times in history? Does this poetry seem to have a political activist ring?

THE COMMONERS

The city is the same, dear Cyrnus, yet how different are its fold
Who in days gone bye knew naught of justice of the law,
But wore to shreds upon their naked flanks the skins of goats,
And grazed as sheep without the town far from the city's walls,
Yet now, O son of Polypus, these are termed the Good. For those
Of yesteryear, our noble sires, are now considered scum.
Who can behold such things — to see them smile upon each other in deceit
Knowing the character of neither good nor ill.
Make none of these, your townsmen, son of Polypus, your friend;
Let not your heart be thus destroyed, even for your need.
Yet let your tongue give forth to all the tender words of love,
Withholding from them ever all matters of importance and concern.
For you will truly know the hearts of miserable men
That there's no trust, no, not a jot, in any of their deeds
Since they have learned to love deceit and treachery and guile
And in their souls they recognize the nature of the lost.

Translated by George Tracy[9]

MARRIAGE

Cyrnus, in rams and asses, as in the horse, we seek
The thoroughbred and everyone desires the best breed of each sort.
Yet no man, not e'en the good, when money is in question,
Hesitates to wed the evil daughter of an evil sire.

Translated by George Tracy

[9] The two elegiac poems by Theognis were translated by George Tracy, Head of the Classics Department at St. Paul's School, especially for this text. I would like to express my thanks to him for this help.

Simondes of Chios died in 467 B.C. He had been patronized by
many rulers from Hiero, the tyrant-dictator of Syracuse, to the
Athenian democrat, Themistocles. He was noted for his pathos
and for the fact he made money out of his poetry. He wrote verse
in all the known styles. Compare this poem with the ones above.
What is its spirit? These are limited examples but do the poets of
the time seem to be involved or affected by the politics? Is this
true today for our writers?

ON THOSE WHO DIED AT THERMPOYLAE[10]

Of those who at Thermopylae were slain,
    Glorious the doom, and beautiful the lot;
Their tomb an altar: men from tears refrain
    To honor them, and praise, but mourn them not.
Such sepulchre, nor drear decay
Nor all-destroying time shall waste; this right have
    they.
Within their grave the home-bred glory
    Of Greece was laid: this witness gives
Leonidas the Spartan, in whose story
    A wreath of famous virtue ever lives.

Translated by John Sterling.

Pindar is perhaps the most famous of the Greek poets. He died
c. 440 B.C. We have about 1/4th of his works most of which are
hymns of praise to athletes. This seemed to be his finest inspiration
and reflects again the mood of Greece. You may recall the interest
in athletics seen in Black Figure vase painting and recall the importance of athletics to the Greeks. Pindar loved Olympia and the
Olympic Games held there and this selection is the final stanza of
a long ode in praise of Hiero of Syracuse who had won a chariot
race. What does this passage set forth as the ideal of the Age of
Pericles?

The first, the greatest bliss on man conferr'd
    Is in the acts of virtue to excel;
The second, to obtain their high reward,
    The soul-exalting praise of doing well.
Who both these lots attains, is bless'd indeed,
Since fortune here below can give no richer meed.

Translated by Gilbert West.

[10] Thermopylae (480 B.C.) was a famous battle of the Persian War in which
the Spartan forces led by Leonidas were all killed rather than surrender to the
Persian army. The battle was considered a high point in Spartan history and
an example of great bravery.

Clearly, the poetry reflects many attitudes and viewpoints. War, patriotism, love, old age are all written about as they are today. There is a connection between the political and economic situation and the poetry in the case of Theognis and Tyrtaeus but others seem to be oblivious to these conditions. You might want to make a list of these poets and write after each a phrase that would sum up your impression of each.

The great dramatic playwrights of the 5th century who wrote plays to be performed at the annual festival of Dionysius in Athens are probably the most interesting Greek writers to read. As in the case of Herodotus and Thucydides, the difference in style and theme between Aeschylus who wrote c. 470 B.C. and Euripides who wrote c. 420 B.C. is great. Aeschylus deals with themes from the great legends and tells of noble qualities of men and heros in such works as the Oresteian Trilogy which deals with the murder of Agamennon and how it was avenged. The structure of the play reflects its origins as a part of Dionysian religious ritual in which a priest recited lines and a chorus of believers responded. Aeschylus introduced three actors in place of the one priest and developed dialogues between two of them. He used the chorus to comment on the action and to fill in details of the story. The plays are beautifully structured. This should recall the idea of order and balance we discussed in regard to 5th century sculpture, architecture, and pottery. Aeschylus' works were contemporary with the Poseidon (sculpture number nine). They must be seen on the stage to appreciate the full significance of these facts.

Sophocles wrote his great plays about the Oedipus legend in the middle of the 5th century. His *Oedipus Rex* and *Antigone* are perhaps the two best known Greek tragedies. They both pit individuals of strength and pride against their fate and the law of the community. The questions raised are profound ones relating to the human situation. The struggle of Antigone between the law of the state and her own individual conscience guided by a higher law than that of the state is a story that is extremely timely and raises a basic issue that each individual living in a human society must face. It is a work well worth reading to see how the issue is resolved. The subject matter is reflective of the growing democracy of Athens and the interest in the individual.

Euripides, the last of the great tragic dramatists, wrote plays full of emotion, often with heroines, an interesting situation in a society that was so male oriented. His *Medea* is one of the finest psychological studies ever written of a woman thwarted by a man. *Hippolytus* tells the story of the love of Phaedra, wife of Theseus, for her step son. It is an emotional and tragic tale focusing on individuals and not on the grand themes and topics used by Aeschylus early in the century. The change we see in these playwrights is the same we saw in the scenes portrayed on the Red Figure pottery and the shift we saw in the sculpture as the balanced, idealized works of the mid-5th century move towards the individualized and more emotional work of the 4th century, seen in a sculpture like the Agias (sculpture # 8).

It is hoped that every student will want to read some of the Greek tragedies. There are many excellent translations and it can be very enjoyable to act out scenes from various plays for the class. Reading the parts aloud with a little action can produce a sense of the work that no silent reading can do. Aeschylus' *Oresteian Trilogy,* Sophocles' *Oedipus Rex* or *Antigone* and Euripides' *Medea, Hippolytus* or *The Trojan Women* are suggested.

Reading the great philosophers, Thales, Pythagoras, Plato, as he presents his own ideas and those of Socrates, and Aristotle is very valuable. Often the student finds the reading difficult and it is not recommended until after one is familiar with Greek attitudes and Greek history.

Section V—*Summary and Chapter Review*

Three important matters were considered in this chapter. You should have your own ideas on each of them. First, the question of whether art reflects the attitudes and values of an age or leads an age was discussed. By considering the Greeks or a society with which you are more familar, you should have developed a theory on this point. Your theory can be tested as you study more history.

The second matter considered was the way Greek art styles changed between 800 and 323 B.C. The changes were studied in sculpture, architecture, and pottery. In literature, the variety of interests of lyric poets was presented, and the changes in the style of the dramatists and historians was mentioned. You should be able to trace the changes in style or interests in one area of the arts.

Finally, it was mentioned in the chapter that the art was presented at this time in order to provide a framework for the study of the remainder of ancient Greek history. This framework was not specifically detailed for you but the general points were stated many times. From this presentation you should realize that the changes in artistic style follow a similar pattern in all areas. As part of your chapter review, you should make a brief outline of these changes and then be prepared to see how they relate to the history presented in the next chapters. It is suggested you use a few dates in your list to provide the "coathooks" upon which to hang other historic events. You may wish to use the chronology in the Appendix to set a few of these "coathook" dates.

As indicated in the chapter, one can learn many things about a society from the art it produces. Poetry and sculpture may seem far apart but they can each teach us about their creators and the age in which the work was produced. For many people the study of the arts and art history is much more interesting and rewarding than the study of political or military history. The author is biased in his belief that the arts are of more significance historically than the *details* of political history. This bias is reflected in this chapter and particularly in its use as an introduction to the political and military history of fifth century Greece. You should keep this bias of the author in mind as you review this chapter. It is hoped you, the reader, will become interested in the history of the arts and that you will pursue art history.

The following questions will help you to gain a mastery of the details presented in the chapter.

1. Review the questions on Greek statues and be certain you can answer them. Consult Appendix B for specific information.
2. Make a sketch of the front of a Greek Temple in the Doric Order and label the various parts.
3. Describe the Temple of Hera at Paestum (the Basilica).
4. Why is the Parthenon considered one of the most remarkable buildings conceived by the human mind?
5. Describe a Doric, an Ionic, and a Corinthian Order column capital.
6. List in order of development the Greek pottery styles.
7. Describe in detail *one* pottery style.
8. What different attitudes are reflected in the poetry of Trytaeus, Sappho and Theognis?
9. Copy the name of the following authors and after each write a phrase summarizing his style and subject matter.
   (a) Herodotus
   (b) Thucydides
   (c) Aeschylus
   (d) Sophocles
   (e) Euripides
   (f) Pindar

10. What experiment did Pythagoras conduct which gave him an idea of how the world was constructed? In a sentence indicate Pythagoras' view of the world.

Essay Question: Pick one of the periods listed below and in an essay indicate how the sculpture, pottery, architecture, and literature reflect the same and/or different characteristics or attitudes.
(a) c. 600 B.C.
(b) Golden Age of Athens (Age of Pericles c. 470-430 B.C.)
(c) The fourth century B.C. (c. 404-323 B.C.)

The following words are used and defined in the text. You should be able to give the meaning of each
(a) agora
(b) caryatid
(c) stoa
(d) tholos
(e) incise
(f) slip
(g). orientalizing
(h) post and lintel

Innumerable books have been written on Greek art. Many have superb photographs. There are also many translations of the Greek authors. This bibliography provides a sample of the variety of works you may consult for further study of this topic.

Aristotle, Plato, Demosthenes, and all other Greek writers. Loeb Classical Library, London, Wm. Heinemann.
Aeschylus, Euripides, Sophocles. *The Complete Greek Tragedies,* ed. D. Greene & R. Lattimore. Chicago, Univ. of Chicago Press, 1959.
Agard, W. R. *The Greek Mind.* Princeton, N.J., D. Van Nostrand Co.
Boardman, John. *Greek Art.* New York, Praeger, 1964.
Bowra, C.M. *Greek Lyric Poetry.* Oxford, Clarendon Press, 1961.
Devambez, Pierre. *Greek Painting.* London, Contact Books, 1962.
Flaceliere, Robert. *Daily Life in Greece at the Time of Pericles.* N.Y., Macmillan Co., 1966.
The Horizon Book of Ancient Greece, ed. Horizon Magazine. N.Y., American Heritage Publishing Co., 1965.
Kitto, H. D. F. *Greek Tragedy.* N.Y., Barnes & Noble.
Lucas, F. L. *Greek Poetry for Everyman.* Boston, Beacon Press, 1956.
Lullies, Reinhard. *Greek Sculpture.* N.Y., Larry N. Abrams, Inc., 1960.
MacKendrick, Paul. *The Greek Stones Speak.* N.Y., St. Martin's Press, 1962.
The Portable Greek Reader, ed. W. H. Auden. N.Y., The Viking Press, 1948.
Wright, J. W. *Masterpieces of Greek Literature.* Cambridge, Mass., Houghton, Mifflin & Co., 1902.

CHAPTER IV

SIXTH CENTURY POLITICAL DEVELOPMENT

Section I—*Introduction*

In Chapter III we took an overview of the period 600-323 B.C. and the point should have been clearly established that many changes took place in Greek life during those years. If we look back to the "Dark Ages" we can realize how many changes took place in the Greek world in the 200 years after Hesiod. In Chapter II many of these changes and their causes were explored. In this chapter we will look at the political changes of the 6th century in some detail and then briefly consider the overall history of the century.

We have discussed the political organization of the "Dark Ages" and the establishment of the rule of an aristocratic class in the years following 750 B.C. You will recall that some of these changes were reflected in Hesiod's *Works and Days* and that many of them were stimulated by the expanding population and the need to cultivate new lands in the hill areas to feed the population. Aristocracies, small groups of like minded individuals who were considered the best, ruled basing their power on their land holdings and their military activity since they could afford horses at the time when cavalry was important. These aristocrats introduced the use of hoplite military tactics. They did not realize that including the average man in the armed forces might undermine their own privileged position. They also encouraged trade and the founding of new colonies again not realizing what the results of these two activities would be for them as a class. What happened politically in the major trading cities after 650 B.C. can be illustrated by the following exercise in which we will consider several leaders of the city of Athens. What is presented here specifically for Athens could be applied to many other Greek city states during the late 7th and the entire 6th century.

Section II—*Political Responses to Changing Conditions*

In 594 B.C. the following program was carried out in the city of Athens by the elected Archon or chief executive officer for that year, an individual named Solon.[1] The position of Archon changed in authority later on but at this time it was the most powerful one in the city.

Solon accomplished the following:

1. Ended enslavement for debt.
2. Reduced the amount of all debts.
3. Limited the size of the estates an individual could hold but he did not confiscate the land already held.
4. Restored land to those who had lost it for indebtedness.
5. He bought back with state funds those citizens who had been sold into slavery abroad.
6. Encouraged industry by requiring each father to teach his son a trade.
7. Encouraged industry by bringing foreign craftsmen, especially potters, to Athens.
8. Encouraged industry by emphasizing the growing of olives and grapes for the production of olive oil and wine for export. The Athenians were thus encouraged to trade and not to attempt to be self-sufficient in supplying their needs.
9. Reformed the state politically by adding to the three existing citizen classes, which were based on wealth in land, a fourth class, the Thetes, who had no landed property but who could vote in the Assembly (Ecclesia) and serve in the law courts (Heliaea). They were not allowed, however, to hold offices in the government.
10. Reformed the state politically by allowing the Ecclesia or Assembly to nominate 40 candidates for Archon (executive position) who would be responsible to the new law courts upon retiring from office for all their actions while in office. From the 40 candidates chosen, nine Archons were chosen by drawing lots to hold office for the year. (According to the Greeks, decision by lot left the decision to the gods.)
11. Reformed the state politically by creating a new Council of Four Hundred, one hundred from each of the four traditional tribes of Attica (the name of the territory around Athens) to prepare the business for the Ecclesia. The new class of Thetes could vote for but not serve in this council.
12. Reformed the state politically by instituting new law courts, the Heliaea, and reducing the power of the old aristocratic council and law court, the Areopagus, giving it only vaguely defined powers of

---

[1] The history of Athens is full of famous individuals. Many are noted for political changes in the city. Solon ranks among the most important. Others who you may read about are Draco, Peisistratus, Cleisthenes, Themistocles, and Pericles.

In Chapter VII some students will be asked to research the city of Athens and they should certainly be familiar with these six men. Students researching Sparta at that time will need to know about Lycurgus who is known as the law giver for that city state.

control over the agenda of the Ecclesia or Assembly. The nine Archons upon leaving office at the end of their year's term became permanent members of the law court of the Areopagus. This added nine new members who had been chosen by the entire citizenry to this aristocratic court each year. The membership of the Areopagus was thus no longer based solely on inherited positions.

Consider these reforms for a moment. When changes are made in a society, it is in response to a set of demands or needs. What were the demands or needs of the Athenians in 594 B.C. as understood by Solon when he took these actions? Read over the list of reforms again and make a list of the conditions that the actions must have been designed to correct. Your list will include those issues Solon must have considered when he instituted these changes. When you have completed your list, see if any of the items seem familar to you. Are there similar conditions today that need reforming? What are the major differences and similarities that you see between what is needed today and what was needed or done by Solon? Be prepared in class to discuss two things. First, what the conditions were in the Greek world that you think Solon wished to change by his reforms. Second, how the need for reform in ancient Athens compares to what you think the need for reform is in the world today. Be certain you complete your lists and have some ideas on these two points *before* you read on.

Solon has been considered the father of Athenian democracy and since many scholars believe the concept of democracy originated in Athens, the father of democracy. On the basis of the reforms listed and your consideration of Solon, do you think he deserves the title father of Athenian democracy? In other words, did these reforms establish democracy in Athens? It should be clear that Solon took measures to help the common man and the poor man to gain a position within society based on legal understandings. He made slavery of citizens for economic reasons illegal and he encouraged economic activity so that each individual could have work to do.[2] He limited the amount of land an individual could acquire. He limited some of the authority of the aristocratic class but he did not take it all away and he certainly did not give much power to the non-landowning class although he did include

[2] It must be noted that these actions were for the citizens of Athens, i.e. men born in the city-state and not for foreigners. Slavery was common in the Greek world of this time and slaves were considered the property of the owner and he could treat them as he wished. Slaves were usually acquired as a result of war or from trade with the people living on the edges of Greek colonization.

them in government activity. The power of the aristocracy was clipped, economic activity based on trade was encouraged, and the concept of citizenship and involvement of all in the government of the polis was stressed in these reforms. Obviously, the reforms abolished the aristocracy's power to enslave citizens in its striving for power and agricultural wealth. The concept of trade in the Greek world was encouraged and this was to lead to the dominance of Athens in the following century. Trade was to bring in new wealth to the city further weakening the political power of the aristocrats. The reforms established new political organizations and allowed for more participation of citizens in the government of Athens. Considering the system of government in other parts of the ancient world, it is clear there was more democracy in Athens than in other areas of comparable size but there were still many reforms needed to make Athens truly democratic.

These reforms of Solon were achieved peacefully in Athens. Similar changes were being made in other cities around the Aegean at this time. Often the changes were brought about only after civil war in the city. No one in Athens was satisfied with Solon's reforms but they did avoid civil war for a generation. Upon completing them, Solon is supposed to have left Athens for an extended trip around the eastern Mediterranean. In later generations he was considered one of the wisest men of Greece. He was born an aristocrat, worked as a merchant, became a lawgiver, struggled to be a poet (the little poetry we have of his reflects his love of the city and people), and ended a traveler. He died in Athens but not until a new reformer had taken authority in the city. The new political leader was Peisistratus and he was much more typical of the political reformers of the 6th century B.C. than was Solon.

Unlike Solon who was elected Archon for just one year, Peisustratus ruled Athens almost continually from 560 to 527 B.C. and was succeeded by his two sons, Hippias and Hipparchus. This fact should make you realize that something happened to the political reforms of Solon since certainly no one could be chosen by lot that continually. Peisistratus came to power by military force and retained his authority in that manner. He is typical of the rulers of the age—the "Age of the Tyrants."

Tyrant has a negative connotation in our society. It did not have this connotation for the Greeks in the 7th, 6th and 5th centuries. The meaning of the word seems to have shifted during the 5th century to mean one-man dictatorial and sometimes oppressive rule opposing the rise of democracy. In the 5th century B.C. the word was connected with the Persian monarchy and the type of power held by the Monarch which was against Greek ideas. The 6th century Greek tyrants, however, styled themselves as champions of the poor and of the new classes who had made fortunes in trade and economic activity and who were not members of the old landed aristocracy. Since the aristocracy continued to rule the city states with their own interests at heart, tensions developed between them and the new merchant trading class and the tensions often ended in conflict. This was true in Athens.

Three distinct social and economic elements had developed in Athens and although Solon delayed the conflict by his reforms, his compromises only delayed the final conflict. The Plain, led by Lycurgus,[3] wanted to retain the oligarchy based on wealth and land. Its members were the old aristocracy and the name derived from the fact they held large land holdings in the fertile plain area of Attica. The second group, led by Megacles, was the Coast and as its name suggests its members were those who had developed wealth through coastal trade and business. The final group, the Hill, was led by Peisistratus and consisted of the dispossessed, those whose land holdings were up in the poorer hill country and those few who had made money in exploiting natural resources.

The Hill was a motley group looking for a leader. Peisistratus made the most of his speaking abilities, his great daring and affrontery, and the fame he gained fighting in small wars to become leader of the Hill.[4] Peisistratus, like most tyrants, was an aristocrat

---

[3] The names of more and more individuals are known to us as we approach the 5th century and the Golden Age of Greece. The fact we know individuals and that they were recorded everywhere from on vase paintings to tombstones indicates how much emphasis this civilization put on individuals. We will mention many individuals but it is up to each reader and teacher to determine how many names should be memorized. The emphasis in the text will be on a few outstanding individuals while many others will be only mentioned.

[4] Herodotus in *Persian War* (Book I paragraph 59-64) has some very interesting tales about Peisistratus and his family. Peisistratus gained power three times, first by duping the people into granting him a body guard when he claimed he had been attacked in the countryside. With the guard he seized the acropolis and thus the city. When he was thrown out a few years later, he again duped the people by riding back into the city with a very tall woman dressed as Athena in his chariot. He claimed he was appointed by her to rule and with help from Megacles gained power again. He was forced into exile a second time and this time used military force to return.

One son, Hipparchus, while ruling Athens was killed in a plot led by Harmodius and Aristogeiton. The assassins became great heroes of Athens and were known as those who overthrew the tyranny but the basis by birth. He had gained wealth by exploiting gold mines in Thrace. But this was not enough for him and he sought fame and fortune in political action. The reforms that Peisistratus instituted in the city of Athens reflected the conditions of the mid-5th century. Read these and compare them to the reforms of Solon. What conditions appear different? What does Peisistratus seem to be concerned with the most? Do these reforms appear as significant as those of the Archon Solon? Do these reforms seem to appeal to any class or group? Read these over and then refer back to the reforms of Solon before you read on.

Peisistratus accomplished the following:

1. Built an aqueduct to bring more water to the public fountains in the city.
2. Planned the building of a huge Doric Temple to Olympian Zeus that was not completed until Roman times. Improved the temples on the acropolis and added a new colonnade to the temple of Athena.
3. Encouraged artists and sculptors. Red Figure vase painting began during his rule as did the use of marble rather than limestone for sculpture.
4. Developed the Panathenaic Festival thus encouraging participation in the arts (it is believed the *Iliad* and *Odyssey* of Homer were first written down at this time).
5. Rebuilt the Theater of Dionysios at the foot of the acropolis and encouraged dramatic presentation there.[5]
6. Established a lavish court in Athens and invited artists and poets from different areas to visit and to settle in Athens.
7. Sent a military expedition to the Hellespont which captured the fortress of Sigeum and gave Athens control of the area and thus the sea route to the Black Sea.
8. Encouraged the founding of a colony in Thrace near the Hellespont by Miltiades, a leader of the Plain.

of the plot according to Aristotle was not liberty but the fact good looking Harmodius rejected the advances of the young tyrant's half brother who then made unpleasant remarks about Harmodius in public. The two lovers, Harmodius and Aristogeiton, then planned the murder of both Hipparchus and Hippias but the plot was only partly successful. The date was 514 B.C. The story is significant in indicating the tyrants were not overthrown because of their oppressive tyranny and in revealing the ethical code of the age in Athens.

[5] Drama originated as a dance of satyrs before the alter of the god Dionysus (in mythology, satyrs were half-human, half-goat: in the dance people dressed as satyrs). The leader wrote the song the satrys were to sing. During the age of Peisistratus, the leader began to talk to the satyrs apart from their singing. The leader later put on a costume to indicate who he was. In Chapter III we discussed how Aeschylus developed this basic form into the great dramatic plays of the 5th century.

9. He cleansed the holy island of Delos by removing the bones of all of those buried on the island. He claimed for Athens the leadership of the Ionian people by this religious act. This leadership claim was very important later in Greek history.

10. Arranged for the nomination as Archons (chief elected executive officers) of individuals friendly to him thus assuring these leaders' support of his actions.

11. Distributed to his landless supporters the lands seized from his enemies who fled from Athens. The new owners paid a land tax of 1/10th of the produce.

It should be obvious that the actions of Peisistratus are much less important and basic than the reforms of Solon. There seems to have been little attempt made to legally change the structure of government. Instead the outward structure established by Solon was kept but the real authority was exercised in a manner not anticipated by Solon. How often changes take place this way in which the form is left but the real basis is very different than what was originally assumed! Can you think of examples where this has taken place or is taking place now?

Peisistratus had his henchmen in office. He did not hold any elected position but could exercise power through his men. He made military moves to support the growing trade of Athens. As the city concentrated on her specialties of wine and olive oil, wheat had to be imported to feed the people. At this time in history the best source of wheat was the Black Sea region of southern Russia. By securing Athenian control of the entrance to the sea, cheap wheat was assured for the populace and wealth for the importers. This newly wealthy group in the society then gave strong support to the rule of Peisistratus.

The building of the aqueduct was a clever move to gain support from the masses in the city where water was in short supply. The construction of the aqueduct required high engineering skill and clearly indicates how far the Greeks had come in their recovery of the lost skills of the Mycenaeans.

The main concerns of Peisistratus were with the arts. The foundations for the greatness of the Age of Pericles were laid by him and his court. Without the 6th century foundations, the 5th century would have been far less glorious. Certainly drama, vase painting, architecture, and sculpture were all encouraged by the wealthy tyrant. This fact should make one wonder if the arts are a luxury that only flourish when supported by the wealthy. There was plenty of money for the arts in the 6th century as there was when Pericles used the money from the Delian League to beautify Athens after 447 B.C. Peisistratus got his money from exploiting gold mines in Thrace and from the new 10% tax on farm produce.

The tyranny encouraged the arts and encouraged the young men of aristocratic families to find pleasure in them and in other diversions. The palestra and gymnasium flourished as the interest of the noble youths were diverted in directions that would not focus on the lack of political freedom and would keep them from attacking the tyranny. The middle class could now provide the soldiers needed for hoplite tactics and, although military service was required of all citizens, the leadership role of the traditional aristocracy was fading. The new wealthy citizens were pleased with the tyranny as trade flourished and the new colonies assured a fine future. Athens grew tremendously in the century and by mid-century had replaced Corinth as the most important trading nation of the time as indicated in Chapter II. In many ways the tyranny was good for Athens.

Late 7th and 6th century tyrannies had been good for other city states also, unlike the tyrannies that developed in the 5th and 4th century. These latter clearly indicate a shift in the concept and aims of tyranny. The 4th century tyrants that ruled many of the city states of Sicily ruled solely with their own interests at heart and these interests often did not coincide with what was best for the citizens of the city state. In Sicily tyrants had body-guards that abused the citizens and the story is told of one tyrant, Phalaris of Agrigentum, who roasted his enemies alive in a bronze bull. Whatever the facts,these later tyrannies were different from the earlier ones in that the policies followed by the individuals in power did not benefit any of the people.

It seems tyrants first appeared in the Ionian city states and it is thought the idea originated there as a copy of the form of government practiced in Sardis, capital of Lydia. The kings of Lydia were extremely rich and as said in Chapter II, they were the first to coin money. They encouraged trade and established an elaborate court where the arts were supported. Thrasybulus of Miletus is the most famous of the Ionian tyrants but tyrannies were established for varying lengths of times in all these city states. Under Thrasybulus Miletus flourished in trade and the arts. He was responsible for the establishment of several of the Black Sea colonies of Miletus which gave the city dominance in that area. As seen in Chapter II, Miletus was one of the leading colonizing cities of the Greek world and tyranny, by reducing the power of the aristocracy and encouraging the merchant class, aided the economic and cultural growth of the city.

The fact that many nobles were exiled and some lost their lives; the fact that there were small wars between different city states (these paved the way for later Persian domination of the coast of Ionia as only Persia could control the fighting and establish order in the coastal area); the fact that the common men did not rule and were often exploited must not be overlooked in evaluating the good effects of these tyrannies. It should be noted, however, that the nobles had been oppressing the common men and the merchants and that warfare was common among the Greek city states. Finally, after the overthrow of tyrants democracy appeared in several cities allowing more rule by the average man than had ever existed before. We must avoid judging these tyrants of the 7th-5th centuries by our standards of good government, as their contributions varied greatly and the needs of people were often met effectively by their acts.

There was at least one tyrant ruling somewhere in the Greek world from the 7th century until the Romans conquered the Greeks. In later history the Greeks looked at tyrants as bad. In the "Age of Tyrants," the benefits they brought outweighed the disadvantages. Tyrants based their power on force and not on a legitimate claim to authority as do hereditary kings or elected leaders. This fact opposed the Greek sense of both freedom and order, those two conflicting forces in Greek life. Constitutional development was slowed by the tyrants as you can see from the list of actions taken by Peisistratus but other benefits were great. The tyrants are closely linked to the growth of trade and colonization. For instance, Cypelus established a tyranny in Corinth by overthrowing the ruling clan of nobles in 657 B.C. Cypelus stimulated the growth of Corinthian colonies and brought the island of Corcyra under Corinth's control, a break with the usual relationship of mother city and colony.

Cypelus' son, Periander, took over the tyranny and is the most famous of all the 6th century tyrants. He continued to encourage colonization and established an alliance between Corinth and the tyrant of Miletus, Thrasybulus. Periander established contacts with Pharaoah Psammetichus II of Egypt and brought Corinth into that rich market soon after Miletus entered it. He planned to cut a canal across the isthmus of Corinth thus connecting the Corinthian and Saronic gulfs but did not have the resources to complete the undertaking. The concept indicates his support of the merchants. He encouraged the pottery trade and a great quantity was produced but the quality suffered which paved the way for the later domination of Athenian pottery. It was under the tyranny that roof tiles were developed at Corinth allowing for new techniques in the Doric architecture. One of the earliest Doric temples in Greece, a temple to Apollo, was built at Corinth. Periander encouraged the arts and a new poetry form was developed in Corinth at this time. Look over the acts of Periander and make a list of them. Now, turn back to the list of the acts of Peisistratus. How do the two compare? Can you make a generalization as to what actions tyrants undertook? Can you now summarize the changes that took place in Greek economics, art, and government either instituted or encouraged by tyrants or by elected reformers in the 6th century?

Were these reforms universal in the Greek world of this time? Obviously not. Each polis developed in its own unique way during the age of tyrants. We can, however, set a general picture of what was happening although we must realize that there were many variations on the generalized development.

To return briefly to the 6th century Athenian history, after the murder of Peisistratus' son, Hipparchus, by Harmodius and Aristogiton, for whom there was little public sympathy at the time, the surviving brother, Hippias, instituted a harsh policy of repression fearing that others were involved in the plot. How often this happens in history as fear drives men to acts they soon regret. Can you think of other examples? The harsh measures undertaken such as arrests and exile affected the former supporters of the tyrants. The time was ripe for overthrow.

Cleisthenes, a member of an old and important noble family, the Alcmaeonid, that had been exiled by Peisistratus, led the revolt and with the help of the Delphic Oracle, got the support of Sparta in the overthrow. Hippias and his family fled. The reforms of Solon were reinstated and then Cleisthenes left the country the way Solon had.

Soon strife broke out between conflicting Plain, Hill and Coast groups. Sparta intervened again. This was a mistake. The Athenians rose up as a people and threw out the Spartans. Sparta was no lover of democracy and feared its growth in Athens but she could have done nothing to support its growth more strongly than to invade Attica. The antagonism of these two cities had its roots earlier but this aggravated the situation and set the basis for the struggles between the two cities in the 5th century which culminated in the disastrous Peloponnesian War. Cleisthenes returned and Athens underwent a political reform—more basic than anything so far in her history. It was this reform that set the basis of 5th century democracy in Athens.

THE GOVERNMENT OF ATHENS

ASSEMBLY

[Ecclesia]

All Citizens

Determined policy and laws

Council of 500
[Boule]
chosen by lot for one year
— 50 from each of the 10 **— CITIZENS —**
Tribes. Prytany rotated for
1/10th of year among
tribes.
*Prepared material for con-
sideration by Assembly —
Responsible for daily operation of the city as mem-
ber of the Prytany
(Presidency)*

Jury
[Heliaea]
Chosen by lot from volun-
teers over age 30.
Jurors were picked from
the pool to form a jury for
each case.
*Decided law cases for
Athens and Delian League*

EXECUTIVES

Generals [Strategoi] Elected by vote of citizens each year *Commanded military Other indirect powers*	Special Boards usually 10 on a board elected by lot for one year *Supervised special functions*	Nine Archons Elected by lot for one year *Presiding officers for trials, etc.*	Priests and Treasurers Some by inheri- tance; some by lot; some elected *Various traditional and administra- tive functions.*

What do you think was the heart of the trouble in the city of Athens as far as sound and stable government by elected officials might have been in 508 B.C.? As you read the following, decide if Cleisthenes focused on the key problem. Be prepared in class to discuss the issue. Remember he had the populace behind these reforms because they had a foreign foe and this unified them for the moment. Common enemies have often united people.

Cleisthenes decided the main problem was the three parties, Plain, Coast and Hill, that coincided with geographic areas and also formed the basis for representation in government. Cleisthenes abolished the old tribes that went back to the days when legendary Theseus unified the plain of Attica and which had little relation to the political situation in Attica. He established ten new tribes in their place. These tribes were made up of units from each of the geographic areas. To achieve this Attica was divided into many small geographic units called demes. A citizen, only males were citizens in Athens, was born in a deme, and was registered there for life. Even if he moved he still belonged to that deme. Demes from each geographic area were assigned to one of the ten tribes. A man thus belonged to a deme and to a tribe. A man did two things as part of his tribe—he fought with it and he voted with it. Thus each tribe developed a sense of brotherhood in military actions and of common interests politically. The effect of the change would be similar to a complete abolishment of the state borders in the United States and setting a pattern so that a new state consisted of people from every one of the old states. These people would vote together thus eliminating regional commitments. The South would no longer exist as a unit for voting and the Middle West would disappear as would all our regional divisions. Men from all these geographic areas would get to know each other by serving together in the army. Of course, this is an impossibility for a nation the size of the United States but Athens was small enough, it worked. The result in Athens was a much greater sense of unity for the city and less for the old geographic regions.

To go along with the new tribes Cleisthenes changed the Council of Four Hundred and it became a Council of Five Hundred, fifty elected by lot from each of the new tribes. The Council members served for a year. The outgoing council had the duty to eliminate any incompetent members chosen by lot for the new council. All magistrates or law enforcement officers and executives were responsible to the new Council of Five Hundred and were chosen by lot from its membership.

The only positions in Athens in the 5th century that were not chosen by lot were the ten generals or strategoi, one from each tribe, who led the army. These were elected and could hold office in succeeding years. Cleisthenes' reform put the power of the government in the hands of the citizens of Athens and it was this democratic government that ruled the city in the 5th century. Pericles, who gave his name to the last half of that century, was one of the generals. He, as one strategoi, was elected to office year after year while all the other government positions in Athens were filled by lot.

In Athens by the end of the 5th century, tyranny had given way to democracy and this pattern was followed in varying degrees in other cities. The impact of changing economic conditions created by the growth of trade and colonization had led to this new political situation. The new colonies had established the worth of the individual—he could conquer the wilderness—and now government in mainland Greece reflected this attitude also.

Consider how this shift is reflected in the scenes on the vase painting done in Athens before and after 500 B.C. The end of the frontier opportunity which was discussed in Chapter II helped precipitate many of the changes which occurred on the mainland.[6]

We have mentioned the city state many times and earlier we stated that the Greek word was *polis* and that it really could not be translated yet we continually do so. What was this organization we have been discussing? How did it function?

Section III—*The Polis*

The polis was many things to the Greek living within it. The organization fulfilled many of the functions of society that are filled by separate organizations in the United States. The relationship between the individual and his polis was so intense and important that Aristotle, the great 4th century philosopher, defined human beings in terms of the polis. He wrote that man was a creature who lived in a polis. When you analyze the state-

---

[6] You may wish to consider again the parallels between the U.S. and its frontier experience and that of the Greeks. See Chapter II for comments on the work of F. J. Turner on the frontier in American History.

ment, it means that what distinguishes man from other creatures, animals and birds, is that he lives in a particular type of social arrangement. This statement of Aristotle's has often been translated, 'Man is a political animal', but this really is not what Aristotle says. Certainly from the Greek viewpoint man was a political animal and any one who knows the modern Greeks know they still are, but Aristotle did not focus only on the political aspect of the polis—he had in mind the many other aspects of the organization which also set man apart from all other creatures.[7]

The polis as we will describe it functioned for several centuries in Greece. As with all institutions, it changed gradually over the years. The form it took about 500 B.C. was different from what it had been about 750 B.C. We will generalize about the polis of 500 B.C. because it reached a peak of development then. At the end of the book we will ask you to consider what major changes in its form and function must have taken place by the time of Alexander the Great.

The polis about 500 B.C. fulfilled the religious, recreational, educational, cultural, military, unifying, economic, patriotic, and political needs of the people within it. There was an olympic diety that was the chosen god or goddess of each polis. The goddess Athena was the patron and protectress of Athens. Many of our examples will be chosen from Athens because we have more information about Athens but the principles apply to all poleis (plural of polis). Athena's temples on the Acropolis were a focus of the religious life of the Athenians. Other gods had their temples and special ceremonies and each family had family gods they worshipped but the city was held together by the worship of Athena. The form of the worship and the role of the protecting god or goddess varied from place to place. In Athens, Athena was considered both the giver of the olive signifying support of the peaceful activities of the city and also the warrior goddess signifying support of the military operations which defended the city from attack.

The minor Athenian Panathenaic festival held every year was both a religious and a recreational activity and shows how the functions of the polis often overlapped and were closely interrelated. Think for a moment how the United States as a political entity becomes involved in the religious and recreational life of the citizens. Keep this comparison in mind as you read on and see what similarities and differences you can spot.

[7] The fact that the word politics has the Greek word polis as its root confuses the matter greatly. Politics was a crucial part of the polis but not the only part as we shall see.

The games of the Panathenaic festival are an example of the recreation provided by the polis. So are the dramatic festivals instituted by Peisistratus in Athens. The same type of activities can be found in other poleis. During the tyrant's rule, the gymnasium became important. This was a place for training the citizen in both physical activities to keep him fit for military service and intellectual activities to inform him what was expected of him as a citizen of the city.

In a famous speech reported by the historian Thucydides, Pericles referred to Athens as the "School of Hellas." Pericles believed Athens taught Greece what was best by example just as the polis taught its citizens by example and induction. The polis was the training ground for the individual and it was as a participant in the affairs of the polis that a person learned the meaning of virtue and proper conduct. There were no public schools in Athens paid for by the city but a person lived his whole life in front of his fellow citizens, many of whom he knew or knew him, and his conduct was always subject to their approval or censure and in this way the entire polis was the school.

The cultural life of the city was common to everyone and later in Athens, citizens were given free tickets to the theater so that even the poorest could attend and be enlightened. The theater was like our T. V. today. Instead of paying income taxes as in the United States, wealthy individuals in the city provided the funds for the production of the plays and it was a great honor to have sponsored the winning play at the festival of Dionysus.

Every male citizen at age 18 had to give two years of military service to the Athenian polis. This activity helped to train him as a citizen and it also provided the basis for the defense of the polis. After the two years of training, the citizen until age 60 was on call in case of need. The older men were on home guard duty and the younger fought in the hoplite ranks because this new military tactic had created a need for every citizen to be a soldier. Hoplite tactics required more men and special training in close order drill. A few citizens served in the cavalry if they were able to afford it. Each one of the ten tribes established by Cleisthenes had to provide a cavalry unit and a hoplite unit so service was evenly spread through the polis in case of any military activity. The numbers in each unit depended upon the military action. Thus in Athens, the defense of the polis was integrated into the life of each citizen.

Sparta also had a tight relationship between the citizens and the defense of the polis. There each boy at age 7 was started on his military training and his whole life both educational and religious was tied to the polis. He was not allowed to marry or vote until age 30 unlike Athens where the voting age was 18 and marriage was a private affair arranged usually by the families. Spartan men lived in army barracks and had no individual home life—a great contrast to Athens but a clear indication of the importance attached to the polis which could control the life of the individual as the polis determined.

Other city states had variations on the military service required but no other polis went to the Spartan extreme. Can you imagine what it would have been like to live in Sparta? Would you like to live that way with no individual decisions to make and no chance to marry or influence the government until 30? Most of us find the Spartan way of life distasteful but many Greeks admired Sparta for her clarity of national goals and admired the way she lived up to these goals. An important attitude of the Greeks was to pursue arete—which we loosely translate as excellence—in whatever was undertaken.[8] To many Greeks, Sparta achieved arete better than any other polis since she set her ideal of excellence and then led her citizens to live up to the ideal. Many Greeks disagreed with the ideal but they admired the way it was pursued. This again gives us a clear insight into a function of the polis.

The economic life of the polis was self-sufficient in the earliest days of its development. As each polis grew, trade and colonization developed and a man such as Solon who encouraged specialization by his reforms in Athens helped to break down this self-sufficiency. The new trade helped give each polis its identity as poleis concentrated on certain products. As we have seen in Athens, trade precipitated political changes that involved more citizens and not just the aristocrats in the government of the polis. While ultimately the introduction of outside influences through trade led to the decline of the polis, it took several hundred years. The disappearance of self-sufficiency combined

---

[8] Arete meant more than excellence. It meant doing what you did as well as you could with full devotion and exertion. Achilles, the hero of Homer's *Iliad*, provided an example of arete for all ancient Greeks who studied the *Iliad*. He fought against the Trojans superbly but he also displayed his anger fully when he felt he was wronged and he exhibited his grief in the extreme when his closest companion was killed. Arete entailed living to the utmost, doing to the fullest, supporting to the extreme, and abiding by the best. It provided a noble ideal, one hard to attain, but one which the ancient Greeks strove for and greatly admired particularly in the 6th and 5th centuries.

with the growth of specialization in trade intensified a feeling of identity with the local city and led to a feeling of antagonism towards other and especially neighboring poleis. Interdependent trade never created a feeling of unity among the Greeks. Instead each Greek thought first of his polis. This intense patriotism for the polis and a lack of national feeling is an important characteristic of Greek history. Are there other illustrations in history of this sense of localism at the expense of national unity? How does the Greek view compare with that of the United States? How did it happen that we have developed a national unity out of 50 different states? How does modern Europe compare with the ancient Greeks? with the United States?

The manner in which Athenian writers referred to their city provides us information on the function of the polis. Besides Pericles saying the polis was the "School of Hellas" playwrights used the term in many ways. For instance, the playwright Sophocles, refers to it as a ship brought safely through a storm. This simile, the ship of state, is now common in the western world but for Sophocles it had a special connotation. He thought of the polis as an entity like a ship that needed to be steered and guided by the citizens and the rulers.

Aeschylus in his play, *The Oresteia*, referred to the polis as the means by which law is fulfilled. To the Athenians law was king and the polis, not some individual King or pharoah, expressed the law. The law changed in Athens but it was changed by the citizens of the polis as it was debated by these citizens in the ecclesia (assembly) and put into practice in the law courts where all citizens served as jurors chosen by lot. Every citizen had to know the law because he never knew when he might have to defend himself in court or serve as a juror.

To later Greek philosophers the polis was the culmination of a long development and the great contribution of the Greeks to civilization. It was the source of order in the relations of men and we have already considered how important order was for the Greek. Aristotle was particularly impressed by the polis and, as indicated above, felt it was the polis that set humans apart from animals and which in turn made the Greeks better than other men all of whom were called barbarians by the Greeks. The word barbarian did not have quite the connotation for the Greeks it has today. To them it meant a person who did not live in a polis and enjoy the benefits provided by this form of organization.

Finally, the polis was the focus and center for all political activity. Whether ruled by a tyrant or by the people as in Athens, the unit ruled was the polis.

Aristotle believed that the ideal polis would be small enough for each citizen to know all his fellow citizens. It would operate best under these conditions of intimacy. In this day of the super powers it is an interesting concept. How does it appeal to you? Would you like to live in a country small enough where you could know all the voters?

Having considered the way the Greeks view a polis, what does it remind you of? Think back over the above description and see if anything comes to mind that is similar in our society. Two institutions come to my mind. The first is the boarding school and as a teacher in a church school, the similarity between it and the ideal polis has always struck me. The school is small enough so that all members can know each other. It has a religious life that dominates the place and all members are expected to worship together. There is a close knit quality about the school — a type of patriotism that unites students whenever another school is mentioned. They defend the school not in war but in athletic contests for which they prepare by intense training organized by the school. All its members must participate in these contests. Cultural activities are a function of the school and visitors and trips away are planned. Recreation, from dances to movies, is organized by the school. The school is governed by the members. Some have more authority than others, which was typical of poleis other than Athens, but all school members vote for student and faculty representatives to a council and they all serve on committees. The school is a self contained economic unit with its kitchens, electricians, roads, heating plant, and jobs for all community members.

The aim of this organization is to create a certain type of person and although there has been a decided move away from the standardized prep school graduate in recent years, there is still something distinct about the "preppie". There was something distinct about the citizen of each polis when he went out into the world and you could expect certain actions from an Athenian or a Spartan just as you could and often still can from a St. Paul's, an Exeter or an Episcopal High graduate. A small college has some of these characteristics but it is not as easily identifiable and the college does not control as much of a person's life.

The other institution that comes to mind is the summer camp run by groups such as the YMCA or the Scouts. There is a unity among the members that is similar to that created by the

Greek polis but because the members are together for such a short time, the parallels do not seem as great as those between a boarding school and the polis.

We asked above what comparisons there were between the United States and the polis. What ideas have you developed? Do you see any similarities? any differences? Can you state what the greatest difference is between the two forms of social/ political organization? Think about it and then write down your idea. What are the strengths and weaknesses of each type of organization? Be prepared to present your views. You may be asked to divide up into small groups in class to develop your ideas.

One way of analyzing the Greek polis is to diagram its functions. This has proven helpful to students in the past and it allows for an interesting comparison to the United States. Such a schematic presentation appears in this section. You will note that there is one box into which all the functions of the polis are fitted. In the case of the United States, these functions can not be fitted into one box because for one thing the Constitution requires the separation of Church and State. In fact, our society breaks these functions up into many different boxes some of which overlap and some of which are entirely separated. This clearly points out the unifying force of the polis within the society—a force that you personally might consider stultifying but which proved not to be so for the Greeks as we know from the Age of Pericles. On the other hand, perhaps one of the major difficulties of our lives is the fragmentation involved and the difficulty we have in committing ourselves to anything when we have so many choices. We also find it difficult to affect the results in any one area since we must spread our effort about in so many different boxes in order to have a full life. It is hoped that you will have a chance to discuss these two diagrams in class and to consider the impact of both the polis and the United States on its citizens. Athens, as the United States is, was a democracy. We have many things in common and we owe many of our ideas about government to the Greeks but there is a major difference as we have discovered. How do you think this difference affects us?

In summary, the polis was at the heart of Greek life and history. It is a most important institution and one that must be understood if the Greeks and their contributions to the civilization of the west are to be appreciated. The Greeks were ready to fight for their polis against all others, especially against their fellow

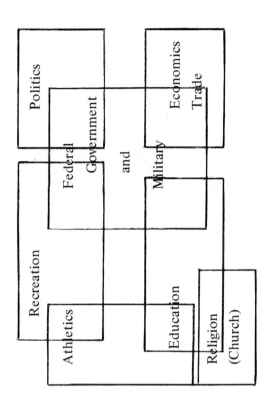

THE UNITED STATES

THE POLIS

Greeks. This fact was at the root of much of the history of the period 545-323 B.C.

Section IV—*Chapter Review*

The questions and suggested exercises below will provide a good review of the most important material in this chapter. The chapter has as its focus the political history of the Sixth Century. Events and ideas that relate to the economic and intellectual history of this period have been presented elsewhere and your teacher may ask you to write a paper putting all of the information together.

The important concept of the polis was introduced in the chapter. It is essential in gaining an understanding of the ancient Greeks, and perhaps most importantly an understanding of their contributions to western civilization, that the polis and what it meant and how it functioned is understood. The concept was introduced in the chapter on political history since the polis is usually translated as city state and its political function is stressed. It should be understood, however, that this function is only one of many filled by the polis and its total impact and affect on the ancient Greek must be understood to appreciate Greek history. The polis served a religious, recreational, educational, cultural, military, unifying, and economic as well as political function. The polis encouraged the Greek to live a full life and to participate actively in the life of the city. This attitude has had an important effect on western civilization as it has led to an emphasis upon the individual and his role in society. Within some poleis the Greeks developed ideas of democracy and these ideas have influenced the west particularly in the past four hundred years.

Some of these questions were included in the text and others are added here to aid you in mastering the chapter.

1. What were the needs of the Athenians in 594 B.C. as understood by Solon? Did his reforms instituted to meet these needs establish democracy in Athens?
2. To what group or class of people would the reforms of Peisistratus have appealed?
3. Compare the actions and reforms of Peisistratus and Periander. As a result, what generalizations can you make about 6th century tyrants?
4. Did Cleisthenes focus on the key problem(s) facing Athens when he made his reforms? Explain your answer in a short essay.

   5. What was the function of the Greek polis?
   6. Would you have liked to live in Sparta? Why?
   7. Would you like to live in a country small enough that you
      could know all the voters? Why?
   8. What parallels and differences do you see between the U.S.
      and the polis? What are the strengths and weaknesses of
      each type of organization?

The following people are mentioned in the chapter. You should
be able to connect each with a country or polis and indicate at
least one thing of significance that he did.

a. Cleisthenes   d. Cypelus
b. Hippias   e. Periander
c. Peisistratus   f. Solon

The following terms are used in the chapter and should be
understood before going to the next chapter.

a. areopagus   d. ecclesia
b. archon   e. heliaea
c. arete   f. thetes

There are many projects that could be developed based on the
information in this chapter. For instance, you might organize your
class according to Cleisithenes' reforms and hold an election
according to Athenian election methods. You may wish to pursue
the comparison between the polis and a boarding school. The
class might divide up aspects of life in the U.S. and then discuss
how these overlap and how they are separated. The diagram
included in the chapter could then be analyzed with more insight
and understanding. Some students might make a report on scenes
on Greek pottery of the 6th century and what they show of
the life of the age. Many Greek vases have scenes of athletic
activity and several books have been written describing Greek
athletics based on these scenes. A student might be interested in
reporting on life in the gymnasium or on one athletic activity
such as jumping or wrestling.

The following bibliography will help you in any research projects you undertake.

Agard, W. R. *The Greek Mind.* Princeton, N.J., D. Van Nostrand Co., 1957.
Aristotle, Plato, and all other Greek writers. Loeb Classical Library,
   London, Wm. Heinemann.
Burn, A. R. *The Lyric Age of Greece.* New York, St. Martin's Press, 1960.
Burn, A. R. *Persia and the Greeks: The Defense of the West 546-478 B.C.*
   Minerva Press, 1968.

Bury, J. B. *History of Greece.* London, Macmillan, 1963.

Gardiner, E. N. *Greek Athletic Sports and Festivals.* London, Macmillan Co.

Greece: Myths, Gods & Heroes; Greece: The Birth of Reason; Greece; The Golden Age; Greece: Pride and Fall. Life Education Program — Reprints Time, Inc.

Harris, H. A. *Greek Athletes and Athletics.* Bloomington, Ind., Indiana University Press, 1966.

Herodotus, et. al. *The Portable Greek Historians.* ed. M. I. Finley. N. Y., Viking Press, 1959.

Kitto, H. D. F. *The Greeks.* Baltimore, Md., Penguin Books, 1951.

CHAPTER V

THE IONIAN REVOLT and the "AXIAL PERIOD"

Section I—*Highlights of Greek history from c. 700 B.C. to 495 B.C.*

The major events in the history of the 6th century have already been touched upon so far in this text. The end of overseas colonization as a major activity, the rule of tyrants, the growth of democracy in many poleis, the expansion of wealth and trade throughout the Greek world, the change in art styles moving towards presentation of an idealized individual or god in sculpture, the development of pottery skills allowing superb reproductions of the human being in Red Figure vase paintings reflecting the life of the age in the scenes portrayed, and the increase in engineering ability as seen in aqueducts and greater refinements in the Doric and Ionian styles. We have indicated at length the influence of other regions on the developments of the Greeks and we have noted that Egyptian influence was particularly strong in the late 7th and 6th centuries. We have, however, said little specifically about the internal relations of the Greek city states.

Two developments on the mainland are important to note. First, was the intervention of Sparta in the overthrow of the Athenian tyranny and her continued intervention after the tyrant Hippias had fled. This action at first gained Sparta support in Athens but by trying to prevent the growth of democracy under Cleisthenes, Sparta created a distrust among Athenians of her motives and way of life which had developed so differently from that of Athens. The second development was the establishment of Sparta as the dominant polis in the Peloponnesus and of Athens as the dominant polis north of the Isthmus of Corinth. Sparta in the course of the century defeated her neighbors to the north and in 550 B.C. defeated Argos to the north east. She organized a league of all Peloponnesian states except two, Argos and Achaea. Even Corinth joined the league for sound economic reasons, as did Megara at the northern end of the isthmus of Corinth. The league supported aristocratic oligarchies. It made Sparta the most powerful polis in Greece. The league came into conflict with both tyrants and growing democratic states. Peisistratus, however, kept good relations with the league and with powerful Argos in the Peloponnesus who was not in the league—a clever action of keeping support in two camps which strengthened Athens.

Athens' position was also strengthened when she captured the island of Salamis which controlled the sea route to both Athens and Megara. Whichever city controlled the island had a great advantage for trade and growth over the other city. The acquisition of Salamis was essential if Athens was to grow. Peisistratus gained fame in the fighting which gave the island to Athens. Settlers were sent to the island and although the inhabitants were never made Athenian citizens, possession of the island laid the foundation for Athenian supremacy on the sea. She now controlled the bay of Eleusis and no longer had to fear her neighbor Megara.

Other important events of the century having to do with Greek political and military history had connections with the Near East. During the century Persia rose to be the greatest power in history to that date with an empire that stretched from Egypt, through Anatolia to the borders of modern Pakistan. Assyrian power had been overthrown by the Medes and Chaldeans in 612 B.C. The Medes consolidated with their kinsmen, the Persians, and proceeded to conquer the northern part of the old Assyrian empire and attacked Lydia in southwestern Anatolia. An eclipse of the sun which was interpreted as an act of the gods stopped the opponents and a treaty was signed that preserved the Lydian empire for a generation. The daughter of the Lydian king married the Persian king and Lydia prospered because of the extensive trade she had with the Greek world and the Near East. The Lydian King, Croesus, became noted in ancient history for his wealth.

The Persian king who had signed the treaty with Lydia was overthrown by Cyrus of the Persian Achaemenid family. Under these conditions, King Croesus of Lydia decided to attack Persia after consulting the Oracle at Delphi.[1] He was defeated by Cyrus in 545 B.C. The Greek city states along the Aegean coast of Anatolia, which had been under Croesus's domination, were now brought under the influence of the huge Persian empire. They were unable to exercise any control over the direction the Persian King would take unlike the days when the Greeks had many

[1] The famous report of the Delphic oracle to Croesus is typical of the oracle's statements. Asked if Croesus would win if Lydia went to war against Persia, the oracle replied that if Croesus attacked, a great empire would fall. The empire was not named leaving it up to the interpreter to decide what was the meaning. Croesus, of course, thought the great empire would be Persia. He attacked and found the great empire that fell was his own. He was spared by the Persian King and lived at his court for many years.

friends at the Lydian court and viewed the Lydians more like Greeks than like barbarians. In fact, King Croesus had given fabulous gifts to Apollo's shrine at Delphi and he followed many of the ways of the Greeks. The Persians were very different and were considered barbarians by the Greeks.

The organization of the Persian empire and especially the Royal Road that linked the Ionian coast with the capital at Susa aided trade as did the standardization of the coinage effected by Darius. The Persian coin was always known to the Greeks as a Daric named after Darius. Life under the Persian rule was certainly tolerable to the Ionian Greeks but it was not as easy as it had been under Lydian influence.

The predecessors of Darius had established the Asian and African limits of the empire. Darius turned to Europe to extend Persian control over Thrace, into the Balkans, and along the shores of the Black Sea in order to insure access to the Black Sea and to avoid attacks by nomadic tribes. He organized an expedition calling on support from the Ionian cities. With this help, he bridged the Bosphorus, the water that separates Europe from Asia, and in 513 B.C. attacked Thrace. The Greek historians presented a very distorted version of the expedition but discounting their bias, we learn that it was very successful. Darius held territory in the Balkan peninsula for over fifteen years. He marched across the Danube and made Persian power felt there as he tried to gain control of the gold mines in what is now Rumania. He failed to establish permanent control in these areas, however.

On returning to Anatolia he found that several Ionian Greek poleis had revolted and he crushed the revolts and brought the cities under Persian control. Those Ionian cities ruled by tyrants had remained loyal and they retained more freedom. The tyrants were clever.

In 509 B.C. the tyrant, Hippias, son of Peisistratus, was thrown out of Athens and democracy was established by the reforms of Cleisthenes. For the next decade, peace seemed to rule Persian and Greek worlds. It is possible that the example of Athens inspired the next crucial event in Greek-Persian relations— the revolt against Persian control by the cities of Ionia. This revolt eventually led to the Persian War between the loosely united Greek cities of the southern mainland and Peloponnesus and the Persian barbarians. This war set the tone for all 5th century Greek history.

Section II—*The Ionian Revolt*

The origin of the Ionian revolt is presented in detail in Herodotus and is interesting to read with its many details of personal intrigue, frustrations, and ambition. The impact of the individual on the course of history is often overlooked, but this revolt clearly points out how the desires of one person can lead to major shifts in history. The story briefly is as follows. Darius planned to reward Histiacus, tyrant of Miletus, for his part in the expedition against Thrace. Histiacus asked for a site on which to build a colony that might have threatened Persian power. Instead of getting the reward he asked for, Darius, feeling threatened, took him to his capitol, Susa, as a captive. His son-in-law, Aristagoras, ruled in Miletus instead and he got the idea of a major expedition against the islands of the Aegean which would build up his own glory and make him as important as his father-in-law had been. The satrap or Persian governor of the area, Artaphernes, and Darius approved. A fleet sailed to Naxos but the Persian admiral and Aristagoras argued. The Persians then warned the Naxians of the attack and the Naxians withstood the attack. Aristagoras had not become a hero and to redeem himself, plotted a rebellion against Persia by the Greek cities of Ionia. Sparta refused to aid the revolt just as she had refused to fight against the original Persian conquest, but Aristagoras gained limited support from Athens which sent twenty ships, and Eretria. Eretria was the little town that fought with Chalcis the first recorded war in Greek history, remember? This Athenian and Eretrian support provided Darius a reason for his attack on mainland Greece in 490 B.C. which began the Persian War.

The Ionian revolt of 499 B.C. was well coordinated and involved the overthrow of the tyrants in all the cities—the reason why the action of Athens in throwing out the tyrant Hippias may have inspired this revolt. There were many reasons why the time was ripe for revolt and certainly many citizens were delighted to get rid of the tyrants but the idea for the revolt and its organization was in the mind of Aristagoras. Its motivation was his ambition and his need to prove himself better than his father-in-law.

Darius sent the father-in-law, Histiacus, to crush the revolt but he joined the rebels and later became a pirate at Byzantium and was captured and crucified by Artaphernes the satrap. In the meantime, Aristagoras had attacked Sardis, former capitol of Lydia, and burned the city. While he was returning to Miletus,

Amphora "Two Warriors"

Courtesy, Museum of Fine Arts, Boston

a Persian army attacked his Greek force and defeated it. As a result, the Athenians withdrew support and Aristagoras fled and was later killed. Thus died an individual whose ambition was to make himself known, to gain a high reputation. Aristagoras is known to history for these acts but they led to a great war and many killings. It is hard to judge him favorably. The idea of establishing democratic rule in the city states and getting rid of the tyrants was a fine one by our standards but the root inspiration of the idea seems less than noble. How often do we find this the case in our lives when we do a good act but for the wrong motive? How much better the actions of Aristagoras would appear if his motivation had not been purely personal ambition? Yet do humans need this sense of accomplishment and reward to take the lead in any action? These two questions are continually before us when we deal with the role of the individual in history.

Artaphernes, the satrap, led the crushing of the revolt but it took several years to re-establish Persian authority in the region. Darius was angry that the Athenians had become involved. He planned revenge on them. To remind him of this project, it is reported Darius had one of his slaves repeat to him at dinner each day, "Remember the Athenians." It is also reported that Darius did not even know who the Athenians were at the beginning of the revolt.

Such is the material of history, an ambitious man gaining support from an insignificant city to attack a great empire created the conditions for a protracted war that made the insignificant city one of the most noted and important in the history of the western world. We will briefly outline the Persian War at the start of Chapter VI. Before we turn to that, there is one other development of the 6th century that must be noted. It is an intellectual development that may be the most important in the history of the human race.

Section III—*The Axial Period—750-450 B.C.*

Karl Jaspers has referred to the period of c. 750-450 B.C. as the "axial period" in history. By this he means that before this period the known civilizations had many points in common, pantheistic religion that established rituals without any or very limited ethical content, centralized bureaucratic political administrations that organized the food production for a region and developed writing for record keeping, economic life that was largely agricultural providing self sufficiency for a region, limited trade that provided only a few luxuries for the upper classes, social hierarchies with slavery at the base and a small ruling class on top with family and family ties very significant in preserving the way of life and the future, a technology that provided increasingly complex weapons as stone gave way to bronze which in turn gave way to iron. These characteristics were found in China, India, the Near East and Greece—all the regions that have indications of advanced civilizations at this era. Then, during the "axial period," matters changed in all of these regions and by 450 B.C. a new set of conditions were present everywhere. Why? What made this age one of such change and produced such important individuals as Amos and the other Hebrew prophets in the Near East, the Buddha in India, Confucius in China, Zoroaster in Persia, and the pre-Socratic Greek philosophers in Ionia?[2] We may find there was a development of cosmic rays that mutated the human mind but that seems too much like science fiction so the reasons need to be searched out in history. Three suggestions have been offered that make sense and you should decide which one appeals to you or work out an agreement between the three or develop your own theory. Reflect on these before class and in class be prepared to present your ideas.

One idea is that the growth of civilization reached such a point in this era that there was enough knowledge accumulated that it could be reevaluated in new ways. For example, the Babylonians and Chaldeans had been collecting observations on heavenly bodies for centuries and these observations could be studied and interpreted now whereas without this data, predictions about the movement of the heavenly bodies, information that made it possible for the Greek Thales of Miletus to predict an eclipse in 584 B.C., were impossible. Empires had risen and fallen and the knowledge of the past was now available for use. For example, Assyrian kings built libraries where the knowledge was collected. The prophets knew over two hundred years of national history in the chronicles and understood over 1000 years of Hebrew tradition. With this background, they made ethical judgments on the present and future conditions of their nation. Examples of this use of knowledge can be found in the life and times of all the great individual thinkers mentioned above.

[2] Amos and the other prophets gave a new direction to the Hebrew religion and paved the way for Christianity. Buddha, Confucius, and Zoroaster all founded new and very important religions and the pre-Socratic Greek philosophers introduced a new manner of thinking.

Another suggestion is that the technology of iron following that of bronze set the stage for new situations. Bronze was useful to a few who could gain military control through its use but iron meant power to more people as stronger ploughs were made and new military techniques were developed. All the civilizations of the known world entered this new technological era at about the same time. It is similar to the entrance of the world into the Atomic Age or earlier into the Age of Steel and Coal. New technology starts in one or two places but it spreads rapidly, more rapidly today than in 700 B.C. The new iron technology made conditions of greater wealth possible. According to this theory the development of coinage was necessary to keep up with the growing economic possibilities. With greater technology and wealth came demands for better conditions for everyone and not just for the few. As a result, we have the emergence during the "axial period" of new religious concepts with strong ethical and moral bases demanding the protection of the weak and the punishment of the wicked. The growth of democratic rule in Greece and even in Persia where the empire was organized under satraps so that power was distributed around the empire and not centered with the King, indicates a growing interest in a better life and more power for more people. Although there was a continuation of slavery and social hierarchy, the prophets called for an awareness of the common man and social justice. Others of the great religious thinkers of the "axial period" had similar messages. The idea of the punishment of wickedness either in a next world if not in this one or by reincarnation as a lower type being is an idea common to Confucian China, Buddhist India, Periclean Athens, and Zoroastrian Persia. With the development of these concepts, world history changed and civilizations emerged based on new ideas.

A third possible explanation is that the new ideas especially in religion developed in one region and were spread to the others so that there was a link between the great religious thinkers of the "axial period". For instance, perhaps the conquests of the Persian King spread the ideas of Zoroaster to many regions and they affected the ideas of individual thinkers. Whatever the explanation, it is certain that something important happened in the entire world of Asia and the Near East during the "axial period" and that it changed the course of history in many areas.

What happened in Greece during the 6th century that reflects this age and makes the "axial period" a topic to be considered at this time? We have already mentioned the development of the ideas of political democracy that grew during the age and the individualism seen in the art work of the century. We have mentioned Pythagoras and both his scientific experiments and general philosophy of harmony. His philosophy affected Greek thought as the teachings of Confucius and Buddha affected China and India. Pythagoras asked new questions about the universe and man's relations with it. Accumulated knowledge helped him to provide answers. But what led to the asking of the questions? He was not alone in asking them. Thales, mentioned above, who a generation earlier had predicted the eclipse of May 28, 584 B.C. (not using that date), had laid the foundation of European science and philosophy. Thales asked the question of what substance is the world made? He was seeking a unifying principle and a way to create order out of the chaos of the universe. Thales was seeking order in the same way that Hesiod was when he wrote the *Theogony*[3] but the answer each provides indicates a total change of attitude and thought. Hesiod c. 750 B.C. asked how was the world created and the order of the universe established? His answer was the gods created the world by mating and by their battles and family struggles finally brought order from chaos when Zeus established his rule over the gods and the earth. Thales asked what would unify the world and create order and his answer was the world was made of one substance, water, and it appeared in many forms. Consider a moment what a great difference there is in the two answers. Consider which is closer to us and perhaps the importance to us of Greek thought and the Greek approach to life will become clear. The difference also illustrates what happened during the "axial period."

The Egyptians in the Middle Kingdom c. 2000 B.C. had begun to ask some of these questions but they did not actively follow through on them. Perhaps the time was not ripe. A combination of individuals and circumstances create history and the combination wasn't there in Middle Kingdom Egypt to redirect the "How" of history. The combination was present throughout the eastern hemisphere in the "axial period." Some ideas developed during the Middle Kingdom, were written into Egyptian wisdom literature and Thales of Miletus who studied in Egypt may have called on the accumulated knowledge of Egypt in his work which set the way for a new approach to life and science.[4]

Thales was followed by a group of thinkers in Miletus and the

[3] For information on Hesiod's *Theogony* see Kellogg, *Out of the Past,* Chapter VI.

[4] The Middle Kingdom is discussed in Kellogg, *Out of the Past,* Chapter XIV. In Chapter VI there is mention of several of the followers of Thales.

cities of Ionia where access to the knowledge of Persia, the Near East, and Egypt was easier than on the mainland. These pre-Socratic Greek philosophers combined a seeking of positive knowledge with an ability to speculate that characterizes all great scientists and philosophers.[5]

For example, Anaximander of Miletus created the first map using mathematical principles applied to an observed area of the earth and his contemporary, Hecataeus, wrote a geography to go with the map. He used scientific observation to relate the details. Anaximander not only made maps but rejected Thales concept of water as the unifying principle and suggested an undefined term, the "unlimited" as the organizing principle that took different forms and thus created the world. Another contemporary, Xenophanes, developed a whole theory of the universe based on a god who is without form. He was also a geologist who read fossils with great ability. Heraclitus presented a doctrine of flux to explain the universe and Parmenides and Xenophanes each developed a system which rejected the senses as a guide to the universe.

The impact on future thinkers and on Pythagoras who is probably the most important of these early philosophers and scientists was great. Greek history is not a political history alone but is full of other matters that have had great impact on us. This 6th century B.C. was crucial in the history of the Greek world and in the growth of western thought but it was part of a greater development throughout the eastern hemisphere and we wish we knew more of the interconnections between the areas during this crucial "axial period."

Sixth century Greek philosophy used reason and analysis to find answers to the great questions of existence and of purpose in the world. In opposition to this approach many societies have turned to emotion and mystery to provide answers. As we have indicated before, the Greeks were fully aware of these two forces in this world and in their lives. They had a place for the mysterious, the mystic, the erotic, and the emotional but with the introduction of the rational approaches of Thales and the pre-Socratic Greek philosophers who emphasized the rational tendency of the Greek mind, this mystic side was not allowed to dominate.

[5] Socrates was the great philosopher who lived in Athens in the 5th century. Plato recorded many of his ideas. The philosophers, such as Thales, Anaximander, and Xenophanes who lived before Socrates are grouped together as pre-Socratic philosophers. This designation reflects both a time period and certain type of questioning of the universe.

There was mysticism in Greece in the 6th century and it found its expression in various religions such as the Orphic mystery cults and the Eleusian Rites. There was an aspect of this mysticism in the pronouncements of the Delphic oracle controlled by the priesthood. In the Near East and Egypt priesthoods had developed which capitalized on the emotional and irrational side of man's nature to gain the support of the rulers and become adjuncts of despotism. This was certainly the case in New Kingdom Egypt. Greek tyrants might have benefitted from such priesthoods and several tyrants supported the emotional religions of the day. For example, Peisistratus supported the Festival of Dionysius in Athens, but the growing interest in scientific and rational thought precipitated by the pre-Socratic Ionian philosophers made the dominance of mystery cults impossible in Greece. They were always present and were an important part of the fullness of Greek life but they did not dominate it.

In fact, those statements that are often quoted as being typical of the Greek attitude towards life were developed by men who followed the pre-Socratics and later philosophers. The English in the last century were particularly impressed by these statements ascribed by legend to the "Seven Sages of Greece." "Know Thyself" and "Nothing in Excess" are the two most famous rational guides offered by Greek philosophers to help men understand the world. We must not allow this emphasis of 19th century English writers on Greek rationality to blind us to the wholeness of the Greek mentality and to their understanding of the irrational side of life.

The philosophers, both the pre-Socratics and later Socrates, Plato and Aristotle, made great contributions to western and world thought as did the other great thinkers of the "axial period." The foundations of Greek rationalism laid by the Greek philosophers during this "axial period" have had a profound impact on patterns of western thought. To be logical and scientific in some peoples' definition is to be "western." The root of this rational approach can be traced to the impact of the Greek philosophers, especially Plato and Aristotle, on the Christian church leaders and of Plato on the thinkers of the Renaissance. In the mid-twentieth century there has developed some distrust of this rationalism and perhaps it is long overdue since what we have often understood and been taught as the Greek way, has been a distortion and one-sided emphasis on one aspect of Greek thought patterns and understanding. We may be entering a better understanding of what man is if we can combine the emotional with the best aspects of rational and logical thought as the Greeks did.

In conclusion, the "axial period" is a helpful idea to connect the many changes that were taking place throughout the civilized parts of the eastern hemisphere between 750 and 450 B.C. The impact of these changes was great on each civilization but the developments in Greece are of particular concern to members of so-called western civilization. This is because the rational, scientific foundations of our civilization were laid at that time by Greek philosophers and many ethical and moral concerns of the west were considered then in Greece and elsewhere, especially in Israel.

Section IV—*Chapter Review*

As the title of this chapter suggests, two important areas are included in the chapter. First, the origin of the Persian War was presented in the story of the ambition of Aristagoras and the Ionian Revolt. He organized the Ionian revolt against Persian power in 499 B.C. This is one indication of the impact an individual can have upon history and the chapter includes other evidence of the individual's role in history. We will consider the individual and history further in the text, but the actions of Solon, Peisistratus, Cleisthenes, Thrasybulus, and Periander mentioned in Chapter IV and the actions of Aristagoras, Darius, and Histiacus as well as the ideas of Thales or Pythagoras mentioned in this chapter give evidence of the importance of the individual in history. You should be aware of the actions of these people and of their ideas so you can discuss their importance in history. For this chapter, however, if you can answer the question, "How did the Ionian Revolt begin?", and identify the following individuals and places you should have control over the material on the Ionian Revolt.

Aristagoras	Athens
Artaphernes	Eretria
Darius	Naxos
Histiacus	Sardis
	Sparta

The other area introduced was that of the "axial period." The idea that intellectual changes of great significance took place throughout Asia between 700 and 450 B.C. is important. But for this text the questions asked by the pre-Socratic Greek philosophers during this period and the answers they provided are more crucial than the moral and ethical contributions of the religious thinkers of Asia. These philosophers answered their questions in a manner many consider laid the basis for western rational and scientific thought. Certainly historians of the last two hundred years have emphasized the rationalism of the Greeks, often at the expense of understanding the manner in which the ancient Greeks actually viewed life.

These questions will help you review the information on the "axial period."

1. What might have caused the "axial period"?
2. What are the characteristics of societies of the pre-"axial period"?
3. What are the characteristics of societies of the post-"axial period"?
4. Who were the pre-Socratic Greeks? What type of questions did they ask?
5. What other parts of the world were affected by the "axial period"?
6. Who were the leaders of thought during the "axial period"?
7. How would you characterize the ideas developed during the "axial period"?
8. Identify the following: Anaximander, Pythagoras, Thales, Xenophanes.

There are many projects that could be developed based on the information in this chapter. For instance, you might read the sections in Herodotus in which he describes the events leading to the outbreak of the Ionian revolt. You might try to identify examples of his bias.

Another project would involve the pre-Socratic philosophers. Look over the brief descriptions of the Greek thinkers and see what points you think are most important then pick one of the individuals mentioned and try to find out more about him. This exercise could effectively be spread around the members of a class or friends might get together to work on one individual. Your goal would be a report that relates the similarities and differences in the approaches of the philosophers and the specific contributions to thought made by each individual studied.

Another project that would focus on the "axial period" involves extensive research. The text assumes there was such a period but you might research the period. To begin you might ask if there was such a thing as an "axial period" or was it just one of the interesting coincidences of history? Wouldn't it have been interesting if the men mentioned in the text had had a chance to meet and discuss their ideas? As part of your project, plan a class presentation in which each person plays the role of one of these thinkers and you discuss issues together such as: What is the basic substance of the universe? How do you go about finding out? How should men treat each other? What should be the guidelines or rules for relations among men? If you do not have a class presentation, you might write a conversation in which two or three of the people mentioned discuss their philosophies.

The following bibliography will lead you in the different directions suggested in the chapter. There are several works included on the Persians as well as on different aspects of Greek thought and philosophy.

Agard, W. R. *The Greek Mind.* Princeton, N. J. D. Van Nostrand Co., 1957.

Aristotle, Plato, and other Greek philosophers. Loeb Classical Library, London, Wm. Heinemann.

Burn, A. R. *Persia and the Greeks: The Defense of the West 546-478 B.C.* Minerva Press, 1968.

Collins, Robert. *The Medes and Persians: Conquerors and Diplomats.* N. Y., McGraw-Hill Book Co.

Culican, William. *The Medes and the Persians.* N.Y., Praeger.

Dodd, E. R. *The Greeks and the Irrational.* Berkeley, University of California Press, 1951.

Freeman, Kathleen. *The Pre-Socratic Philosophers.* Oxford, B. Blackwell, 1953.

Greece: Myths, Gods & Heroes; Greece: The Birth of Reason; Greece: The Golden Age; Greece: Pride and Fall. Life Education Program—Reprints, Time. Inc.

Guthrie, W. K. C. *The Greeks and their Gods.* Boston, Beacon Press, 1950.

Hamilton, Edith. *Greek Mythology.* N.Y., New American Library, Mentor Book, 1969.

Herodotus, et. al. *The Portable Greek Historians.* ed. M. I. Finely. N. Y., Viking Press, 1959.

Kirk, G. S. and Raven, J. E. *Presocratic Philosophers.* Cambridge, Eng., Cambridge University Press, 1957.

CHAPTER VI

THE PERSIAN WAR

Section I--*Introduction*

We now come to the Fifth Century B.C. in Greek History, a century about which volumes have been written and high praises have been sung. It is called both the Age of Pericles and the Golden Age of Greece and to some historians and philosophers, the highest degree of human civilization ever was achieved in that century. Is this enthusiasm and praise deserved? What do people see in the developments of that century that make them feel so enthusiastic about it? Has this age that many consider so great affected the development of the west politically or intellectually? We have already taken an overview of the century through the art. We have set the stage in the last chapter for the chronological development of the century and for the intellectual and political flowering. The next three chapters are devoted to fifth century Greece. In them we will do five things. First, we will briefly trace the events of the Persian War and take a quick look at the major events in the years 479-435 B.C. focusing on the actions of several individuals. Second, we will present a scheme for analyzing a society that has been developed by individuals trained as sociologists. This will give us a tool to use in investigating the century. Third, we will present information on the three most important political units of the time in the Aegean area and suggest a way of comparing them to gain insights into why the century is so significant in the eyes of many people. Fourth, we will analyze the outbreak of the Peloponnesian War and try to decide if it could have been avoided. Finally, we will briefly consider the Peloponnesian War and its aftermath.

The Fifth Century naturally falls into three parts. The first covers the years 499 to 479 B.C. and includes the revolt of the Ionian cities from Persian rule and the great war, the Persian War, that followed. The second period is 479-435 B.C. and constitutes the years when Athens passed Sparta as the most important polis in the Greek world. The years are noted for Athenian imperialism, democracy, and intellectual developments—an amazing combination when first listed but, if you consider the 20th century A.D.

and the United States, perhaps the three developments will not seem so incompatible as they do on first reading. During these years in Sicily tyrants ruled who gave brilliance to that island so the glory of the century is not confined to the Aegean Greeks. The third part of the century from c. 435-399 B.C. constitutes the period of the Peloponnesian War between Athens and Sparta which changed the entire situation in and way of life of the Aegean area. In many ways the century was as full of events and changing conditions as our own century has been for Americans. An eighty year old American today has seen two world wars, a cold war, the introduction of the age of flight, of radio and T.V., of atomic power, and artistic developments ranging from the atonal musical works of Schoenberg to the rock musicals *Hair* and *Jesus Christ, Superstar*, and he has followed the changing fortune of his nation as a great power. The Athenian born in 491 B.C. who lived to be ninety lived through two world wars, a cold war, artistic developments in sculpture, in architecture, and in drama, the introduction of new military tactics, and he watched the changing fortune of his polis that brought it to the peak of world leadership and down to near total destruction by the end of the century. Perhaps this listing alone is enough to indicate why so many have studied the age and found it fascinating. Many people believe we can learn a good deal from fifth century Greece.

Section II—*The Persian War*

In the last chapter we considered the revolt of the Ionian city states led by Aristagoras, in 499 B.C. and the crushing of the revolt by the Great King of Persia, Darius. The daily reminder given to Darius by a slave kept Darius alerted to the idea of an expedition against the Greek peninsula to punish Athens and Eretria for their part in the revolt. An attack was made in 492 led by Mardonius, son-in-law of the king. He brought Thrace and Macedonia, the country that was to bring ruin to Persia in the next century, under Persian control but the Persian fleet was badly damaged by a storm and the expedition did not invade Thessaly or the southern part of the peninsula.

Darius was not to be stopped and proceeded to plan another attack this time by sea across the Aegean. His fleet subdued the Aegean islands, sparing the holy shrines of Delos, a clever move if the purpose was ultimately to have the support of the Greek

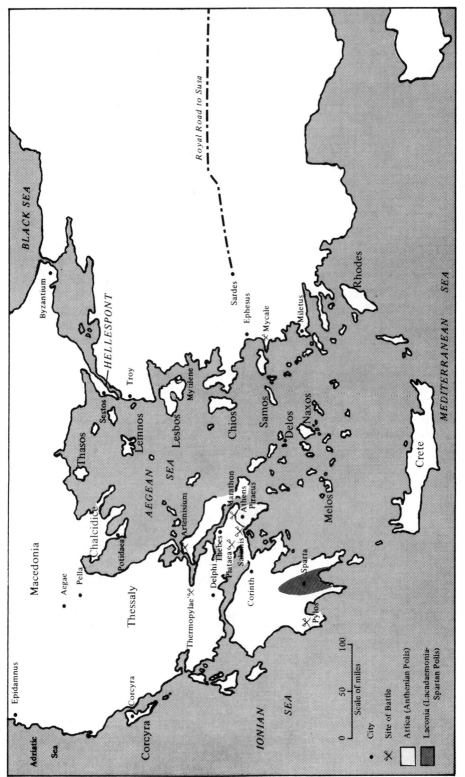

Greece During the Persian and Peloponnesian Wars

people, and in 490 B.C. his army landed on the island of Euboea and attacked Eretria. The city fell in a week because of traitors. Throughout the Persian War the Greeks were hindered by traitors, an indication of the selfishness of individuals, intensity of feelings among Greeks on political issues, and the great lack of unity among the Greek poleis.

There had been no plans made for a common defense of Athens and Eretria yet they had known for several years that an attack was inevitable. Many Ionians had fled their homeland and were living in Athens and could easily have warned them of coming events. These Greeks did introduce intellectual stimulation but no unity. At the time of Darius' invasion the military leader or polemarch of the Athenian forces was Callimachus, but he took advice from Miltiades who has been given the credit for the Athenian actions. Miltiades had ruled as tyrant in the Chersonese and he had fought against Persia in the Ionian revolt. When the revolt was going against the Greeks, he fled to Athens and gave to her two islands he had captured, the islands of Lemnos and Imbros. These islands became the starting point for the later Athenian empire. Miltiades knew more about Persian tactics than anyone else in the city. He had several good reasons to fight against the Persians. First, he had lost his land. Second, Hippias, the son of the Athenian tyrant, Peisistratus, was fighting for the Persians. Miltiades' father had been killed by Peisistratus. Third, Miltiades had been forced into exile by this event. Thus, there was introduced into the battle a very personal element and this must have been a driving force for Miltiades. He got the Athenians to fight at Marathon, a small plain on the coast of Attica across from Euboea, and not wait to be attacked at Athens. This move was crucial in the first great battle of the Persian War. Athens moved her army to Marathon where her only ally was the neighboring polis of Plataea, who sent 1000 troops. Athens had asked Sparta for aid. Sparta should have sent it as in 490 B.C. Athens was a member of the Peloponnesian League under Sparta's leadership but when Athens asked for aid after the fall of Eretria, Sparta replied she would come but because of a religious ceremony, she was unable to send troops until after the full moon. By then the need had disappeared. In this day of alliances and troops stationed overseas to support allies, one wonders what would have happened in Greek history if the alliance of Athens and Sparta had been stronger and Spartan troops had been available in Athens to withstand the Persian attack. Even without her aid, Athens won at Marathon. It was a well planned attack by

Miltiades and the Athenians fought well. Geographic features were well used and the Athenian losses were small whereas Persia lost heavily. It was an important victory but later legend made it much more than it actually was.

Later interpretations made Athens the savior of Greece against the Persian power and this supported Athens' claim to imperial leadership later in the century. The parallel to our interpretation of the Battle of Bunker Hill or Lexington Green is strong. These battles were actually not very important as battles but what they have come to mean to us as Americans is part of the myth which supports our understanding of ourselves and our role in the world as the defender of freedom and the fighter for freedom and democracy against great odds. Marathon fulfilled a similar place in Athenian myth.

After their defeat at Marathon, the Persians sailed around to Athens but seeing the Athenian army already there after a quick march from Marathon, the Persian commanders, Datis and Artaphernes, withdrew and the second attack of Darius against the Greek supporters of the Ionian revolt ended. It was Darius' last attempt as he had to deal with internal disorders and then died in 485 B.C. before the next expedition could be planned. His successor, Xerxes, after crushing a revolt in Egypt planned a great expedition against Athens. His plan was to cross the Hellespont on a bridge and march along the coast with his fleet following along offshore. To avoid the danger of sailing around the peninsula of Mt. Athos in the open sea, a canal was dug so the fleet could sail along safely. The account of the expedition given by the Greek historian, Herodotus, clearly indicates how well it was planned and what a large army was involved. Herodotus reports that when the army stopped at night the men and horses would drink the streams dry. Although it might not be true, it gives us a very vivid picture of what an army can do to the countryside. The Greek cities in Macedonia and Thrace, which had been conquered by Darius, gave earth and water to the army of Xerxes signifying their surrender. Thessaly surrendered without a fight when her Greek allies decided not to fight at the passes on her border.

During the ten years between the attack of Darius and the major expedition of Xerxes, the Athenians made plans for defense. These were the ideas of Themistocles whose plan was to make Athens a great sea power and not rely on the strength of the army. The change was a major one in determining the history of the Aegean area. Before Marathon, Themistocles had persuaded the

Athenians to fortify the harbor of the Piraeus, a necessary step if there was to be a large fleet.[1] The attack of 490 B.C., held up his plans as did a war Athens fought with Aegina, but by 481 B.C. walls from Athens to the Piraeus had been built. He also had persuaded the city to spend the recently discovered silver found in city owned mines on the building of warships and 200 new triremes had been built by the time Xerxes attacked.

There had also been some changes in the functioning of the government in Athens that brought more democracy to the city. The polemarch, or military leader, was replaced by an elected board of 10 generals, or strategoi, one being elected by each tribe to be that tribe's leader in warfare. All other offices in the city were now chosen by lot and one could not succeed oneself in office. The strategoi, however, could be elected year after year, a technique that makes great sense when the growing complexity of military affairs is considered. It also allowed for continuity in military planning in Athens and provided an elective office which could supply leadership for the city. Another instrument of democracy, possibly designed by Cleisthenes, but now used for the first time, helped reduce the possibility of a tyrant taking power. The instrument was ostracism and it allowed the citizens to vote each year for the one person they felt had too much power and constituted a threat to the democracy of the city. This individual was then ostracised or forced to leave the city for a period of ten years. Athens was thus prepared to meet the threat of Xerxes' authoritarian Persia with her new democratic concepts and her newly built fleet.

Also, the two major cities of Greece, Sparta and Athens, were preparing a joint defense. Sparta preferred to make the defense line across the isthmus of Corinth thus abandoning Athens to the Persians. Athens wanted the defense line north of her borders and Thessaly asked that the line be on her northern borders. This was too far north for the Spartans. Finally, Thermopylae, an easily defended pass on the mainland opposite the northern tip of Euboea and just south of Thessaly was decided upon as the place to make the stand against Persia. Again the entire Spartan force was not sent for religious reasons but a "band" of 1000 men under the leadership of King Leonidas was sent. They with some allies stopped the Persian advance at Thermopylae until they were betrayed. A Greek showed the Persians a narrow trail

[1] Athens is located several miles from the coast. The Piraeus is her nearest natural harbor with coves and high land that can easily be defended.

over the mountain that allowed them to attack the Spartans in the rear. When it was clear the situation was hopeless, the other Greek forces withdrew and the Spartans remained to die to the last man creating one of the great stories of military warfare and providing an example of the Spartan way of life for all the Greeks.

Meanwhile, the Persian fleet had been damaged in a storm and by an attack of the Athenian fleet off Artemesium, a promontory on the north end of the island of Euboea close to Thermopylae. The Persian fleet was not destroyed. The Athenians fled homeward upon hearing of the betrayal at Thermopylae.

At this point in the war the main Spartan force set up the Greek defensive line across the isthmus of Corinth thus abandoning Athens. Themistocles arranged for the evacuation of most of the citizens of Athens to the island of Salamis or to Troezen in the Peloponnesus. A few citizens remained to defend the Acropolis but it soon fell and the Persians burned the city of Athens. This was the high point of Xerxes' attack. Many a city state would have surrendered to the enemy at this moment. Themistocles, however, was able to rally the Athenian fleet, although Herodotus reports he had to resort to trickery to keep the fleet together and to force them to fight between the Piraeus and the island of Salamis, a location selected by Themistocles to give the Greeks the advantage.[2] When the Persians attacked at Salamis, the Athenians and their Greek allies won a spectacular victory. There was little space in which the Persians could capitalize on their greater numbers and the highly maneuverable Greek boats took a heavy toll. Xerxes was watching the battle from a hillside. During the battle he realized his chance for victory that year was gone and after the battle he left for home leaving his commander, Mardonius, to spend the winter in Greece and renew the attack the next year.

In 479 B.C. the Spartan and Athenian forces attacked the Persians at Plataea, a little northwest of Athens and north of the Isthmus of Corinth, and defeated them in one of the major battles affecting the course of western civilization. At about the same time in 479 B.C. the remainder of the Persian fleet was attacked at Mycale off the Ionian coast and the Greeks won another decisive victory which ended the immediate Persian threat. Persia

---

[2] The story is he sent word to the Persian commander to block the other entrance to the Bay of Salamis where the Greek fleet was. With escape impossible, the Greeks had to fight.

was still a tremendous military, economic, and political power but the Greeks had stopped the immediate threat of a conquest of the Greek peninsula. This was a great credit to the Greek spirit but Greece was not completely safe. Athens, with her new fleet and great interest in trade, felt the threat more directly than Sparta. She organized a defensive alliance which she controlled for the next fifty years. The organization and activities of this alliance, the Delian League, is the focus of the political and military history of the middle period of the fifth century B.C.

At the same time that the Greeks of the peninsula were stopping the advance of Persia, the Greek cities in Sicily were fighting the power of Carthage, the colony founded by Phoenicians. Carthage was the single most powerful state in the western Mediterranean and was a threat to the Greek cities there as Persia was a threat to the Greeks in the Aegean and on the mainland. Carthage invaded the island of Sicily in 480 B.C. and, according to Greek historians, on the same day as the Battle of Salamis, they were defeated at the Battle of Himera. The cities of Sicily were thus free to develop in their own ways, and in the next century they flourished in trade and cultural developments under a series of tyrants. The Etruscans of northern Italy still were a threat but they were defeated by Hieron, tyrant of Syracuse, at the Battle of Cyme in 474 B.C. After this defeat the Etruscans stayed in northern Italy and the Greeks of Sicily and Magna Graecia (southern Italy) were free to develop with little threat from non-Greek peoples.

The contributions of these western Greeks to the total history of the Greek speaking peoples and their distinct yet important development is a very interesting subject. Unfortunately, we do not have time in this work to develop this area of Greek history. Any student interested in the unique history of the Greeks in Sicily and southern Italy is encouraged to do research on this topic. The focus of such research might be the difference in the history of the Greeks in the Aegean and those in the west. Topics of particular interest might be: (1) the tyrants of Syracuse; (2) the part played by Syracuse in the Peloponnesian War; (3) the wealth of the Greek cities of Italy; (4) the impact of the Greeks on the Etruscans and Romans.

With the Greek naval victories of Salamis and Mycale and the land victory of Plataea, the immediate threat of the Persians to mainland Greece ended. Persian power was still great and the resources at her command in Asia were tremendous so the possibility of a renewal of hostilities was present. How the Greeks

met this threat is discussed below. Before these details are presented
it is important that one realizes the emotional impact of these
victories on the Greeks and especially the Athenians.

Athens had been burned in 480 B.C. and the citizens returning
from the safety of Salamis and Troezen were faced with the task
of rebuilding their city. The Athenians, more than the other
victors, realized the power and threat of Persia and this colored
their actions in the years ahead. Anyone who is aware of the
antagonisms between the Irish and the English or the Israelis and
the Arabs over the years will have some idea of what the feelings
of the Athenians for the Persians must have been.

Besides an awareness of destruction the Athenians had an
awareness of victory and their own power. It is difficult to capture
or describe what must have been the spirit of the Athenians. The
victory of the Greeks had been a cooperative effort and a Spartan
had commanded both the navy and army, but the Athenian
fleet had played a crucial role and the victory at Marathon in
490 B.C. was an Athenian effort.[3] Here was the small polis of
less than 300,000 people which had defeated the greatest empire
the world had seen to that moment. It would be as though a
nation the size of Italy were to defeat the Soviet Union. The
situation has similarities to the North Vietnamese withstanding
the power first of France and then of the United States. You are
probably aware of the spirit and tenacity generated in the Vietnamese. On a more personal level the situation of 479 B.C. recalls what happens when the odds on favorite at a football
game is beaten. When the underdog wins, the excitement and
spirit is hard to contain. So it was in ancient Greece. This spirit
of exuberance and self-confidence filled Greece and especially
Athens. It was a crucial element in the flowering of Athens in the
Golden Age and allowed her to take the leadership of the Aegean.

Section III—*Sparta and Pausanius*

Although the Greek victories in 479 B.C. ended the immediate
Persian threat, the Greeks realized the Persian Empire was still

[3] An indication of the significance of this event to the Athenians is seen
in the story of the tomb of Aeschylus the great Athenian playwright. We
remember him as the originator of western drama but there was no mention
on his tombstone of that fact but instead it reported he had fought as a
citizen at Marathon. This fact to Aeschylus and to many of his contemporaries
was the most important event in his life.

strong and powerful and might renew the attack at any moment. Before the Persian War began the Greek cities were badly divided but there was a very loose confederation of several cities of the Peloponnesus plus Athens under the leadership of Sparta. During the war cities fought together but the cooperation was far from strong. In fact there had been squabbles as to the leadership of the forces and several cities refused to fight under Athenian leadership. Sparta, therefore, supplied both the commander in chief for the army and the navy in spite of the fact Sparta had no navy. You might like to recall and consider this point when Athenian policy of the following fifty years is considered.

Thus, although the Athenians were crucial to the victories at Salamis and Mycale, Sparta ended the war as the acknowledged leader of the winning cities. The question then was, how would Sparta exercise her leadership?

Traditionally Sparta was a conservative state with a policy of little involvement in foreign or overseas activity. Trade was actively discouraged. Yet in 479 B.C. this isolationist polis emerged as the leader of the victorious coalition or grouping of poleis against the Persian Empire. The situation resembles somewhat that at the end of World War I when the previously isolationist United States emerged as a world leader after the Allies defeated the German Empire. America turned away from the role of leader then. She had a second chance after World War II to exercise it again. Sparta had only one chance in the fifth century B.C. and mishandled it. Sparta then withdrew from Greek leadership which the exuberant, self-confident, and eager Athenians quickly seized. The century became Athens', not Sparta's. How did this happen?

In many ways the story of Sparta's failure is the story of one man and it again illustrates the importance of the individual in history. The Spartan commander at the end of the war was Pausanius. His actions were to determine the future history of Sparta and the Greeks in the Aegean just as other individuals had changed history by their actions in the war; for example, Miltiades of Athens at Marathon, Leonidas of Sparta at Thermopylae, and, most important, Themistocles of Athens at Salamis where his plans to make Athens a sea power were tested.

It is difficult to reconstruct all of Pausanius' actions but what we know would indicate he lacked flexibility in leadership and understanding of human motivation while being personally overwhelmed by power and potential wealth. Pausanius began well by freeing the city of Byzantium from the Persians which indicates how widespread were his actions. The Greek cities on the coast of Anatolia as well as the Aegean islands were cleared of Persian influence. He soon began to act as a tyrant over the Greek cities and when he allowed some kinsmen of Xerxes to escape it was suspected he was planning to marry Xerxes' daughter to further his own interests. Pausanius was recalled to Sparta but nothing could be proved against him. He was removed from leadership but he returned to Byzantium as a private individual. He gained control of the city and continued his plotting with the Persians. In 476 B.C. Pausanius was captured by Cimon of Athens and sent to Sparta with proof of his intrigues. He fled to a Temple but the Spartans stoned him to death for his misdeeds. Thus ended the career of the general who assured the Greeks their freedom by his victory at Plataea.

What would lead a man to become a traitor to his nation in this way? Pausanius is not alone in fifth century history and this fact must reveal something about Greek values and attitudes. Even Themistocles was suspected of taking Persian bribes and when he became too powerful for the Athenians he was ostracised and died at the Persian Court. We've mentioned Hippias, the rejected tyrant of Athens, who fought on the Persian side at Marathon. The most outstanding example is the Athenian Alcibiades who changed sides at least three times in the Peloponnesian War.[4]

These men were not minor individuals but national leaders and the parallel in this century would be if a United States Cabinet member or the Army Chief-of-Staff had joined the Nazis during World War II. Why did these Greeks act this way? What values and attitudes are reflected? We will not investigate all these traitors to their nation but let us consider Pausanius in some detail. After further research on other Greek traitors, you might develop some generalizations on this phenomenon.

One reason given to excuse Pausanius is that his training in Sparta had not prepared him for the intrigue and luxury of international affairs. This puts the blame for Pausanius' actions on the traditions of Sparta and not on the individual. You may ask, "Is it fair to blame society for the errors of an individual?" This is a debatable point and certainly some defenses offered for criminal action would indicate we believe society can be responsible. What do you think?

A second reason given is that Pausanius believed that cooperation with the Persians was more important than Greek indepen-

---

[4]You might like to investigate these individuals more fully. Thucydides in his *Peloponnesian War* has a good deal to say about Alcibiades.

dence. This might indicate that Pausanius held a view of international relations close to that represented today by close cooperation between communist and non-communist nations. This feeling that the international viewpoint—the concept of a cosmopolis—is more important than the national viewpoint—the concept of the polis—developed slowly throughout Greek history. When Alexander the Great conquered Greece, he went on to force the cosmopolitan view on the eastern Mediterranean. Pausanius may represent a forerunner of this type of person. What do you think?

A third possible explanation of Pausanius' actions is that he represented a new attitude among the Greeks in which the individual and his desires were more important than the polis or the society as a whole. In this explanation of his motivation Pausanius emerges as a proto-type for the individual who puts himself above society, who believes he is the sole judge of right and wrong, and who feels responsible only to himself. It can be argued that in Greek history from 490 to 323 B.C. the trend was away from the polis and a commitment to society and towards the individual and a commitment to self. We have seen this trend in Greek statues where the subject changed from the idealized god representing the best in the society to the emotional individual at a moment in time (Agias—See statue #8).

The final explanation and by far the simplest is that Pausanius was a selfish person who wanted wealth. There may be truth in all of these and it is certainly hard to determine exactly what motivated Pausanius. Whatever it was, he was not alone in 5th century history and in many ways he illustrates movements that can be identified throughout the century.

The tragedy of Pausanius was not only personal but national. His traitorous conduct turned the other Greek cities against Sparta and Spartan leadership. The Spartans withdrew from leadership of the Aegean area into comparative isolation and Athens quickly stepped in to fill the gap. Unlike the United States which retreated from world leadership into isolation after World War I only to have a second chance to lead the world after World War II, Sparta never got a second chance to lead the Greeks internationally although she did have a brief moment of leadership on the mainland after the Peloponnesian War. After Pausanius' actions, the Spartan people basically wanted nothing more to do with international affairs; however, Sparta was pulled back into international affairs as Athenian imperialistic action eventually became a threat to her. How did Athens act to fill the leadership void of 478 B.C.? What methods did she use that led to these accusations of imperialism? We'll consider these in Chapter VII.

Section IV—*Chapter Review*

In reviewing this short chapter there are three questions that might provide a focus for the review. First, what were the major battles in the Persian War? Second, how did Sparta exercise her post-war leadership of the Aegean area? Third, what motivated Pausanius to act as he did?

There are a number of individuals and places mentioned in the text. It is suggested you go through the text and be certain you can identify the people and places listed below. Be certain you can locate the places on a map.

Artemisum	Cimon
Carthage	Darius
Himera	Leonidas
Marathon	Mardonius
Mycale	Miltiades
Plataea	Pausanius
Salamis	Themistocles
Thermopylae	Xerxes

An extensive bibliography covering the fifth century is included at the end of Chapter VIII. If you plan to do further research on Greek traitors as suggested in the text, it will provide a good starting place for you. The bibliography will also provide information on many aspects of the Persian War if you wish to investigate certain events further. Several books are also included on the Greeks in the west.

CHAPTER VII

THE GOLDEN AGE OF THE FIFTH
CENTURY—ATHENS, SPARTA, PERSIA

Section I—*Athens and the Delian League 478-433 B.C.*

Athens had suffered more from the Persian War than the other city-states. The Persians had burned Athens and destroyed the temples and walls of the city. The citizens were united in their determination that this would not happen again. While Pausanius was misleading the loosely united Greeks, the Athenians under Themistocles' leadership rebuilt the walls on the Acropolis and refortified the port of Piraeus. They used any material available and today you can see in the walls of the Acropolis column drums and other stones from the destroyed temples which were incorporated in these walls of 479/8 B.C. Archaeologists have studied the misplaced stones and have been able to describe and draw pictures of the archaic temples of the Acropolis from which they came.

The Athenians knew that rebuilding their own fortifications would not be defense enough. When Pausanius was recalled to Sparta, the Athenians stepped into the leadership vacuum. A league or confederacy was quickly organized. All the Greek cities of the Aegean area were potential members and with Persian power still a threat, most joined. In many ways it was similar to the military defense organizations such as NATO and SEATO begun after World War II.

The confederacy, known as the Delian League, was in theory a voluntary grouping of states for their mutual defense. The headquarters and treasury was established on the island of Delos—a place which had been sacred to the Greeks for centuries as the birthplace of Apollo and Artemis, two of the Olympian gods. Delos was a neutral and sacred location and was meant to symbolize the equality and unity of the members of the League.

The purpose of the Delian League was to protect the member cities and especially the Ionian cities from Persia and to raid Persian territory to get wealth to help support the organization. From the beginning in spite of the theory of equality, Athens assumed leadership since she had the largest fleet. Other members were asked to supply either ships or money for the mutual defense. The smaller members found it easier to send money which the League, meaning Athens, used to build ships for the League and to fill other defensive needs. When the council met at Delos, each state was supposed to have an equal voice in the deliberations, but Athens could bribe the smaller states and thus get her way in any policy decision.

The first action of the League was to capture the island of Sestos. Pausanius had fled there from Sparta when he was first suspected of treachery. Cimon, the Athenian leader, captured Pausanius at Sestos, and, as mentioned in Chapter VI, sent him to Sparta with evidence of his mis-deeds. It was there Pausanius was stoned to death.

As you can see, from the very beginning the League did not feel bound to attack only the Persians. Over the sixty plus years of its existence, the Athenians used the League for many purposes always calculated to benefit Athens, although some actions backfired. In 468 B.C. Cimon defeated a Persian fleet and army at the Eurymedon River in southern Asia Minor and this gave the League control of this region. It allowed greater trade opportunities for Athens, it also gave all the members greater security so it appeared to be following the League's stated purpose of mutual defense.

On the other side of the ledger, however, is the case of the island of Naxos which in 469 B.C. announced she was withdrawing from the voluntary league. Under Athenian leadership, the League attacked Naxos and forced her back in. It was evident the League was not to be the voluntary group it started out to be.

In 465 B.C. there was a power struggle on the island of Thasos between men of different political opinions. The League under Athens' leadership this time attacked to suppress those people who disagreed with the democratic political group. As Athens was the leading democratic city of Greece, this action indicated that members of the League, and remember members were forced to stay in, were going to be forced to agree with Athenian political philosophy. What had happened was that the Delian League had become an arm of Athenian policy. While internally, the government of Athens was becoming more democratic, externally the Athenians were pursuing an imperialistic policy of dominating the other Greek city states and using the Delian League to achieve this goal. It is a complex situation and difficult to analyze briefly. The Athenians were dependent upon foreign trade and markets to supply full employment and to support the welfare of her citizens who were now running the government. To many there are parallels between the role played by the United States since World War II and that of Athens after the Persian War. Of course, many conditions are different and history does not repeat itself but maybe you can develop some parallels. If you find some parallels, you might wish to continue looking for other parallels as you read on.

The attacks on Naxos and Thasos clearly indicate that the nature of the Delian League had changed. It was now an arm of Athenian imperialism and member states could not leave. A new type of membership was added to the original two, the tributary subject state which gave money to the League and which was under its control. The defensive purpose of the League was also changed. In 459 B.C. the Athenians attacked Egypt. There had been an important internal change in Athens in 461 B.C. which pushed the city towards greater democracy. Cimon, who was quite conservative, supported Sparta when her Helots (slaves) revolted. He was rebuffed by the voters and ostracized. Ephialtes, the leader of the democratic elements who opposed Cimon, was assassinated. Pericles, whose name we link with the fifth century Golden Age of Athens, was elected one of the strategoi or generals. As stated above, the ten strategoi held the only elected positions in Athens and the only positions which could be held for succeeding years. It was under the leadership of the new strategos, Pericles, that Athens attacked Egypt. It is hard to see this move as defensive of the Aegean area. Egypt was under Persian control and one might argue, of course, that an attack is the best defense. It appears more likely, however, that the attack was simply an attempt to expand Athens' trade and power by the more democratic and liberal new government. Cimon, although using the League aggressively, had been a restraining and conservative influence. With his ostracism and the internal crisis involving assassination, the people of Athens were apparently ready for a major adventure.

During the fighting in Egypt, Athens captured the island of Aegina which is just a few miles south of the port of Piraeus and forced the island to join the Delian League, an act that surely must be considered imperialistic. The attack on Egypt went badly. One Athenian fleet was destroyed and in 454 B.C. the attack was abandoned. The League was militarily weakened and Athens persuaded the League to move its headquarters from Delos to Athens where the treasury would be safer. Athens also established that all law suits involving League members were to be tried in Athens. Athens now had full control—economic, legal, military, and political—over the Delian League. Although a peace treaty was

signed with Persia in 448 B.C., Athens continued to use the League
for her own ends until her defeat by Sparta in the Peloponnesian
War.

The high handed actions of the Athenians were not well
received among the non-member Greek city states. There were
skirmishes against Athens. Sparta emerged as a major opponent.
Limited warfare broke out and Athens lost control of her neighboring city of Megara. In 445 B.C. a treaty, the Thirty Years'
Peace, was signed between Athens and Sparta, to end these
skirmishes. The terms of the treaty called for the status quo
or the re-establishment of things as they had been. Thus,
thirty-four years of almost continual warfare ended, but the
situation in the Greek world was far from peaceful. These conditions will be referred to in the next chapter.

The treaty was not effective in removing tensions and Athens
continued her imperialistic manner. In 447 B.C. she settled
colonists on land bought from city-states in the Cheronesus,
the peninsula that juts into the Aegean and which forms one side
of the body of water called the Hellespont. In places scattered
about the Aegean Athens founded colonies in the following
years. In 440 B.C. the island of Samos revolted from the Delian
League. Following the precedent set at Naxos, the League crushed
the revolt and forced Samos back into the League in 439 B.C.
In 437 B.C. Pericles himself led an expedition to the Black Sea
to show the power of the Athenians. The Athenians helped the
people of Sinope force out a tyrant indicating they were ready
to force their views on Greeks outside the immediate Aegean
area.

Athens appeared aggressive and dangerous to the other city
states. Her trade was large. Her domestic democracy was threatening
to the more conservative and traditionally governed states and her
control of the Delian League was tight. We've indicated how she
exercised this control. With her large fleet, she dominated Aegean
trade and also largely controlled the trade with the Black Sea.
Her merchant class was becoming interested in trade with Italy
and any expansion in that direction meant conflict with Corinth,
who still largely dominated this trade. There were clear warnings
that any imperialistic movements in that direction would lead to
renewed conflict, but the Athenians under Pericles' guidance
ignored them. The result was the Peloponnesian War.

In summary, Athens dominated Greek history of the middle
years of the fifth century. Her foreign policy was imperalistic as
she pursued her own interests at the expense of her allies in the

Delian League. Athens led while the other Greek cities basically could only react to her actions. Eventually, as Athens alienated more and more Greek cities, she was called to account for her actions in the Peloponnesian War.

Section II–*The Athenian Golden Age*

Athens in the mid fifth century B.C. has been considered one of the greatest places in history for the expression and development of the human spirit. As suggested above, it is hard to reconcile the domestic glory of Athens with her imperialistic foreign policy, but this is one of the ironies of the human condition. The government of fifth century Athens was described above. It was a democracy, but participation in the political process was limited to adult males who were citizens.[1] Every citizen could expect to serve in some political office, chosen by lot, during his lifetime. Also, each male had to serve in the armed forces for two years from 18 to 20 before becoming a member of the ready reserve until he was 60. This forced participation and involvement in government and full participation in the life of the polis described in Chapter IV must have reinforced the spirit and enthusiasm generated by the Greek victories of 480/479 B.C. to provide the vitality that made the age golden.

The playwrights, Aeschylus, Sophocles, and Euripides mentioned in Chapter III, were writing their fine tragedies and the people of Athens were able to attend the great performances of these new plays at the annual festival for Dionysius. Herodotus, also mentioned in Chapter III, was writing his history of the *Persian War.*

Athletics and the life of the gymnasium which was so important in the late 6th century, still provided a meeting place for young citizens and training for the active, outdoor life citizens led.

Education of the wealthier boys was done by slaves at home or in small classes. To help train them, boys often had a pedagogue. These men were often well educated slaves captured from other Greek cities. More advanced education was offered by a new type of teacher, the sophist, who, for a fee, undertook to teach young men anything from rhetoric to music. Rhetoric became a crucial

---

[1] Only males were considered citizens and only if both their father and mother had been born in Athens which meant in reality a rather limited citizenship.

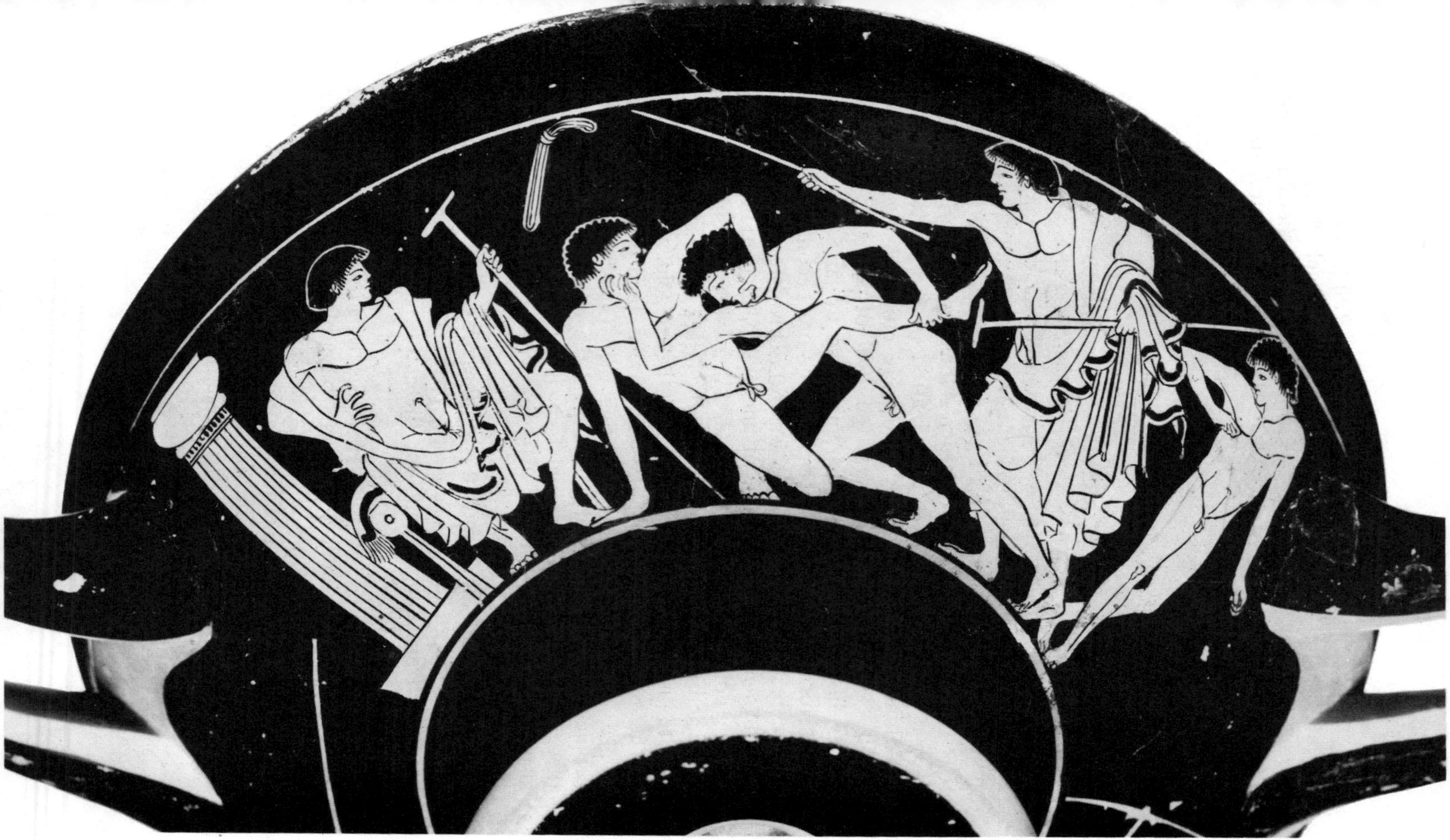

Red Figured Kylix

subject as citizens were expected to speak up in the Assembly and had to defend themselves in the law courts if brought to trial. The polis was still the focus of a person's life, but other concerns were becoming important also. The individual was finding opportunities to express himself in the law courts, in pursuit of education, and in the arts.

The profound questions raised by the pre-Socratic philosophers were popularized by the sophists who often supplied slick and easy answers. Other teachers pursued these questions and others similar to them more thoughtfully. Socrates is the most famous of these philosophers and his philosophical questionning gave philosophy a new direction. Rather than questions on the nature of the universe, he asked questions about the meaning of abstract ideas such as love and justice. He sought answers through dialogues or conversation with any who would listen to him. Many consider him the greatest citizen of Athens and the greatest teacher, but he never charged for his teaching. He claimed he was merely seeking wisdom and truth and welcomed anyone who would discuss ideas with him. He talked in the dressing rooms and covered walks of the gymnasium and in the stoas of the agora or market place. His pupils were among the most noted citizens of Athens and included the traitor, Alcibiades, and the great 4th century philosopher, Plato.

Although democracy, drama, and philosophy flourished in fifth century Athens, what most people probably connect with the age are the buildings, and the sculpture on the Acropolis of Athens— the Parthenon, Erechtheum, and Propylea. Soon after the defeat of the Athenian navy in Egypt and the removal of the treasury of the Delian League to Athens, Athens, under Pericles' instigation, began a great building program. It has recently been suggested that the program was begun to provide employment. These scholars believe Athens was suffering from an economic recession which was intensified by the Egyptian disaster and the building on the acropolis provided jobs while money from the Delian League treasury provided pay. We know Pericles used League money with the justification that as long as Athens defended the member cities, the money was hers to do with what she wanted. This is quite a change from the originally stated purpose and concept of the League.

Whatever the reasons for the construction, the Parthenon, the Erechtheum, and Propylea, discussed in Chapter III, are great contributions to architecture and the sculptures of Phidias on the Parthenon were among the finest produced in the ancient Greek world. If a person has never heard of anything else from Greek history, he may still have heard of the Parthenon. Architecture and sculpture rank among the notable glories of the Golden Age and must be considered when trying to understand the Athenians of the fifth century.

Little mention has been made of women in Greek society and we have just pointed out that only adult males were considered citizens of Athens. Athenian women were expected to stay at home and run the household. They did the shopping but in wealthier homes even this was handled by slaves. Women were secluded and excluded from most of the life of the city although they could attend certain religious functions and festivities. We know little of their daily life and must assume it was devoted to child bearing and training of the young children, to weaving and sewing, to planning and overseeing house jobs and operation, and some social activities that they developed for themselves. Women rarely ate with their husbands and more rarely attended dinner parties. Although marriage was common, it does not appear to have been motiviated by love as we understand it today. It apparently was more a contractual arrangement often planned by parents for economic and social reasons and for perpetuating the family.

Men, according to accounts we have, found their love objects elsewhere, often at the gymnasium, as homosexual love was not frowned upon. There were also common prostitutes in Athens and another class of women, the hetaira, for which there is no parallel in our society. These women participated in the social life of Athens as hostesses and leaders of intellectual circles. They became mistresses but usually did not marry thus avoiding the restrictions placed on wives. The most famous hetaira was Aspasia, the mistress of Pericles. We'll never know what influence she had on him, but if she was as brilliant and attractive as contemporary accounts indicate, her influence must have been great. It is ironic we have so little specific evidence on the influence of women when the man who gave the age his name was connected to such a famous hetaira. Perhaps, in spite of the evidence that fifth century Athens was a male-dominated society, a woman played a crucial role in its great history.

In summary, the arts and politics flowered in fifth century Athens. She carried the democratic experiment further than any society had until then and her artists produced works that still influence the world in the areas of architecture, sculpture, drama, history, and philosophy. Many scholars view the civilization of fifth century Athens as the high mark of the human experience and would like to have lived then. Would you?

Section III—*Analyzing a Society?*

A—What do societies need?

When presented with a question such as "Would you have liked to live in fifth century Athens?", you can approach the answer in many ways. You might give a quick emotional answer based on the "feel" of the age you get from reading about it or looking at pictures of the architecture. Or you might focus on one aspect of the period such as the democratic government and base your decision on that. Many people make decisions without seeking as much knowledge as possible on the subject or investigating other alternatives and options. With the question, "Would you like to have lived in fifth century Athens?", you really need to investigate the society in some depth if you wish to make an intelligent answer. How can you go about investigating or analyzing a society?

Sociology is the social science that deals with society. Sociologists investigate all aspects of societies often breaking up society into segments for intense investigation and analysis. They provide us with tools for analyzing a society. To begin our analysis of a society we can begin with the question sociologists often ask, "What must societies do to survive?" Make a list of those things a society must have to survive.[2] Do this before you read on. You may be asked to discuss your list in class before you read part B of this section.

B—Basic Functions

If you compare your list of items a society must do to survive with the lists of others in the class, you will probably discover you have listed many of the same items. Look at all the lists or your personal list and see if you can consolidate the items under broad categories. For example, if you have listed "find water, grow vegetables and raise meat," you might consolidate them under "provide food." In addition if you have "trade, manufacture, and selling" you might consolidate all of these under the heading of "economic activity." Consolidate the items into as few categories as possible.

[2] For this exercise you must define society. You may wish to make your own definition or use this one from Webster's. "(1) The social order, esp. as a state. . . . or community. (2) A voluntary association of individuals for common ends. (3) An enduring, cooperating social group so functioning as to maintain itself and perpetuate the species." For this exercise you may wish to consider the United States as one example of a society.

Some sociologists have done this and have suggested the five categories below as headings for summarizing what any society must do to survive or as the sociologists phrase it, what functions a society must fulfill to survive.[3] These sociologists believe these five functions fulfill the basic, essential needs of *all* societies regardless of size or whether they are a nation or a sub-group and refer to them as the five basic functions of society. Societies may meet these needs in different ways, and this is what makes the study of mankind so fascinating, but all societies have these needs since they are basic to the survival of human groups. The five basic functions are: a method of replacement of members, a method of supplying economic needs and wants, a method of political organization including protection of individuals from each other and of the society from other societies, a method of educating or inducting new members into the society and, finally, a method of establishing cohesiveness through adherence to common goals and values. In brief, the needs are for replacement, economic activity, political organization, education and cohesion.[4]

The theory holds that societies create institutions to fulfill these needs. An example of an institution would be the family or the market. Some institutions are often connected with buildings. We often think of the education function taking place in a school building, but the institution of school is much more than the building. In Section I we mentioned Socrates who helped fill the education function for Athens but his school had no building so keep in mind that institutions need not be a building. As you use the technique of analyzing basic functions, you will want to look for the institutions that filled the functions in the different societies.

If you have listed other categories or functions, see if you can fit them into these five. If you cannot, ask yourself if the function is truly basic. If you and your class agree it is, you should add it to this list of five basic needs for purposes of evaluating societies you study. All sociologists do not agree with this minimal list and there is *no reason why you must*, but if you and your class

---

[3] See *Family Form and Social Setting* for an analysis of the five basic functions of society in relation to the ancient Hebrews and the modern Israeli Kibbutz. There are other examples of the use of the basic function approach which you may have studied. Not all sociologists agree there are only five basic functions, some suggest more. The concept and *not* the number or the wording of the five or more basic functions is the important thing to comprehend. Function is defined in Webster's as "(1) action, performance, (2) Special purpose, office, duty, or the like."

[4] See Appendix C for further explanation of these five categories.

add to it, be certain you have considered the addition carefully and are clear that it does not belong in one of the other categories as a sub-head.

Now that we have considered this sociological basic function approach to analyzing a society, let us turn back to the original question in this section, "Would you have liked to live in the society of fifth century Athens?" You can see that it is not an easy question if you analyze how the society functioned. How did the Athenian society fill the five basic functions? As you analyze how the basic functions were filled, another complexity will be evident: the basic functions were filled by persons of different classes and the two sexes in different ways and in turn they were affected in different ways by the manner in which the functions were filled. Your decision will, therefore, be affected by whether you would be a male or a female, a slave or a citizen in fifth century Athens. The question is complex. Would you have liked to live in the society of fifth century Athens?

Section IV—*Persia in the fifth century B.C.*

Three societies dominated the life and history of the Aegean area in the fifth century. One was Athenian which we have considered. The other two societies were Persian and Spartan. If we analyze these three societies using the sociologists' technique of looking at basic functions, we can get a much better understanding of the tensions, conflicts, and wars of the century in the Aegean. The Persian War between Greeks and Persians and the Peloponnesian War between Athens and Sparta and their allies were clashes between societies with different ways of fulfilling the basic functions which resulted in or were the result of different values. Although mankind has much in common, there appear moments when the differences appear irreconcilable. These two wars were such times. Let us consider Persia briefly and see if this provides us a fuller understanding of the Persian War and of the events described in Section I and in Chapter VI.

The replacement function was filled in Persia largely by the family unit. The family was usually an extended family including several generations and not the nuclear family (mother, father, children) we are used to in the United States. A man might have several wives and/or concubines. Also, conquests brought in slaves and immigrants from the conquered areas.

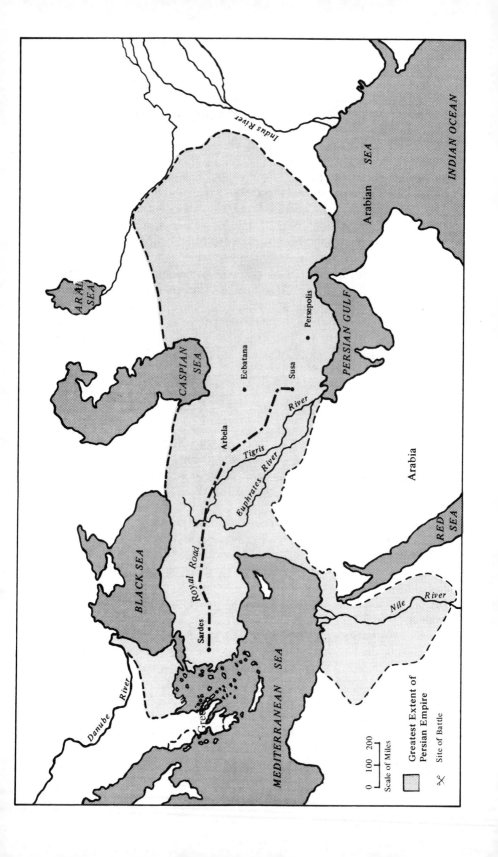

INDIAN OCEAN

Arabian
SEA

Indus River

ARAL
SEA

CASPIAN
SEA

PERSIAN GULF

Ecbatana

Persepolis

Susa

River

Arbela

Tigris

Euphrates River

Arabia

RED
SEA

BLACK SEA

Royal Road

Sardes

Nile River

Danube River

Greece

MEDITERRANEAN SEA

0 100 200
Scale of Miles

Greatest Extent of
Persian Empire

✄ Site of Battle

The economic life was extremely diverse and varied. Specialized craftsmen produced fine armour, pottery, jewelry, and the like. Agricultural activity was carried on both on large estates where slaves-did much of the work and on small farms. A large governmental bureaucracy including soldiers, administrators, and priests and a large merchant class that moved goods about the empire and ran shops added to the complexity of economic life. What institutions are suggested by these activities? An army, an institution of religion, an agricultural institution including organized slavery are among the institutions suggested to me. What other ones are implied?

The political organization differed greatly from the Greeks and particularly from the Athenians. Persia was an empire ruled by the Great King. The empire was divided in satraphies or provinces ruled by satraps or governors appointed by the Great King. The Persian Empire was known for its just rule and efficiently run government. Yet the law was the King's and he could act as he wished. If there was a bad king, everyone suffered. The King's power was so great, many tried to seize the power. Still, the government was well run and even captured peoples were well treated. For instance, it was the Persian ruler, Cyrus, who when he conquered Babylon, allowed the Hebrews to return to Jerusalem.[5]

Little is known about education in Persia. We can assume that most Persians learned their skills at home or by working for a craftsman such as a weaver. The court and the religion required more education and writing must have been taught the scribes at court sponsored schools although the schools may not have resembled our institutions.

Several factors appear to have given cohesion to the society. The first was the unity established by the Great King — the all-powerful ruler. A second and related matter was the mail and road system which tied the great empire together physically. A third and most important factor was the state religion— Zoroastrianism. The religion was founded by the prophet, Zoroaster, who pulled together many ideas prevalent in the region near the Caspian Sea and elaborated on and interpreted them. The focus of worship was fire and the altars and ritual of Zoroastrianism developed around fire. Zoroaster's basic teachings held that there was a struggle in the world between the forces of light and goodness led by Ahura-Mazda and the forces of darkness and evil led by Ahriman. Man could choose which side to fight on,

[5] See *The Book of Ezra* in the *Bible*.

but naturally would fight for the good. The good neighborly life of a successful farmer was set as an ideal of what was good. The struggle of good and evil would end in a final judgment and good would triumph. There would be a resurrection and rewards for the good and punishment for evil actions. The world was full of good and evil spirits who were also engaged in the struggle. Translated into daily living Zoroastrianism provided a way of explaining both why man must struggle in this world and why there is evil. The teaching of a final judgment provided an ethical and moral basis for good actions. Of course, the decision of what was good in each situation was up to the individual. The priests and/or the government often helped the individual to decide. These teachings, however, did provide a strong unifying force and a system of values for the Persian Empire that was unique among the great empires of the ancient world. The small Hebrew nation, of course, developed a high moral and ethical sense also. The influence, however, of Zoroastrianism on Hebrew thought and ultimately on Christianity is often overlooked.[6]

Considering the above and comparing it with how the Greeks, especially the Athenians, fulfilled the basic functions of society should help you to better understand the Persian War. The difference in the political and cohesive functions appear particularly pronounced. What do you think? Are there other differences we should note? Does this analysis help you understand the clash between Athens and Persia? Now let us turn to an analysis of how Spartan society fulfilled the basic functions.

Section V—*Sparta in the fifth century B.C.*

The five basic functions were filled in Sparta very differently than in Athens or in Persia. The contrast clearly illustrates the great variety of ways humans have devised to meet society's basic needs. The contrast also illustrates how different people can be even when they share such basic points as language and religion.[7]

[6] For instance, the Magi in the Christmas story were Zoroastrian priests. There is limited information on Zoroastrianism, but it is well worth looking at what is available. Several books are suggested in the bibliography.

[7] There is a good deal of information on the social organization of Sparta in Chapter II and IV. Be sure to refer back to it in considering Spartan society and in preparing any comparison between it and Athens.

The population of Sparta was replaced by reproduction. Immigrants were not welcome and the enslaved Helot population made more slaves unnecessary. Family life as we understand it existed for the two lower classes, the Helots or slaves and the Periocei or merchants, but for the upper class Spartiates such family life did not exist. Spartiates did marry and marriage was expected. In fact, if a satisfactory marriage was not arranged, the unmarried men and women of that age group were put in a dark room and were expected to come out paired off. Spartiate babies were inspected for perfect health and if there was a defect, the child was killed. The purpose was to raise fine Spartan leaders for the next generation. Spartiates did not have a home and family life as we understand them. Spartiates ate in community dining halls and male children after age 7 lived together in barracks. The Spartans had a clear goal in mind and the state functioned to achieve that goal. All basic functions were interrelated and one must realize this interdependence to fully understand Spartan society.

Economically Sparta's goal was complete self-sufficiency. She discouraged trade with other poleis. Spartiates were forbidden to be merchants or traders and this work was done by the Periocei class. Spartan coins were of iron rather than of gold to make trade more difficult. Crops were grown by the Helots on state and private lands and, since Sparta included some rich farmlands, she did not need to import food. The Spartan community mess or dining hall was noted for its unappetizing and poor quality meals.

The political system of Sparta was unique. It combined monarchy, oligarchy, and democracy. There were two kings, one of whom commanded the army in the field and one of whom was always supposed to be in Sparta. They had some executive authority and acted as a check on each other. The most important officials were the five ephors. They had to be over 60 and served as censors, chief justices, and executive officers. They were elected by the apella or assembly of all male Spartiates over the age of 30. The two kings and the five ephors planned the agenda for the apella which voted on those laws proposed by them. It was a tight system of checks and balances that worked effectively to preserve the Spartan way of life.

Education in Sparta was state controlled for Spartiates and in the hands of the family for the other classes. Spartiate girls received training similar to the boys but they were allowed to remain at home whereas all boys at the age of seven were taken

Amphora. Blacksmith's Shop

Courtesy, Museum of Fine Arts, Boston

from their mothers to live in the state barracks or dormitories where they received vigorous training. The goal of the education was to raise Spartan soldiers, but music and moral attitudes were instilled also. From age eight to twenty a Spartan boy was under the tutelage of an older citizen who taught the boy all he knew. There were tests to pass. Endurance and strength was emphasized in very brutal ways including beatings. At twenty the young man went on active military duty for ten years and at thirty he became a citizen and member of the apella. His formal education institutionalized by the state prepared him to serve the state and its goals.

The Spartan military forces had a great reputation in Greece and were for many years considered invincible. The intense training of the youth made the phalanx an effective military weapon. In the phalanx each hoplite depended on the other as they moved forward locked together with spears protruding from the front three ranks. The Spartan phalanx must have looked like a porcupine as it advanced as a solid, prickly mass towards the enemy. The Spartans also had cavalry, but the phalanx was their main unit of battle.

As suggested above, the Spartan way of life had a clear goal and it was to create an orderly, conservative society in which all units worked for the preservation of the state and Spartan traditions. Change was not tolerated and extraneous matters, such as the arts, were not encouraged although before 700 B.C. Sparta had produced as fine sculpture as any place in Greece. Spartan poetry, the Spartans liked music and poetry, was directed towards supporting the state and it emphasized the virtues of bravery and of devotion to the polis. Several selections from Spartan poetry were included in Chapter III.

We believe that what motivated the Spartans to adopt their way of life was fear of the Helots. The Spartans had conquered their neighbors about 680 B.C. and enslaved them. They became the Helot class. After crushing a twenty-year rebellion of the Helots in the late 7th century, Sparta lived in fear of another such struggle and organized her whole society to prevent it. Many Greeks admired the Spartans for their devotion to an ideal and the way they lived by it. This admiration and this commitment to an ideal reflects the Greeks' idea of arete. Many Greeks who admired Sparta would not have liked to live there. How do you feel? Would you have liked to live in fifth century Sparta?

In 462 B.C. Sparta crushed a Helot rebellion. The rebellion

shows the Helot threat was real. This particular rebellion had effects on Athens and was one step on the way to the Peloponnesian War. Cimon, the Athenian leader, sent aid to Sparta to help crush the rebellion and in doing this, Cimon lost support in Athens. He was ostracised. Cimon's successor, Pericles, had no love for Sparta and this showed clearly in the development of Athenian-Spartan relations.

To summarize, in this chapter we have presented information on Athenian, Persian, and Spartan society. By using the sociologists' basic functions, we have established a technique for analyzing and comparing these three societies. Using this technique should make these societies more understandable. The technique should allow you to focus on the chief similarities and differences between the three societies which influenced fifth century history in the Aegean. In turn, this should help you to better understand the conflicts of the fifth century, especially the Persian and Peloponnesian Wars. We began considering basic functions by indicating that all societies had to fill certain functions to survive, yet we end by finding how differently peoples can fulfill these functions. What similarities can you find in the ways these three societies filled the basic functions? What might your observations indicate about peoples and nations and finally, about international relations?

The Spartans and Athenians were both Greeks. They shared a common language, although their dialects were different, and common gods. In 480/79 B.C. they were able to cooperate in defeating the Persian Empire, yet over the next fifty years they clashed several times and a period of 25 years of warfare between them began in 431 B.C. Why? Why did these two poleis go to war? The societies were both Greek and had the same basic functions to meet. With so much in common, why could they not avoid war? This is one of the great questions for mankind — Why do we have wars when we are all sharing the human condition? Could the Peloponnesian War have been avoided? What do you think? What would have been necessary to have avoided the war? We will consider these questions and the Peloponnesian War in the next chapter.

Section VI—*Chapter Review*

In discussing the society of Athens, Persia or Sparta, one must use a number of words with specific meanings peculiar to that society. You should be certain you can identify and use these words correctly. Among the most important are the following.

apella	pedagogue
archon	Periocei
Court of the Areopagus	phalanx
ecclesia	polemarch
ephor	satraph
heliaea	satraphy
Helot	sophist
hetaira	Spartiate
hoplite	strategoi
ostracism	Zoroastrianism

Several of these terms appear in other chapters where information on Athenian, Persian, and Spartan society was presented. You should refer back to those chapters both to find the meaning of these words and to provide further information on how these three societies fulfilled the basic functions.

It should be clear that any review of this chapter should focus on the basic functions of society. You should understand how we developed this method of analyzing societies and what sociologists mean by the five functions given in the chapter. You should be able to present information on Athens, Persia, and Sparta to illustrate how each of these three societies filled the basic functions. As stated above, you will find information on these societies in other chapters besides this one and you should be certain to refer back to these chapters especially for information on the political and economic functions. Finally, you should be able to indicate what institutions each of these societies developed to fill these five functions. The best review question for this material would be to develop an answer for this question, "In which fifth century society would you have preferred to live, Athens, Persia or Sparta?"

In Section I information is presented on Athenian imperialism and the Delian League. If you understand this material, you should be able to answer these questions:

1. How did Athens fill the leadership gap left by the removal of Pausanius in 478 B.C.?
2. What actions did Athens and the Delian League take in the years 478-435 B.C.?

A good research question is raised in Section I, "What parallels exist between Athenian history in the fifth century and United States history in the twentieth century?" Your class might divide the research according to the basic functions and do a group project rather than each person working on the topic.

A bibliography for fifth century history is included at the end of Chapter VIII.

CHAPTER VIII

THE PELOPONNESIAN WAR

Section I—*Simulation and the Avoidance of War*

In this section a technique will be suggested which may be used to help us develop an answer for the question, could the Peloponnesian War have been avoided? The technique is called simulation and this particular approach to simulation or gaming is a variation on Simulex, an approach developed by the Department of Political Science at the University of New Hampshire.[1] Although Simulex is usually used for current affairs, this particular simulation approach has proven a useful device for analyzing many situations.[2]

In a simulation you are asked to take the position of various participants or play the role of an individual Often a simulation will focus on a crisis situation. You must be as realistic as possible in playing the role of an individual or representing a group that was involved. This requires research on the participants' positions. In simulating the conditions leading to the start of the Peloponnesian War you, as a reader and student, should take either the side of the Athenians or Spartans. In the last chapter a technique was presented for analyzing a society and in the chapter review you were asked to study Athens, Persia, and Sparta and decide where you would prefer to live. Based on that analysis pick your side.

Before you read further, write down briefly in two lists what

[1] Permission to use information on Simulex taken from *Simulex II: Procedures for Inter-Nation Simulation* edited by David L. Larson and copyrighted in 1968 by the N. H. Council on World Affairs was granted by the editor and the copyright holder and is gratefully acknowledged by the author. For further information on Simulex you should contact the N. H. Council on World Affairs, 11 Rosemary Lane, Durham, N. H. 03824; the Department of Political Science, University of New Hampshire, Durham, N. H. 03824; or the author. A computerized version of the gaming procedures is used at St. Paul's School.

[2] There is information in Appendix D on how to set up the Simulex. What is presented in the text is a rather simple version of a simulation involving one person. What simulation amounts to is putting yourself in another's shoes.

you believe to be the values and the goals of the polis you decided to represent. As you read Section II on the steps leading to the Peloponnesian War, decide what actions were taken to achieve these goals. Can you imagine other methods of achieving these goals that might not have antagonized the other city states? What compromises might have worked that would allow your side to attain its most important goals without compromising its values? This is the art of foreign policy—to achieve your goals without compromising your values. In history war has often resulted from this situation. Could it have been avoided? Can it be avoided today?

The point of this simulation is to face the question, "How might a war be avoided between societies that have much in common yet are different?" How much would you as a member of these ancient societies have been willing to compromise to avoid war? This is obviously a question of major concern in our world today and the ancient Greek world had a similar problem. How much has mankind changed since 431 B.C. in the way we feel and think about our way of life as opposed to others who are just as human as we are?

Section II—*Steps leading to the Peloponnesian War*

As mentioned in Chapter III, one of the great writings from ancient Greece is Thucydides' account of the Peloponnesian War. We are very fortunate to have such a high quality account by an eye witness of and participant in many developments of this crucial war. The work should be read by all students of Greek history. Several selections are included below. Thucydides was involved briefly in the war as a general but he lost his post. He was thus deeply involved in the actions about which he wrote and was no doubt present at some of the events described. This first-hand knowledge of events provides a certain authority to the book yet it is not merely a memoir. In fact, many scholars believe it is the best history work of the ancient world. The book is noted for its analytical approach in which both sides of issues are given and the reader is actively involved in judging the actions.

Thucydides, as all historians, had his biases, and one must look for them. In the *Peloponnesian War,* Thucydides applied to historic events the rational analysis of phenomenon and the questionning approach to life which the pre-Socratic Greeks had developed. Thucydides carried the multiple causation and questionning approach of Herodotus, author of the *Persian War* and often called the "father of history", even further. Because of Thucydides we know a great deal about the war but, in spite of his attempts to remain unbiased and to be rational in his approach, we must realize Thucydides did have sympathy for the Athenians but not for Athenian imperialism.

In Chapter VI we discussed the end of the Persian War and the role played by Pausanius of Sparta after the war. The fact that Athens picked up the leadership abandoned by Sparta is certainly one cause of the Peloponnesian War and Thucydides discussed it. Athens' use of the Delian League for her own imperial goals such as the expedition to Egypt in 459 B.C. antagonized the Greeks. Finally, a conflict between Sparta and her allies in the loosely organized Peloponnesian League and Athens and her allies in the tightly controled Delian League broke out in 446 B.C. The immediate cause of the outbreak was a revolt on the island of Euboea against Athenian control. Euboea supplied much of Athens' wheat and it was essential to Athens' existence that she have a guaranteed source of wheat. Sparta supported Euboea's move for freedom but Athens crushed the revolt. A truce, the Thirty Years' Peace, was quickly arranged on the basis of the status quo or restoration of matters as they had been. This really changed nothing and Athens continued to pursue imperialistic designs and even began to turn her attention to the western Mediterranean where Corinth and other states had extensive interests. This shift to the west was regarded by Sparta and her allies as a breach of the Truce which called for the status quo, but Athenian trade apparently had to expand or Athens would suffer economically.

In 435 B.C., ten years after signing the Thirty Years' Peace, the polis of Epidamnus was attacked by her barbarian (non-Greek) neighbors whom the Epidamnian nobles had joined when they were expelled by the democratic party in Epidamnus. This popular or democratic party ruled Epidamnus, an Adriatic seaport on the coast of modern Albania.

The polis of Epidamnus had been founded some years earlier as a colony of Corcyra, the island city state off the west coast of Greece. As was customary, the oecist had been chosen from Corcyra's mother country, Corinth. As Epidamnus was being plundered and overrun by the barbarians and exiled nobles, the democratic party rulers appealed to the mother country, Corcyra, for help. This was in 435 B.C. Corcyra refused. The Epidamnians then went to the Delphic Oracle for advice and, according to Thucydides, they were told to deliver their city over to Corinth, the home of their oecist. This they did and the Corinthians agreed to aid the Epidamnians. The Corinthians had no love of their colony, Corcyra, because the Corcyrans refused to pay the traditional respect to the mother country. Corcyra was one of the wealthiest cities of Greece at the time, and the Corcyrans were very proud. Her location provided Corcyra partial control over the trade to the west and Corinth saw this control as a threat. Also, the Corinthians believed Epidamnus to be as much a Corinthian colony as a Corcyran one. These are the reasons Thucydides gives for the Corinthians' decision to aid Epidamnus. Do you think they are sound? How might this decision have affected the polis, Athens or Sparta, you are studying?

When the Corcyrans learned that the Corinthians were at Epidamnus, they demanded the Corinthians be told to leave but the Epidamnians refused to do so. As a result and feeling that their trade was threatened by having a Corinthian force north of them, the Corcyrans attacked and laid seige to Epidamnus. Corinth then drew up plans for a major attack on Corcyra and it appeared a major war was underway. At this point Corcyra sent envoys to Corinth to seek negotiations indicating they would be willing to let the Delphic Oracle settle the issue. The Corinthians replied there could be no negotiation under pressure (the Corcyran seige of Epidamnus). Corcyra replied they would end their seige of Epidamnus if Corinth would withdraw her troops from Epidamnus. These positions and the charge and countercharge, cause and effect, action and reaction, recall so many moments of peace negotiations since World War II. (The positions and the charges are clearly presented and analyzed by Thucydides.) Which side was right? Why couldn't they resolve their differences without getting into such a military confrontation? What makes nations and leaders act this way? The result of these charges and counter-charges was that negotiations were broken off. War began and Corinth suffered a naval defeat the first year. Corinth then spent the next year preparing a mighty attack and collecting allies. Corcyra, in spite of her victory, wealth, and large fleet became frightened as she had no allies. Corcyra therefore sought help from Athens. A debate was held before the Athenian assembly in which both Corinth and Corcyra presented their cases. Which side would you have supported if you had been present? Thucydides was present and led the groups opposed to Pericles who wanted to support Corcyra and bring her into the Delian League. Support of Corcyra would allow Athens to extend her interests in the west. Athens' intervention would provide an obvious threat to Corinth's western trade. How would you have voted?

The Athenians voted to support Corcyra. Another step towards a major confrontation involving more and more poleis took place. The alliance of Corcyra and Athens combined the two largest fleets of the Greek world creating an awesome power and a potential threat to all other naval powers. Could other poleis allow this shift in the balance of power to take place? How do you think the Spartans felt?

In 432 B.C. a naval battle between Corinth and Corcyra took place. Corinth was winning this Battle of Sybota until, upon the arrival of some Athenian ships, the Corinthians withdrew which brought an end to the battle.

This battle clearly indicated Athens was preparing for a show-down with Corinth. Athens' actions against Potidaea, a city in Chalcidice, made it more obvious. Potidaea was a Corinthian colony founded by a son of the tyrant Periander in the 7th century. Potidaea was under Persian control at the start of the fifth century but revolted after the Battle of Salamis and became a good member of the Delian League supplying first ships and then after 454 B.C. money only. She was also loyal to her mother country paying Corinth the traditional honors that were due. In 433 B.C. Athens demanded that Potidaea tear down her walls. Athens gave several reasons including Potidaea becoming a threat to Athens if captured by the King of Macedonia. In actuality, tearing down the walls would mean, in case of war, Potidaea could not be a Corinthian base for attacks in the Aegean directed at the Athenian trade route to the Black Sea—a route essential to Athens as she was dependent upon wheat imported from the Black Sea area as well as from Euboea. The Athenians had miscalculated their power over Potidaea and the Potidaeans revolted. If you have chosen to be an Athenian, do you think this move was a wise one? Would you have supported it? The Athenians took two years to crush the revolt and a very large force was needed. The revolt also alerted Sparta to the growing danger of Athenian imperialism. If you have chosen to be a Spartan, how would you have felt about the actions of the Athenians, Potidaeans, and Corinthians?

In July of 432 B.C., under pressure from the Corinthians who looked to Sparta as one of the great leaders of Greek opinion, the

ephors or executive officers of Sparta invited any Greek city state
with a grievance against Athens to appear before the Spartan
apella or assembly to state their case. The members of the apella
were divided into two groups, a war party which was ready to
fight Athens and a peace party which had controlled the Spartan
government since the Thirty Years Peace of 445 B.C. In Book I of
the *Peloponnesian War,* Thucydides presents the Corinthian speech
before the apella and the reply of several Athenian envoys who
were in Sparta. Sparta had not been attacked. Up to this time all
the military activity had involved other states. Why do you think
the Spartans decided to become involved?

Read the following excerpts of speeches from Thucydides'
Peloponnesian War.[3] Then, having decided to be an Athenian or a
Spartan, try to work out a compromise that would uphold your
city's values and goals and at the same time avoid war. As you
read these speeches, try to put into focus all you know about the
situation and the poleis involved and try to develop a compromise
that you think would work. At the end of each speech are several
questions to help you focus on the material and to prepare you
for developing ideas for a compromise. This meeting before the
Spartan assembly in 432 B.C. is in many ways similar to what goes
on at the U. N. Security Council.

According to Thucydides, several city states stated their griev-
ances before the apella. Then the Corinthians spoke as follows:

> 'Lacedaemonians![4] the confidence which you feel in your constitu-
> tion and social order, inclines you to receive any reflexions of ours on
> other powers with a certain scepticism. Hence springs your moderation,
> but hence also the rather limited knowledge which you betray in
> dealing with foreign politics. Time after time was our voice raised to
> warn you of the blows about to be dealt us by Athens, and time after
> time, instead of taking the trouble to ascertain the worth of our com-
> munications, you contented yourselves with suspecting the speakers of
> being inspired by private interest. And so, instead of calling these allies

[3] The excerpts are taken from the 19th century translation by Richard
Crawley.   There are many translations and editions of Thucydides'
Peloponnesian War.   The Modern Library paperback edition published by
Random House uses the Crawley translation and there is a new translation
by Rex Warner available in a Penguin paperback.

[4] The territory of the Spartans was known as Lacedaemonia. The capital
of the territory was Sparta. The territory of Athens was called Attica.
The Greeks referred to their land as Hellas which is the name used by the
Greeks today for their country. The Greeks referred to themselves as
Hellenes.

together before the blow fell, you have delayed to do so till we are smarting under it; allies among whom we have not the worst title to speak, as having the greatest complaints to make, complaints of Athenian outrage and Lacedaemonian neglect. Now if these assaults on the rights of Hellas had been made in the dark you might be unacquainted with the facts, and it would be our duty to enlighten you. As it is, long speeches are not needed where you see servitude accomplished for some of us, meditated for others—in particular for our allies—and prolonged preparations in the aggressor against the hour of war. Or what, pray, is the meaning of their reception of Corcyra by fraud, and their holding it against us by force? what of the seige of Potidaea?—places one of which lies most conveniently for any action against the Thracian towns; while the other would have contributed a very large navy to the Peloponnesians?

'For all this you are responsible. You it was who first allowed them to fortify their city after the Median war,[5] and afterwards to erect the long walls,—you who, then and now, are always depriving of freedom not only those whom they have enslaved, but also those who have as yet been your allies. For the true author of the subjugation of a people is not so much the immediate agent, as the power which permits it having the means to prevent it; particularly if that power aspires to the glory of being the liberator of Hellas. We are at last assembled. It has not been easy to assemble, nor even now are our objects defined. We ought not to be still inquiring into the fact of our wrongs but into the means of our defense. For the aggressors with matured plans to oppose to our indecision have cast threats aside and betaken themselves to action. And we know what are the paths by which Athenian aggression travels, and how insidious is its progress. A degree of confidence she may feel from the idea that your bluntness of perception prevents your noticing her; but it is nothing to the impulse which her advance will receive from the knowledge that you see, but do not care to interfere. You, Lacedaemonians, of all the Hellenes are alone inactive, and defend yourselves not by doing anything but by looking as if you would do something; you alone wait till the power of an enemy is becoming twice its original size, instead of crushing it in its infancy. And yet the world used to say that you were to be depended upon; but in your case, we fear, it said more than the truth.

. . . when we contemplate the great contrast between the two national characters; a contrast of which, as far as we can see, you have little perception, having never yet considered what sort of antagonists you will encounter in the Athenians, how widely, how absolutely different from yourselves. The Athenians are addicted to innovation, and their designs are characterized by swiftness alike in conception and execution; you have a genius for keeping what you have got, accompanied by a total want of invention, and when forced to act you never

[5] The Persian War.

go far enough. Again, they are adventurous beyond their power, and daring beyond their judgment, and in danger they are sanguine; your wont is to attempt less than is justified by your power, to mistrust even what is sanctioned by your judgment, and to fancy that from danger there is no release. Further, there is promptitude on their side against procrastination on yours; they are never at home, you are never from it: for they hope by their absence to extend their acquisitions, you fear by your advance to endanger what you have left behind. They are swift to follow up a success, and slow to recoil from a reverse. Their bodies they spend ungrudgingly in their country's cause; their intellect they jealously husband to be employed in her service. A scheme unexecuted is with them a positive loss, a successful enterprise a comparative failure. The deficiency created by the miscarriage of an undertaking is soon filled up by fresh hopes; for they alone are enabled to call a thing hoped for a thing got, by the speed with which they act upon their life, with little opportunity for enjoying, being ever engaged in getting; their only idea of a holiday is to do what the occasion demands, and to them laborious occupation is less of a misfortune than the peace of a quiet life. To describe their character in a word, one might truly say that they were born into a world to take no rest themselves and to give none to others.

'Such is Athens, your antagonist.

. . ., let your procrastination end. For the present, assist your allies and Potidaea in particular, as you promised, by a speedy invasion of Attica, and do not sacrifice friends and kindred to their bitterest enemies, and drive the rest of us in despair to some other alliance.'

When the Corinthians finished, representatives from Athens, who were in Sparta on other business, asked to speak before the Spartan assembly. Their speech, as reported by Thucydides,[6] was as follows:

'The object of our mission . . . is not to combat the accusations of the cities (indeed you are not the judges before whom either we or they can plead), but to prevent your taking the wrong course on matters of great importance by yielding too readily to the persuasions of your allies. We also wish to show on a review of the whole indictment that we have a fair title to our possessions, and that our country has claims to consideration. We assert that at Marathon we were at the front, and

---

[6] One of Thucydides' very effective writing techniques is to include in the body of his history speeches ascribed to various individuals. It is doubtful whether the speeches thus presented are the actual or verbatim words of the speaker. Rather, we believe they are what Thucydides believes the speakers might have said. Scholars do feel they accurately reflect the mood and temper of the speakers if not the actual words.

faced the barbarian single-handed. That when he came the second time, unable to cope with him by land we went on board our ships with all our people, and joined in the action at Salamis. This prevented his taking the Peloponnesian states in detail, and ravaging them with his fleet; when the multitude of his vessels would have made any combination for self-defence impossible. The best proof of this was furnished by the invader himself. Defeated at sea, he considered his power to be no longer what it had been, and retired as speedily as possible with the greater part of his army.

'Such, then, was the result of the matter, and it was clearly proved that it was on the fleet of Hellas that her cause depended. Well, to this result we contributed there very useful elements, viz. the largest number of ships, the ablest commander, and the most unhesitating patriotism. . . .

While for daring patriotism we had no competitors. Receiving no reinforcements from behind, seeing everything in front of us already subjugated, we had the spirit, after abandoning our city, after sacrificing our property (instead of deserting the remainder of the league or depriving them of our services by dispersing), to throw ourselves into our ships and meet the danger, without a thought of resenting your neglect to assist us. We assert, therefore, that we conferred on you quite as much as we received. For you had a stake to fight for; the cities which you had left were still filled with your homes, and you had the prospect of enjoying them again; and your coming was prompted quite as much by fear for yourselves as for us; at all events, you never appeared till we had nothing left to lose. But we left behind us a city that was a city no longer, and staked our lives for a city that had an existence only in desperate hope, and so bore our full share in your deliverance and in ours. But if we had copied others, and allowed fears for our territory to make us give in our adhesion to the Mede before you came, or if we had suffered our ruin to break our spirit and prevent us embarking in our ships, your naval inferiority would have made a sea-fight unnecessary, and his objects would have been peaceably attained.

'Surely, Lacedaemonians, neither by the patriotism that we displayed at that crisis, nor by the wisdom of our counsels, do we merit our extreme unpopularity with the Hellenes, not at least unpopularity for our empire. That empire we acquired by no violent means, but because you were unwilling to prosecute to its conclusion the war against the barbarian, and because the allies attached themselves to us and spontaneously asked us to assume the command. And the nature of the case first compelled us to advance our empire to its present height; fear being our principal motive, though honour and interest afterwards came in. And at last, when almost all hated us when some had already revolted and had been subdued, when you had ceased to be the friends that you once were, and had become objects of suspicion and dislike, it appeared no longer safe to give up our empire; especially as all who left us would fall to you. And no one can quarrel with a people for making, in matters of tremendous risk, the best provision that it can for its interest.

'You, at all events, Lacedaemonians, have used your supremacy to settle the states in the Peloponnesus as is agreeable to you. And if at the period of which we were speaking you had persevered to the end ot the matter, and had incurred hatred in your command, we are sure that you would have made yourselves just as galling to the allies, and would have been forced to choose between a strong government and danger to yourselves. It follows that it was not a very wonderful action, or contrary to the common practice of mankind, if we did accept an empire that was offered to us, and refused to give it up under the pressure of three of the strongest motives, fear, honour, and interest. And it was not we who set the example, for it has always been the law that the weaker should be subject to the stronger. Besides, we believed ourselves to be worthy of our position, and so you thought us till now, when calculations of interest have made you take up the cry of justice—a consideration which no one ever yet brought forward to hinder his ambition when he had a chance of gaining anything by might. And praise is due to all who, if not so superior to human nature as to refuse dominion, yet respect justice more than their position compels them to do.

'We imagine that our moderation would be best demonstrated by the conduct of others who should be placed in our position; but even our equity has very unreasonably subjected us to condemnation instead of approval.

. . . our subjects are so habituated to associate with us as equals, that any defeat whatever that clashes with their notions of justice, whether it proceeds from a legal judgment or from the power which our empire gives us, makes them forget to be grateful for being allowed to retain most of their possessions, and more vexed at a part being taken, than if we had from the first cast law aside and openly gratified our covetousness. If we had done so, not even would they have disputed that the weaker must give way to the stronger. Men's indignation, it seems, is more excited by legal wrong than by violent wrong; the first looks like being cheated by an equal, the second like being compelled by a superior. At all events they contrived to put up with much worse treatment than this from the Mede, yet they think our rule severe, and this is to be expected, for the present always weighs heavy on the conquered. This at least is certain. If you were to succeed in overthrowing us and in taking our place, you would speedily lose the popularity with which fear of us has invested you, if your policy of to-day is at all to tally with the sample that you gave of it during the brief period of your command against the Mede. Not only is your life at home regulated by rules and institutions incompatible with those of others, but your citizens abroad act neither on these rules nor on those which are recognized by the rest of Hellas.

'Take time then in forming your resolution, as the matter is of great importance; and do not be persuaded by the opinions and complaints of others to bring trouble on yourselves, but consider the vast influence of accident in war, before you are engaged in it. . . .

It is a common mistake in going to war to begin at the wrong end, to act first, and wait for disaster to discuss the matter. But we are not yet by any means so misguided, nor, so far as we can see, are you; accordingly, while it is still open to us both to choose aright, we bid you not to dissolve the treaty,[7] or to break your oaths, but to have our differences settled by arbitration according to our agreement.'

The following questions should help you to focus on the issues involved. (1) What are the chief complaints of the Corinthians? (2) What is the basis of the Athenian argument? (3) Can you list any points of disagreement? (These would then provide points on which a compromise would have to be worked out.) (4) Are the Corinthians and Athenians disagreeing on the same issues or the same type of issues? (5) If you were a Spartan and heard these two speeches, would you vote for war or for compromise on the basis of these speeches? on the basis of other information you have?

At this point in history the Spartan assembly was faced with the issue of war or peace. As a nation, the United States has stood for peace. We believe it is the best policy. Assuming that the Greeks felt peace was the best policy (an assumption that may not be correct but which you should accept for the purpose of this exercise), how could peace have been maintained in 432 B.C. between Athens and her allies and Sparta and her allies, especially Corinth? Thucydides indicates there were some people in Sparta who wanted to avoid war and he reports Archidamus, one of the two Spartan Kings, expressed this view as follows:

'I have not lived so long, Lacedaemonians, without having had the experience of many wars, and I see those among you of the same age as myself, who will not fall into the common misfortune of longing for war from inexperience or from a belief in its advantage and its safety. This, the war on which you are now debating, would be one of the greatest magnitude, on a sober consideration of the matter. In a struggle with Peloponnesians and neighbours our strength is of the same character, and it is possible to move swiftly on the different points. But a struggle with a people who live in a distant land, who have also an extraordinary familiarity with the sea, and who are in the highest state of preparation in every other department; with wealth private and

[7]The Thirty Years' Peace which still had 16 years to run.

public, with ships, and horses, and heavy infantry, and a population such as no one other Hellenic place can equal, and lastly a number of tributary allies—what can justify us in rashly beginning such a struggle? Wherein is our trust that we should rush on it unprepared? Is it in our ships? There we are inferior; while if we are to practice and become a match for them, time must intervene. Is it in our money? There we have a far greater deficiency. We neither have it in our treasury, nor are we ready to contribute it from our private funds. Confidence might possibly be felt in our superiority in heavy infantry and population, which will enable us to invade and devastate their lands. But the Athenians have plenty of other land in their empire, and can import what they want by sea. Again, if we are to attempt an insurrection of their allies, these will have to be supported with a fleet, most of them being islanders. What then is to be our war? For unless we can either beat them at sea, or deprive them of the revenues which feed their navy, we shall meet with little but disaster. Meanwhile our honour will be pledged to keeping on, particularly if it be the opinion that we began the quarrel. For let us never be elated by the fatal hope of the war being quickly ended by the devastation of their lands. I fear rather that we may leave it as a legacy to our children; so improbable is it that the Athenian spirit will be the slave of their land, or Athenian experience be cowed by war.

'Not that I would bid you be so unfeeling as to suffer them to injure your allies, and to refrain from unmasking their intrigues; but I do bid you not to take up arms at once, but to send and remonstrate with them in a tone not too suggestive of war, nor again too suggestive of submission. . . .'

What reasons does Archidamus offer for avoiding war? In part of the speech not included here he indicates that a delay in starting war would help Sparta better prepare for it if it did come. Archidamus clearly understood the difference in the military strength of Athens and Sparta—Athens the seapower and Sparta the land power. In his speech Archidamus indicates that war should not be started without a very good cause. To balance this pro-peace position of the Spartans Thucydides included a speech from Sthenelaidas, one of the Spartan ephors. It clearly reveals there were those in Sparta who were eager for war.

'The long speech of the Athenians I do not pretend to understand. They said a good deal in praise of themselves, but nowhere denied that they are injuring our allies and the Peloponnesus. And yet if they behaved well against the Mede then, but ill towards us now, they deserve double punishment for having ceased to be good and for having become bad. We meanwhile are the same then and now, and shall not, if we are wise, disregard the wrongs of our allies, or put off till to-morrow the duty of assisting those who must suffer to-day. Others have much money and ships and horses, but we have good allies whom we must not give up to the Athenians, nor by lawsuits and words decide the matter, as it is anything but in word that we are harmed, but render instant and powerful help. And let us not be told that it is fitting for us to deliberate under injustice; long deliberation is rather fitting for those who have injustice in contemplation. Vote therefore, Lacedaemonians, for war, as the honor of Sparta demands, and neither allow the further aggrandisement of Athens, nor betray our allies to ruin, but with the gods let us advance against the aggressors.'

Why does Sthenelaidas believe Sparta should go to war? Is it a practical or idealistic argument? Would you support Sthenelaidas' or Archidamus' position on war?

Now, taking your position as an Athenian or as a Spartan, write down those issues on which you think a compromise is necessary. Then make another list of areas where you think compromise is possible. Do the lists agree? Pick several areas where they do agree and write down several specific points for a compromise agreement. Now consider your points for possible compromise, but keep one idea always in mind—you must not compromise on issues of vital interest to the society you represent or in ways in which the values and ideals of your city are abandoned. You should be clear what these values are from your previous work of analyzing a society. Do not continue reading until you have considered possible compromise terms. You may be given special assignments for this work.

Section IX—*The War*

Obviously there was no compromise in 432/1 B.C. or there would not have been an event called the Peloponnesian War. According to Thucydides what happened is that after Sthenelaidas' speech the Spartan apella was asked to vote on the issue of going to war to protect Sparta's allies. The vote on the issue was overwhelming in favor of war. The war, with a short interlude of peace, lasted twenty-seven years and the end marked a great change in Greek life-style, attitudes, and political fortune.

At the start of the war Spartan forces invaded Attica, the territory surrounding Athens, and burned crops and farm houses. Those living on the plain of Attica sought protection within the walls which surrounded Athens and connected Athens with the port of Piraeus. The Athenian battle strategy was for the Athenian fleet to supply food from the Black Sea area and the islands in the Delian League for the Athenian population protected within the walls. The analysis of Archidamus appeared true as the Spartan army could not defeat the Athenian navy and vice verse. Pericles apparently thought a military stalemate would result while Athens continued to develop her trade.

One event of great significance occurred within the over-crowded city of Athens which upset this analysis. The best laid plans of men went awry. Bubonic plague broke out and many Athenians, perhaps a third of the population, died including Pericles. His policy had been one of calculated imperialism, but, according to most interpretations of this great Athenian, he understood balance and would not have pressed the war to the absurd lengths it went under the new, inexperienced, emotional, and radical leaders. With Pericles gone his successors more and more appealed to the emotions of the Athenian assembly in making war policy. The result was a radicalization of policy so that what began as a war over noble ideals of what were a nation's international rights—the right to aid allies, the right to trade freely, the right to a position of leadership based on previous exploits—became a war of conquest on the part of the Athenians. Certainly the political successors of Pericles were motivated in part by self-interest. A desire, however, for revenge on Sparta for her invasion of Attica, a fear of oligarchies taking power even in Athens, and the dream of greater opportunities both economic and political in a larger empire also seem to have been motivating factors in changing the character of the war according to Thucydides' account.

Let us focus on one event of the war, the revolt of the Athenian ally, the city of Mytilene, on the island of Lesbos to see how these factors operated in making Athenian policy. In a rebellion an oligarchy[8] seized the government of Mytilene from the democratic or people's party. The oligarch withdrew Mytilene from the Delian League. Under the leadership of Cleon, Pericles' successor, the Athenian assembly debated what to do and voted to send a fleet with orders to capture and to destroy totally the city and its population. In reconsidering the issue the next day, less extreme voices were heard in the assembly and it voted to rescind the

[8] Oligarchy means government by a few. Usually these few have certain things in common such as business interests and rule the state for their own selfish ends. In fifth century Greece oligarchies opposed the rule of the people or democracy.

order. Fortunately for Mytilene and her inhabitants the ship sent with the new orders arrived before the city was destroyed. The city was captured. The oligarchs were forced out and Mytilene was forced to remain in the Delian League. The idea of the democratic assembly of Athens voting to kill the entire population of another Greek city clearly indicates how war can affect the people and how far the Athenians had moved from following the Pythagoran philosophy of balance, order, and harmony. The affair of Mytilene has its parallels in many wars, the most recent being the massacre at My Lai in Vietnam where fear and the horrible conditions of warfare led freedom-loving, democratic Americans to kill defenseless women and children. Thucydides' account of Mytilene and of the whole Peloponnesian War provide many incidents where we can learn how war affects humans and particularly humans organized in a democratic society.

After ten years of war the Athenians successfully landed troops at Pylos on the southwestern coast of the Peloponnesus and defeated a Spartan army. Sparta offered terms of peace. It was a tremendous shock to Sparta to have an army defeated and Spartans were immediately concerned about a helot uprising. Sensing a possibly greater victory, an indication of the emotionalism and greed of war, Cleon and the Athenians rejected the terms. Soon after Cleon died and after several Athenian defeats, a peace, the Peace of Nicias, was negotiated in 421 B.C. It was a shaky peace. Nicias, successor of Cleon, tried to follow Pericles' policies but he was an ineffective leader.

With the emergence of Alcibiades as leader of the democratic party in Athens, the peace was soon broken. The Athenians then embarked on a clear path of conquest attacking Syracuse on the island of Sicily. The expedition, 415-413 B.C., was a disaster. Alcibiades, who had great ability, might have conquered Syracuse. Instead the assembly recalled Alcibiades to Athens and accused him of religious profanations. This accusation indicates a great deal about this Athenian leader, a student of Socrates, and about the mood of the Athenians after sixteen years of war. Alcibiades was accused of attending a religious rite reserved for women and together with several drunken friends, of damaging many of the herms or carved religious stone markers which stood outside of most Athenian homes. Some Athenians viewed this as an outrage to the gods. Others saw it as an opportunity to take away Alcibiades' power and advance themselves politically. Others saw it as further evidence of the degeneracy of the youth brought on by the radical teachings of the sophists and philosophers. The action and reactions to it reflect the great change in morals and in feelings for the polis that had overtaken Athens. It is hard to conceive of any 6th century Athenian showing such disrespect for the institutions of the polis. Yet Alcibiades was not just an ordinary citizen. He was a student of Socrates, the nephew of Pericles, and the political leader of the democratic faction in Athens. His actions would be similar to a President of the U. S. blowing up the National Cathedral in Washington and then, dressed as a woman, sneaking into the Supreme Court to spy on the secret deliberations of the judges. Alcibiades reflects great changes in Athens and many suggest these changes came about as a result of imperialism, too much democracy, and the stress of war. Do these ingredients of drastic change seem familiar to you? Do you see a parallel between wartime Athens and other societies in history? Do you think it is fair to suggest one man may represent the values of an age so that you can learn of an age by studying the actions of an individual?

Alcibiades did not return to Athens for a trial. Instead he turned traitor—one of the most famous in this century noted for traitors—and fled to join the Spartans, another reflection on his values.[9] The Athenians at Syracuse were defeated. The army was imprisoned in the stone quarries at Syracuse and few ever escaped. The fleet was also destroyed.

The war dragged on until 404 B.C. After the smashing defeat in 413 B.C., Athens was unable to fully recover from her imperialistic attack on Syracuse. If peace had been made after the Sicilian expedition, Athens might have recovered and regained some of the glory of the mid-century. As it was, when peace finally came the Spartans were bitter. They forced Athens to tear down her walls and imposed an oligarchic government on Athens. It only lasted a short time before the Athenians regained control of their government, but this government lacked vision. The people were unable to reassert the power of Athens and looked for scapegoats to blame for her defeat. In 399 B.C. they turned on the philosopher, Socrates, and accused him of misleading the youth and of a failure to acknowledge the gods. Plato, often considered the greatest philosopher in history, was a student of Socrates and recorded the trial and Socrates' defense in his *Apology*. Socrates had been a teacher in Athens for years. Among his pupils,

[9] Alcibiades had a most complicated career. He is a fascinating individual to study and you might like to do a research project on him.

taught free in the stoas of the Agora, were as varied a group as you might wish—from Alcibiades, the traitor to Plato, the philosopher. His technique, which we refer to as the Socratic method, was to question his students exploring all aspects of the issues under consideration. Plato records many of these dialogues in which Socrates seeks knowledge of what is truth, justice, love, and other abstract ideas. This questioning approach reflects what was best in Periclean Athens, an openness to explore life and meaning, a desire to pursue knowledge, a sense that man had great potential and should develop it.

Socrates was found guilty. He was asked to suggest his own punishment, a technique in Athenian courts. It was thought he'd suggest exile. Instead Socrates suggested he be made a hero of the state for his noble work. This was a display of too much arrogance for the Athenians. He was given hemlock, a deadly poison, and died. His death is also recorded by Plato in *Phaedo*.

Socrates represented what was best in the Greek world of the fifth century, but the democratic leaders of Athens could not tolerate his excellence or his questioning and killed him at the start of the 4th century. In many ways Socrates' death can stand as a symbol of the difference between the 5th and 4th centuries of Greek history. Socrates sought what was best and true. His teachings did emphasize the individual and the individual's seeking of the truth, but it was to be for the good of all, of the whole polis. The philosopher's emphasis on balance and order underlay his approach. Socrates ranks as one of the great men of the Golden Age of the fifth century.

During the fourth century emphasis on the individual, the roots of which can be seen in Socrates' teachings and the actions of his infamous student, Alcibiades, replaced the emphasis on the polis. We saw this in the exercise on sculpture. In that exercise we also commented upon the growing emotionalism seen in the sculpture. We mentioned above the emotional reactions of the Athenian assembly to the revolt of Mytilene and how, as the Peloponnesian War dragged on, emotional decisions replaced rational ones. The accusations against Socrates and his death fit into this pattern.

With the end of the war Athens became a second rate power. Sparta exercised her leadership in the immediate area of the Greek world and soon antagonized her allies. In 371 B.C. Sparta called for a general peace conference among the Greek poleis in Italy, Sicily, and Greece together with Persia and Macedon. The topic seems a very modern one—plans for disarmament among all the states. Sparta refused to let Thebes sign the Treaty for her allies which was a direct affront to Theban power and leadership. Thebes at this time was one of the more important poleis in Greece. Persia, always ready to exploit the divisions of the Greeks for the advantage of Persia, sent money to Thebes and encouraged her to attack Sparta. Later that year Thebes attacked Sparta and defeated her at the Battle of Leuctra. It was a great surprise as the Spartan state was still a militarily organized entity.

The Theban general, Epaminondas, had developed a new use of the phalanx which made Thebes the chief city of Greece for a brief period until Epaminondas was killed fighting at the Battle of Mantinea in 362 B.C. Athens then was able to reassert her power but she never again achieved the strength and imperial power of the Golden Age. It was clear no Greek polis could unite the Greeks by arms and the previous centuries had proven that the Greeks would not unite willingly. The first sixty years of the fourth century confirmed this as Sparta, Thebes, and Athens all tried unsuccessfully to dominate Greek politics.

Persia benefited the most from this intra-Greek warfare and was able to play a dominant role in many decisions of the fourth century affecting the Greeks. In 387 B.C. Persia forced on the Greeks the Peace of the Great King. The Ionian city states, whose revolt had precipitated the Persian War, were returned under Persian control and Persia was consulted on Greek affairs. Finally, about mid-century, the country of Macedonia in the north eastern part of the Greek peninsula emerged as an important force in Greek politics. In 359 B.C. Philip II succeeded to the throne of Macedonia and he and his son, Alexander III, called the Great, wrote the last great chapter in ancient Greek history. We will consider these two outstanding individuals in the next chapter.

Section III—*Chapter Review*

The basic issue raised in this chapter is the question, "Why do nations go to war?" In the nineteenth century the German scholar Von Clauswitz in analyzing warfare called it the extension of a nation's foreign policy. He viewed it as the ultimate weapon a nation used to achieve its goals. His analysis was very important for helping people to understand war.[10]

In recent works Konrad Lorenz and Robert Ardrey have sug-

[10] See Karl Von Clauswitz *On War* for a development of this thesis.

gested territorial and aggressive drives are as basic to man's human nature as is the sex drive. Sigmund Freud had suggested sex as the most basic drive of man at the turn of the century. Lorenz and Ardrey's studies include behavioral psychology, anthropology, and biology. Their works may help us to better understand aggression.[11]

These authors are well worth reading. Their theories may help us to avoid warfare in the future. The exercise on the outbreak of the Peloponnesian War in this chapter should also provide insights into man's aggressive nature. Do you think the Peloponnesian War could have been avoided? Do you think war between nations committed to values and attitudes can be avoided? What must be done to avoid such wars? These are questions that you should consider in reviewing this chapter. You should deal specifically with the outbreak of the Peloponnesian War but do not neglect the Persian War dealt with in Chapters V and VI in analyzing these questions. Finally, you may wish to consider other wars you have studied and, more importantly, situations in which wars were avoided. It is important for a study of Greek history to understand the Peloponnesian War—its causes, its course, and its affect on Greek history. Since the war is an excellent example of the impact of war upon society and human beings, it also provides an excellent opportunity to consider war in a large context. Playing the game of, "What might have happened?," is fun but not often productive for gaining knowledge. It would seem, however, that it is worth asking in the case of the Peloponnesian War. What might have happened if (1) Athens had not joined Corcyra, (2) Sparta had followed the advice of Archidamus and delayed going to war (3) Corcyra had supported Epidamnus when aid was requested (4) Pericles had not died of the plague (5) Athens had not attacked Potidaea. Would Greek history have been very different thus changing the whole history of Rome and the development of the Graeco-Roman root of our civilization? These questions are worthy of speculation.

The following questions will allow you to focus on the content of the chapter. If you can provide specific answers to them, you should have a good mastery of the material in the chapter.

1. Was the attack on Epidamnus the cause of the Peloponnesian War?

---

[11] See Konrad Lorenz *On Aggression* and Robert Ardrey *Territorial Imperative* for information on the aggressive and territorial drives.

2. Why did Epidamnus ask for help from (a) Corcyra, (b) Corinth?
3. What were the arguments presented by Corinth to the Spartan assembly which moved Sparta to declare war?
4. What were the arguments presented before the Spartan assembly by the Athenians to justify their actions?
5. Why were the Athenian victory at Pylos and her defeat at Syracuse important?
6. How did the Athenian assembly deal with the revolt of Mytilene? Why is this important? What does it illustrate of changing values and attitudes among the Athenians?
7. What happened to Athens at the end of the Peloponnesian War?
8. Who was Epaminondas?

In the chapter you were asked to focus your attention on either Athens or Sparta. You should be prepared to present a statement as to what the values of your chosen society were and how the polis was governed. In actuality this is the best summary you can make of the material in the last three chapters which cover the fifth century B.C.

If your class participated in the simulation of the outbreak of the Peloponnesian War, you should be able to summarize what happened in the simulation. You should also be able to state briefly why you were able or not able to prevent the outbreak of war in the simulation.

Throughout the chapter mention is made of places and individuals. Although they are not listed for you here, you should realize you need to know where they are or who they were. Finally, two very unusual individuals, Alcibiades and Socrates, are discussed in the chapter. It was suggested that events in the life of each reflect very important aspects of the fifth century. You should be familiar with these events and you should be prepared to indicate the way they reflect the age. You should also consider consider the question again of the relationship between an individual and the age in which he lives. Is it fair to say that an age or period of time can be summarized or reflected in the life of a man? We considered the impersonal concept of society in the last chapter. To what extent is history the story of society and to what extent is history the story of the impact of men such as Pericles, Alcibiades, and Socrates on society? Your further study of history might well focus on this question. The next chapter of this text centers on the actions of one of the great and contro-

versial individuals of history. The next book in this sequence of
books on ancient history published by the Independent School
Press centers on the role of famous men of the Roman period.
It provides an excellent study to follow this work and to help
you pursue this question.

The following bibliography is an introduction to the great variety
of books available on fifth century Greece. This list should help
you begin further research on any topic suggested in the last
three chapters. Many of these books include bibliographies of
their own which will provide further direction for your research.

Burn, A. R. *Pericles and Athens.* N.Y., Collier Books, 1948.

Burn, A. R. *Persia and the Greeks: The Defense of the West 546-478 B.C.*
_____, Minerva Press, 1960.

Collins, Robert. *The Medes and Persians: Conquerors and Diplomats.*
N.Y., McGraw-Hill Book Co.,

Culican, William. *The Medes and the Persians.* N.Y., Praeger,

. . . . *Democracy and the Athenians,* ed. F. J. Frost. N.Y., John Wiley &
Sons, Inc.

Ehrenberg, Victor. *The Greek State.* N.Y., W. W. Norton & Co., Inc. 1964.

Flaceliere, Robert. *Daily Life in Greece at the Time of Pericles.* N.Y., Macmillan Co., 1966.

Forrest, W.G. *A Short History of Sparta.* N.Y., W.W. Norton & Co., Inc. 1968.

Freeman, Kathleen. *Greek City States.* N.Y., W. W. Norton, Co., 1963.

Glotz, Gustave, *Ancient Greece at Work.* N.Y., W.W. Norton & Co., Inc. 1967.

The Horizon Book of Ancient Greece, ed. Horizon Magazine. N.Y., American
Heritage Publishing Co., 1965.

Jones, A. H. M. *Athenian Democracy.* Oxford, Basil Blackwell, 1957.

Jones, A. H. M. *Sparta.* Cambridge, Harvard University Press, 1967.

Kagan, Donald. *The Outbreak of the Peloponnesian War.* Utica, N.Y., Cornell
University Press. 1969.

Kitto, H. D. F. *The Greeks.* Baltimore, Md., Penguin Books, 1951.

Lang, Mabel. *The Athenian Citizen.* Princeton, N. J., The American School
of Classical Studies at Athens, 1960.

Plutarch. *The Lives of the Noble Grecians and Romans,* Trans. by John
Dryden. New York, The Modern Library,

Zimmern, Alfred. *The Greek Commonwealth: Politics and Economics in
Fifth-Century Athens.* N.Y., Oxford University Press, 1961.

CHAPTER IX

PHILIP II AND ALEXANDER III
OF MACEDONIA

Section I—*The Individual and History*

The question of the importance of the individual in history was raised in regard to Greek leaders of the Golden Age. This question must be raised again when we consider the period of the rise of Macedonia under the leadership of Philip II and his son, Alexander III. The latter is better known as Alexander the Great, and whenever an individual has been honored with the epithet of "The Great," we can be certain historians have felt he had an impact on the course of human history. What was the impact of this father and son on history? What did this pair from the northeast region of the Greek peninsula do? What were they like as people?

Briefly, they ended a period of history, the Late Classical period of Hellenic history, and introduced a new period, the Hellenistic. In the Hellenistic Age, c. 323–c. 30 B.C., what we have studied as Hellenic culture, the culture of mainland Greece and the Aegean, was fused with Near Eastern and Persian culture, the culture of the eastern Mediterranean. The synthesis or combination is called Hellenistic. Hellenistic culture was spread to the entire Mediterranean area and western Europe by the conquests of Rome. This Hellenistic culture affected Roman history, changed it, and ultimately it has affected us. The synthesis of the Greek and the eastern cultures and the widespread distribution of Hellenistic culture greatly affected the development and diffusion of Christianity and these two concepts, Christianity and Hellenistic Culture, form the two major roots of our own Western culture. Perhaps the same results would have been achieved without Philip II and Alexander III but historically we can trace the beginnings of Hellenistic culture to these two men. Certainly these two individuals have had an impact on history. But what were they like as individuals? As you read about their actions and lives, try to picture what each man was like as a person. Would you like to have known them? Would you like to have had them as a friend?

Section II—*Philip II, King of Macedon, 359-336 B.C.*

Philip became King of Macedon in 359 B.C. at the age of 23. The land he ruled was considered barbarian by most Greeks although the Macedonians spoke a Greek dialect. The Greeks acknowledged there was some form of relationship since the King of Macedon was allowed to participate in the Olympic Games, an action forbidden to all non-Greeks. It was said the royal family was descended from Dorian princes who invaded the peninsula centuries before. Whatever the historic origins of the Macedonians, since the repulse of the Persian invasions of the fifth century, Greek artists and poets had been welcome at the Macedonian court. The Macedonians were rugged farmers and herders, but by Philip's day there were small cities in Macedon and the rudiments of Hellenic culture had been established.

As a youth, Philip had spent three years as a hostage in Thebes. A bright and able youth, he had studied carefully the military formation and tactics of the great Theban leader, Epaminondas. His use of the phalanx gave Philip ideas which Philip later used to conquer Greece. Philip improved on Epaminondas' idea. He opened spaces in the files of the phalanx so it was more maneuverable and he developed cavalry for use on both flanks of the phalanx thus creating an extremely maneuverable and potent force. The Macedonian army was well protected by armour and the spears held by men of the phalanx were twenty-four feet long making it hard for opposing troops to get close to the body of Macedonian troops. Philip and Alexander also developed extensive seige weapons such as catapults and battering rams which allowed them to attack beseiged cities and not merely to blockade them. They also, unlike their opponents, were ready to fight any time of the year. The farmers of Macedonia provided rugged and effective troops for the phalanx. It was the spirit of these fighting men inspired by their king's leadership that made the Madedonian conquests possible.

While in Thebes Philip witnessed the incapacity of the Greek city states to unite. He determined to create Greek unity under Macedonian hegemony or leadership. Throughout their history the city states of the Greek peninsula were unable to unify for effective political action. In spite of the many original political ideas developed by the Greeks which have been incorporated in the western tradition, the idea of a united state under a federal administration was not a Greek concept. Independence and freedom were valued more highly than unity by the Greeks. Macedonians were Greek enough to appreciate much of Greek life, but they were under other influences as well. One of these was the semi-barbarian tribes to the north. Philip's ancestors had had to unite the Macedonian tribes to withstand their attacks. This background led Philip to think of a unified Greek world. He saw himself as the person to unite all Greeks—the Ionian cities, the Aegean islands, and the peninsula—under one rule. He may have viewed this unity as a power to counter-balance Persian power, but this is uncertain.

Philip needed an opportunity to become involved in the petty fights of the Greek city states. Once involved, he believed he could, through diplomacy and military action, create his desired union. An argument over the control of the sacred shrine of Apollo at Delphi broke out between Thebes and Phocis, the city state next to Delphi. The arguments were involved and neither side had a clear case. Since the shrine was so important to all Greeks, the poleis began to take sides. Athens supported Phocis. Thebes then appealed to Philip for support and Greek history took a new turn. Philip posed as the champion of Apollo and soon was included in the deliberations of the Greeks not only over the shrine at Delphi but on other issues. By 338 B.C. Philip had established himself as a force in Greek internal affairs.

Apparently few people in the poleis realized Philip's goal was to change the political pattern and to create a basis for united action. In Athens one man, Demosthenes, realized what was happening and in a series of famous speeches warned the Athenians and all Greece of what Philip was doing. These speeches, *The Philippics,* are among the most famous in history, but Demosthenes was not able to rouse the Athenians. Philip had a group of supporters in Athens led by Isocrates. He and the pro-Macedonian group hoped Philip would lead the Greeks in a conquest of the Ionian city states, which were back under Persian control as a result of the Great King's Peace of 387 B.C., and Asia Minor. They believed such a conquest would open up many economic opportunities.

Philip's plans were not progressing rapidly enough for him. In 338 B.C. he turned from diplomacy to military action and marched south through Thessaly into Greece. Many of the smaller cities were ready to receive him. Athens finally listened to Demosthenes and abandoned her ally Phocis which welcomed Philip. Athens joined with Thebes to oppose Philip's advance southward. Philip was nearing Thebes when he met the combined forces of Athens and Thebes at Chaeronea, a small town on a plain north of Thebes. Philip attacked. Both sides fought well. The heart of the Theban army, the Sacred Band of three hundred especially chosen young men pledged through love of each other to fight together, died to a man. Philip won the Battle of Chaeronea. The victory dramatically changed the political situation in Greece. It made Philip master of Greece as the other poleis, except Sparta, surrendered. The Greek poleis had a common leader as a result of a military attack. Philip could now turn his attention elsewhere.

Alexander, age 18, fought as one of his father's commanders at Chaeronea. After the victory, Philip sent him to Athens with the ashes of the Athenian dead and with the terms of peace. Philip offered easy terms to his foes—acknowledge Philip as commander-in-chief of the Greeks and Macedonians in a war to free the Greek cities of Asia Minor, send troops and supplies as needed for the campaign, accept a small Macedonian garrison in some cities, allow each city to retain its own form of government. The Athenians were delighted with the terms and quickly accepted. They entertained Alexander royally on this his only visit to the cultural center of the Greeks. We wish, as we will find is so often the case with Alexander, we knew more about his visit. What did Alexander do in Athens? Was he impressed by the architecture and history of the city and its people? How did the visit affect his future actions? We'll never know and yet when dealing with individuals in history it is questions of this type to which we would like answers.

After Chaeronea, Philip toured Greece and at the end of the year called a pan-Hellenic or all Greek conference at Corinth. The Greek poleis, except Sparta, acknowledged Philip as commander-in-chief and began planning the joint expedition to conquer Asia Minor. Philip had achieved half his goal—the poleis of the peninsula were united in a loose organization, the League of Corinth, with a common goal. For the first time in history the Greek poleis were united not just temporarily for defense. Philip returned to Macedon to prepare for the attack on the Persian Empire which controlled the Greek cities of Asia Minor. His plans were progressing well. He had already sent the advance troops to set up the bridgehead in Asia when, at the theater during his daughter's wedding celebration in the summer of 336 B.C., Philip was killed by an assassin.

Philip's assassination climaxed a long series of domestic quarrels at the Macedonian court in Pella. The historian Plutarch says the young murderer, Pausanius, had been encouraged to commit the act by Philip's first wife and Alexander's mother, Olympias. Olympias was a princess from Epirus, modern Albania, and not a Macedonian or Greek. She is reported in all the histories as being violent, wild, and savage with strong emotions that often broke through her thin veneer of civilized manners. Olympias believed in magic and practiced it with strange rites. She worshipped Dionysus, whose worship we have mentioned before as being erotic and emotional.

The year before his assassination Philip had renounced Olympias as his queen, but not as his wife. He had married a young girl, Cleopatra, daughter of one of his Macedonian generals, Attalus, and made her the new queen. When Cleopatra bore a son to Philip, the succession was brought into question, and as the baby was of pure Macedonian blood, it is thought Alexander's position as heir was jeopardized, as he was only half Macedonian and his mother was no longer the queen.

To compound the domestic confusion even more, Alexander was not at ease with his father. He did not readily participate in the drinking and carousing at the palace and the generation gap even included a hair problem. Alexander preferred to be clean shaven and would not wear a beard as was the Macedonian custom. And finally, Alexander was close to his mother and was strongly influenced by her.

At the time of Philip's marriage to Cleopatra, Alexander had felt insulted by Attalus' toast that their child would be a "lawful successor" to the throne. He threw his wine cup at Attalus who ducked. Philip attacked Alexander but was so drunk he fell. Alexander and Olympias fled to Epirus. Philip was persuaded to send for Alexander by a trusted advisor who pointed out how could the Greeks be united by a man who couldn't unite his own household.

These facts have led some people to suspect Alexander as well as Olympias was involved in the assassination. The evidence is not clear and the decision depends on the individual's interpretation of the character and personality of Alexander. Again, we would certainly like to know more about the event in the history of Macedon.   The assassin, Pausanius, however, was killed by Philip's bodyguard, and Alexander age 20 immediately proclaimed himself King as Alexander III of Macedon. Although there was some opposition by Macedonian nobles, two of Philip's generals, Antipater and Parmenio, supported Alexander, and the army quickly rallied to Alexander who had been trained as one of them. Cleopatra, her baby son and her father, General Attalus, were killed as were several other members of the court. Thus, in bloodshed and violence began the reign of one of the most remarkable and significant individuals in history, Alexander III of Macedon, called the Great.

Section III—*Alexander III—King of Macedon 336-323 B.C.*

A. Childhood and Adolescence

Historians agree on what Alexander did militarily but there is little agreement as to his political aims and even less agreement on what he was like as a person. To many people the interpretation of Alexander's aims, character, and personality is challenging. This man had a tremendous impact on the ancient world but we actually know little about him. As so often in history when we consider individuals, we are forced to deal in terms of their impact on society, of how they commanded armies and the like yet we know each individual has a unique personality formed by his family, education, friends, environment, and traditions. The historical novelist creates these personal events. Often the person presented by the novelist is more real than the actual historical personage we meet in the pages of history. Yet we know each person in the history books had a childhood, played games, loved, was educated in some way, had fears and illnesses, experienced little successes and failures as well as those big ones that are mentioned in history books. Think of this as you read about Alexander. You may be asked to write an account of what you think he was like as a person.

Legends about Alexander abound and he has been the subject of many studies and books. We have no contemporary account of his life although Alexander was careful to have records kept and many of his contemporaries including several of his generals wrote accounts of his life and conquests. These are all lost now but these accounts were available to five historians who wrote histories of Alexander during the years of the Roman Empire. It is from these five historians and their quotations from the lost earlier accounts that we learn of Alexander. The five, Plutarch, Arrian, Diodorus, Curtius, and Justin, disagree in their interpretations of Alexander's personality as did his contemporaries.

We will present several of the childhood events that appear in most accounts of Alexander. As you read, try to picture this young man who became King of Macedon at age 20 when most young people today are sophomores in college and who at the age of 23, when most young people have just graduated from college, had conquered the greatest empire the world had seen to that moment. What was Alexander like? Would you like to have known him?

History is full of tales of the unusual events surrounding the birth and childhood of great men. From Sargon II of Akkad to Moses in ancient times and from G. Washington to A. Lincoln in our own history, men have created tales of their hero's childhood. Alexander is no exception.

Alexander was born in Pella, the Macedonian capital, while Philip was campaigning. One story reports that Philip received three, a number with magic qualities to the ancients, good messages at one time that day: first, that his race horse had won at the Olympic Games; second, that his general had defeated the neighboring tribe; and third, that his queen, Olympias, had borne a son. Another story reported that the great Temple of Artemis at Ephesus burned down while Alexander was being born that summer of 356 B.C. It was said the goddess, Artemis, was too busy bringing Alexander into the world to protect her temple. For the ancient world tales of supernatural or coincidental events had magic power and these tales were used to illustrate what a unique life Alexander would have.

We've mentioned Olympias, Alexander's mother, who worshipped Dionysus, and her use of magic. She charmed snakes and even slept with a pet snake in her bed as protection. Apparently Philip married her both for her beauty and for political reasons, but was soon repulsed by her strange customs of worship and her domineering nature and lack of conscience. She was headstrong and stopped at nothing to get her way. Historians agree there was a struggle between Olympias and Philip for Alexander's affections from the time of his birth. In fact, Olympias claimed a god, Zeus–Amon, and not Philip was Alexander's father. Alexander was apparently brought up on this tale as well as that he was descended through his mother from the great Greek warrior of the Trojan War, Achilles. These stories helped form his personality and must have led to the antagonism between father and son mentioned above.

In spite of the antagonism Alexander was educated to be his father's successor. His early training at the palace was under direction of Leonidas, a kinsman of Olympias. All accounts agree he was a stern disciplinarian. He did not let Alexander eat the fancy palace food and he trained Alexander well for the military hardships he was to face. Alexander had a quick temper which Leonidas tried to curb. Alexander became a superb swordsman under his training. Alexander, of medium height and build, had great natural athletic ability which was highly developed. He ran and hunted, rode the chariot and practiced leaping from it when going at full speed. He was an excellent horseman riding bareback as was the custom then. By the age of thirteen he was well developed and prepared physically for his military career.

Philip then hired the great philosopher, Aristotle, as Alexander's tutor to train his mind. Philip knew wisdom as well as physical powers would be needed if Alexander was to succeed him after Philip's plans for Greek unity had been achieved. The antagonism between Olympias and Philip may have been involved in this change of tutor as Leonidas was a relative of Olympias.

Plutarch tells a story that illustrates both Alexander's wisdom and physical ability. Philip was interested in buying a black horse, Bucephalus, but decided not to as the horse appeared too vicious and unmanageable. Alexander said he could manage the horse. Philip took him up on it and promised him the horse if Alexander could control him. Alexander had noticed Bucephalus was afraid of shadows and taking account of the sun's position Alexander calmed him, mounted him, and rode him. Alexander trained Bucephalus and rode him on all his conquests. When Bucephalus died on campaign near India, Alexander named a city after him. Bucephalus became one of the most famous horses in history.

The three most famous Greek philosophers were Socrates, Plato, and Aristotle. Aristotle was Plato's most famous student. Aristotle is noted for his interest in nature and in logical thought processes. He trained Alexander in both and on his campaigns Alexander sent samples of the fauna and flora back to Aristotle in Athens for his study. Aristotle tutored Alexander for three years. We know little of those years, how hard Alexander worked, what was covered in the lessons, who else, if anyone, studied with Alexander. It is probable that Hephaestion, who was Alexander's life-long companion and closest confidant, also studied under Aristotle. We suspect that in those teenage years Alexander's temper exploded often, but he came to control it as he experienced the usual teenage developments.

It was customary in Macedonia to kill a boar as a sign of

manhood, and Alexander did this earlier than his companions. What other events occurred to affect his later life or to give him political or economic understanding we do not know. Certainly few kings or leaders have had the educational opportunities provided Alexander.

When Alexander was 16 Aristotle returned to Athens and Philip placed Alexander in the army to learn the military art with the troops. He must have learned quickly for soon Alexander was being taught the administrative system of Macedonia in Pella. At 17 he was left in charge of Macedon while Philip went on campaign to the east. Alexander learned quickly and even crushed a minor rebellion of Thracian tribes while Philip was away. On Philip's· return he must have realized Alexander at age 18 was well trained for leadership. Philip made him an army commander before the Battle of Chaeronea and Alexander proved his ability there. The trip to Athens concluded Alexander's education. Would you think he was well prepared for Kingship at age 20? What weaknesses might exist in the young man's training?

Alexander collected around him a number of young men of whom Philip disapproved. For what reasons we are not sure. It may have been jealousy or the conflict with Olympias. In any case Philip exiled several of Alexander's close friends. What the impact was on Alexander we do not know, but as soon as he was king, Alexander recalled them. They took high places in his empire, but no one took the place of Hephaestaion. Nearchus became his admiral, Herpalus his treasurer, and Ptolemy one of his greatest and most loyal generals. No mention is made of any females, but perhaps this is not surprising when we consider the role of women in Macedonian society and the place Olympias held at the court.

Besides family, education, and friends, one's environment and the society's traditions strongly influence a person's personality and character. We've mentioned Macedonia as a rugged country of shepherds and farmers with a few towns under Greek cultural influence. The ruggedness of the life and country surely affected Alexander, but recent excavations at Pella reveal a great palace full of beautiful mosiacs and fine marble rooms. Alexander knew beauty but also coarseness. The Macedonians were noted for their drinking and wild parties. Those must have taken place in the beautiful palace setting.

Philip and Macedonia were dependent on the army. The environment of the army camp on campaign and the palace full of soldiers and generals must have dominated Alexander's childhood. The personality traits and characteristics this atmosphere required were the ones so well illustrated by Alexander, physical strength, military ability, ruggedness, temper, and wisdom to analyze and understand the situation quickly.

The Macedonian tradition of military activity, violence, palace intrigue, and an interest in things Greek come together in Philip's assassination and Alexander's ascent to the throne in 336 B.C. At age 20 violence had made him king. He was heir to Philip's plan to fight the Persian Empire in order to free the Ionian Greek cities. How well was Alexander prepared to carry on his father's plan? Had Philip brought him up well? What do you think? How would the recently united Greek poleis react to this sudden change of leadership in Macedonia? An affirmation by the Greek cities that they would follow Alexander was the first step in continuing Philip's design of conquest and unity. Would you, as a Greek, have been ready to follow the twenty year old Alexander?

B. Conquests

Upon hearing of Philip's death the Greek cities began to withdraw from the League of Corinth which constituted their commitment to Philip. Demosthenes spoke against Alexander in Athens, but many Greeks realized very little had changed as long as the Macedonian army was loyal to Philip's successor. Alexander set out to prove they were and decided on a march through Greece against the advice of his generals who felt he should first consolidate his home position. Everyone agrees Alexander was a brilliant general and this first campaign illustrated the fact. He led his army over donkey paths along the rocky coast of Thessaly bypassing their army. He thus cut Thessaly off from the rest of Greece. They immediately rejoined the League. Athens and Thebes asked for terms and Alexander marched triumphantly, to Corinth where the League was reaffirmed.

While Alexander was away, northern tribes attacked the borders of Macedon. Alexander led a small part of his army after them. He left his generals at Pella as he apparently felt the need to prove his ability in the field. Perhaps this need can be easily understood when we realize he was then 20 and had never planned a campaign alone. He chased the tribes north and across the Danube River which he crossed without bridging it. Instead, he constructed rafts out of wood, straw, and leather tents. This feat, his first as king, so shocked and surprised the northern tribes that they didn't attack Macedon again for fifty years. Alexander's military life is full of such feats.

Again while he was away the Illyrians (near modern Albania) revolted. Alexander marched his army to crush them. His forces were trapped while beseiging the fortress of Pelion, but by maneuvering his troops on the field before the Illyrians he so distracted them that when he wheeled his army in a brilliant move he was able to break out of the trap. He then turned and crushed the Illyrians, but Alexander received a blow on the neck. Rumors quickly spread that the blow had killed him.

Demosthenes immediately called on Athens to break with Macedon, but she didn't. Thebes, however, seized the Macedonian garrison stationed there. Alexander was furious and moved his army 300 miles in 14 days, quite a record when you consider the terrain but typical of Alexander's military moves, and appeared before Thebes. When he asked for their surrender, they jeered and Alexander attacked. The city was destroyed and all the citizens killed or sold into slavery. Why did he do this? What does it say? about Alexander the man and about ancient warfare? If you realize Alexander had been continually on the move trying to consolidate his authority since he had proclaimed himself King and that this was the second time Thebes had revolted, perhaps Alexander's motives become clear. He certainly could not attack Persia with the possibility of being attacked in the rear while away.

Two events that occurred at Thebes reveal other aspects of Alexander's character. First, it is reported he spared the house of Pindar, one of the great Greek poets. Was Alexander a sensitive, cultured gentleman as well as a warrior? Second, he spared a woman and her children. The woman was the sister of the Theban commander at Chaeronea and she admitted she had murdered one of Alexander's officers who had broken into her home. Alexander let her go free. Was Alexander a sentimental, emotional lover as well as a general? Throughout his career Alexander was noted for his kind treatment of older women. It provides an interesting side of his personality and makes one wonder if Alexander's relations with Olympias had anything to do with his attitude towards women. We'll later learn how he treated the Persian Queen when he captured her. When we are considering individuals in history, we so often do not consider how leaders react to individuals. These two stories as well as his treatment of Thebes may give us some idea as to how Alexander would have ruled his great empire if he had lived.

After the destruction of Thebes, the Greek poleis reaffirmed their support of the League of Corinth. After two years Alexander had consolidated his rule and controlled the Greek peninsula from the Danube River to the Mediterranean. Alexander at age 22 was ready to move against the Persian Empire as his father had planned. It appears, however, Alexander's dream was not just to unite the Greek world but to conquer and rule the Persian empire. What his ultimate plans were is uncertain, but what he accomplished militarily is not.

Alexander left his general, Antipater, as regent of Macedon, and in April 334 B.C. headed for Asia and the Persian Empire, ruled by the Great King, Darius III. He crossed the Dardanelles and sacrificed to Poseidon, the Greek god of the Sea, as he crossed. On all of his journeys Alexander took special care to sacrifice and to give thanks to the gods. He did not confine himself to the Greek gods, but acknowledged and worshipped those of other peoples wherever he went. Whether Alexander's motivation was a deep religious sense or a superb political scheme, we do not know. But it is certain his tolerance won many to his support as his conquests continued.

Alexander's first stop was Troy, where he again sacrificed at the so-called tomb of his mythical ancestor, Achilles. The Persian generals prepared to fight at the Granicus River. They rejected the advice of a Greek who suggested the Persian army withdraw into central Anatolia pulling Alexander into Asia. The Persians then using their large fleet could invade Macedon in Alexander's rear. The Persian general in Asia Minor rejected this plan. He was certain his Persian army collected from the many peoples of the widespread empire and with its long history of victories, was superior to Alexander's force of 30,000 Macedonians and Greeks. He and his advisors were wrong.

The Persian forces were drawn up along the bank of the river and Alexander saw how he could gain the advantage. He attacked on the right and led his own special mounted troops, the Companions, in a charge on the right where the Persian generals were. Alexander killed one. One of the Companions, Cleitus, killed another general as he attacked Alexander with his sword. With several Persian generals dead, Alexander had the cavalry on the left wing charge as his phalanxes attacked the center. The Persians fled in confusion and the Macedonians then attacked the Greek mercenaries who had never even been committed to the battle.

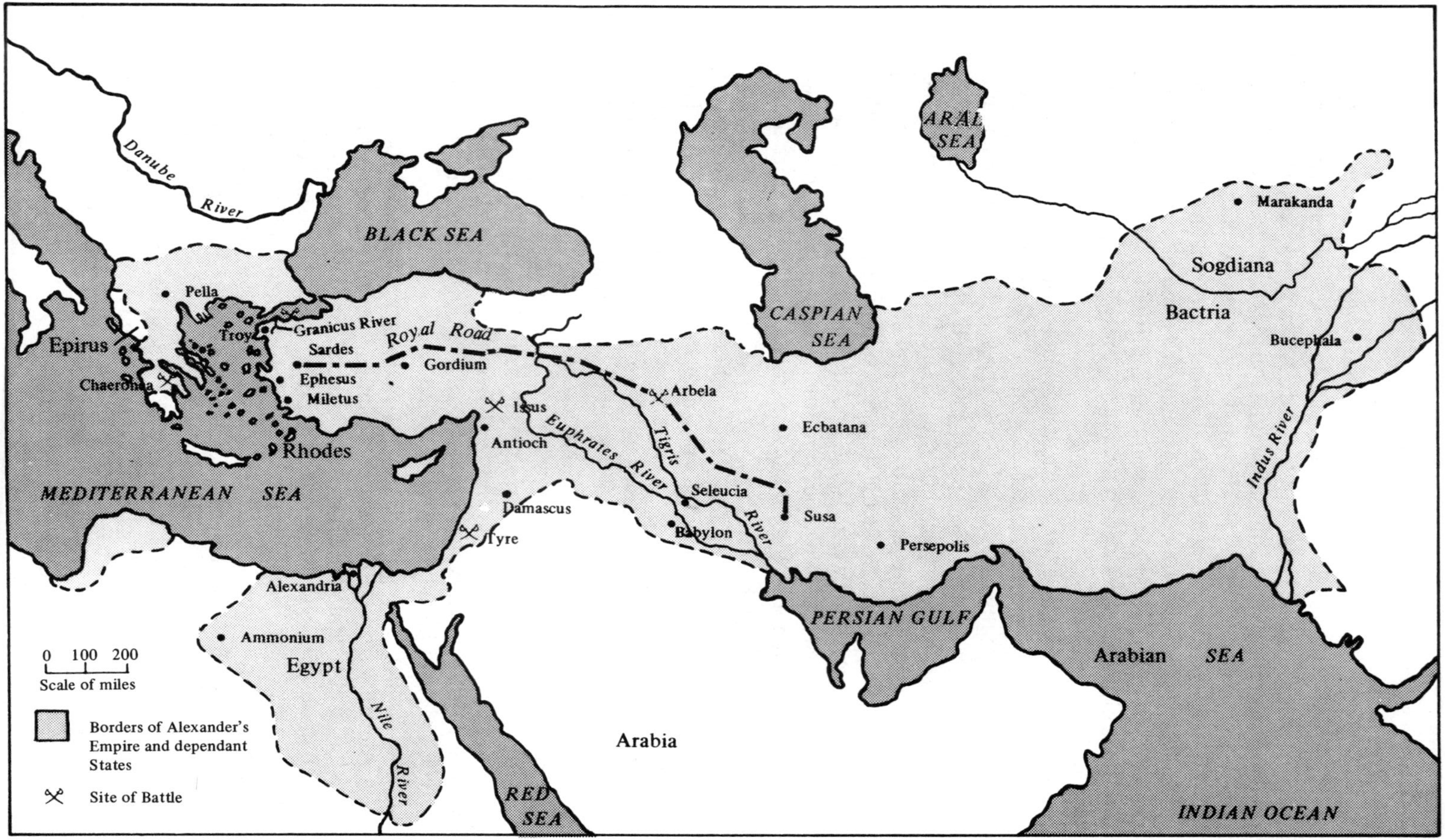
Danube River
BLACK SEA
ARAL SEA
CASPIAN SEA
Pella
Epirus
Chaeronea
Troy
Granicus River
Royal Road
Sardes
Gordium
Ephesus
Miletus
Rhodes
Issus
Antioch
Arbela
Euphrates River
Tigris River
Ecbatana
Seleucia
Susa
Babylon
Persepolis
Damascus
Tyre
MEDITERRANEAN SEA
Alexandria
Ammonium
Egypt
Nile River
RED SEA
Arabia
PERSIAN GULF
Arabian SEA
INDIAN OCEAN
Marakanda
Sogdiana
Bactria
Bucephala
Indus River
0 100 200
Scale of miles
Borders of Alexander's Empire and dependant States
Site of Battle

The victory was ·a total one and the historian, Diodorus, reports the Persian loss as 12,000 slain and 20,000 captured compared to 150 Macedonian dead. The figures are no doubt exaggerated even as our "kill" estimates in recent wars seem exaggerated, but the proportion must have some truth. Alexander's losses in battles were always small as they had to be since his manpower pool was so much smaller than the Persian. As a sign he was over-lord of Greece and that he would not tolerate Greeks who rejected his leadership, Alexander sent to Macedon as slaves the captured Greek mercenaries except the Thebans. Again two actions after the Battle of Granicus show other aspects of his character. First, he freed the Theban mercenaries, perhaps as he felt guilty over the destruction of Thebes. Second, he sent to Athens a gift of Persian armour from the "son of Philip". Perhaps he wanted to be accepted as a true Greek by the Athenians.

After the victory at the Granicus River the coast of the Aegean lay open. He offered freedom from Persia to the Greek cities and Ephesus joined him. He ordered rebuilt the burned Temple of Artemis at Ephesus and, though some freedoms were granted, he put his men in charge of the cities. An organization of the empire similar to that of the Persian was emerging. The city of Miletus refused to join Alexander. He conquered it and destroyed the city. It was clear all Greeks did not want freedom and unity under the hegemony of the Macedonian king. How this affected Alexander's plans we do not know. We do know that at Miletus he added the Greek mercenaries to his own army rather than sending them off as slaves. He was appearing more realistic as to his strength.

Alexander's plan for the conquest of the Persian Empire began to emerge after the capture of Miletus. The Aegean coast would be secured and then inland Anatolia (presently Turkey) by a march through it. He would not follow the Royal Road from Gordium to the Persian capital of Susa but move south into the Mediter-ranean coastal area. As mentioned above, Persia had a large fleet based along this coast. It would be a potential threat to Macedon and Greece if it were left intact. How would you have dealt with the fleet? You may not realize that ships in those days could not stay away from a land base very long. This fact was the key to Alexander's plan of conquest. You can follow Alexander's route on the map.

Darius III, after the Battle of Granicus, took charge of the Persian forces and regrouped at Issus, a narrow pass in the mountains that cut Anatolia off from the Near East. Alexander attacked Darius and again won a brilliant victory. Darius' losses were tremendous and he fled towards Susa, yet Alexander did not pursue him. Darius' camp was captured. Darius' mother, Sisygambis, his Queen, Statira, and two daughters were in the camp. They had been abandoned as Darius fled. They were kept as royal prisoners and always well treated by Alexander. Alexander's way with older women was illustrated in his dealings with Sisygambis. He used to visit her for conversation and he supplied her everything she wanted. When Alexander saw Darius' tent with its gold furnishings, Plutarch says Alexander commented, "This, it appears, is royalty." The King of Macedon had had his first sight of Persian wealth.

After Issus Alexander turned toward Egypt not Susa. The port of Tyre held out for seven months but the remarkable work of Alexander's engineers in building a mole or causeway out to the island where the main part of the city stood and his use of catapults and seige weapons finally forced the city to surrender. Egypt then surrendered without a battle and Alexander entered Egypt in triumph in the fall of 332 B.C. During the winter he planned and laid the foundations of Egyptian Alexandria, the first of the more than 60 cities he founded on his conquests. This first Alexandria became the most important city of the eastern Mediterranean and remains so today.

While in Egypt, Alexander visited the ancient shrine of the god, Zeus–Amon. As he entered, he was hailed as a god. This incident is considered of crucial significance by many yet we know that all Egyptian rulers were considered gods in Egypt. For Alexander, however, being greeted in this way when he was merely making the sacrifices he always made combined with his mother's tales of being the son of the god, Zeus–Amon, may have changed history. Many scholars believe this event gave Alexander ideas of ruling his Asian empire following the Asian tradition of viewing the King as a god and not as a man. In Greece and Macedon it had always been clear that rulers were simply men. Later actions of Alexander indicate he may have felt he was not just an ordinary man but that there was something divine about him. Certainly his military victories were extraordinary and this visit to the shrine of an Egyptian god may have been the crucial event in shaping his personal view of how he was able to win.

Alexander left Egypt in the spring of 331 B.C., marched through Palestine and Syria, and headed for the heart of the Persian Empire.

His rear was secure. The bases of the Persian fleet were under his control as was Egypt. Macedonian military commanders were in charge of the major areas and governors, or satraps, appointed by Alexander carried out the routine administration.

Darius waited for Alexander at Gaugemela in Assyria.[1] Darius had collected a huge force. Alexander attacked and again his generalship proved decisive. The battle was bitter but brilliantly planned and fought by Alexander. Darius fled and the Persian Empire was Alexander's, although he had not yet captured the Great King. Alexander marched to Babylon which surrendered. He sacrificed to Marduk, the god of Babylon, and ordered the rebuilding of all temples destroyed by the Persians. Then he and his troops took a month's leave to enjoy the pleasures and activities of the city.

The empire had to be organized politically. Alexander was ready to adapt ideas from the conquered empires. He appointed a Persian, who had fought well against him, as satrap in Babylon. He appointed Macedonians as treasurer and military commander. He used this policy in many areas combining Macedonian and local administration. A pattern for government organization was emerging and it was combined with an idea of religious toleration, but most accounts of Alexander suggest he had little interest in administration. It must be remembered that up to this point Alexander had not eliminated the Great King, Darius III. According to Arrian, Alexander had sent a message to Darius saying he could have whatever he wished if Darius would acknowledge Alexander as King of Asia. Darius had not done so. He had to be captured. Until then, administration of the empire was secondary.

After the rest at Babylon, Alexander moved his army to Susa. This administrative capital of the empire fell without a battle. The wealth captured was phenomenal. Alexander distributed it among his companions. Some of the Macedonians were overwhelmed and used it for stupid or exotic purposes. There was more gold than any of them had expected to see. Alexander set up Queen Mother Sisygambis in a palace with her granddaughter, Statira. Darius' Queen had died on the march after the Battle of Gaugemela. Again Alexander sent a gift to Athens, the statue of two Athenian heroes seized when Xerxes had burned Athens in 480 B.C.

---

[1] The battle took place between the villages of Gaugemela and Arbela. Therefore this crucial battle is referred to by either name.

Rather than winter in Susa Alexander marched on through the rugged mountains to arrive at Persepolis, the city which had been the home of the Persian Kings. The loot in furnishings was tremendous, twenty thousand mules and five thousand camels were needed to carry it away, and there was more gold than at Susa. Alexander and his troops celebrated. The young man who would not participate in his father's drinking parties was changing. Accounts differ as to exactly what happened, but the result was that Persepolis was burned and totally destroyed. Some say it was a drunken Alexander who set the fires. Others say it was the mistress of general Ptolemy, Thais, an Athenian, who suggested at a banquet it would be a fitting revenge for all the Greek sufferings in the Persian War if Persepolis were burned. Others say Alexander deliberately burned the city in revenge and as an example to the Persians. Would this seem compatible with Alexander's character?

In March 330 B.C. word came that Darius was raising an army at Ecbatana. Always one to attack, Alexander started in pursuit on what turned out to be a six year military expedition. Darius withdrew into Bactria where he was stabbed to death by his Bactrian supporters as Alexander approached. Alexander punished the murderers; he may have been concerned at the precedent Darius' murder would establish. He sent Darius' body to his family in Susa for burial.

Thus in 330 B.C. at age 26 Alexander had no legitimate opposition for the title Great King. He could claim the largest empire the world had known to that time and one of the largest in history. His troops felt the four year campaign of conquest was over and were ready to return to Macedon. From our perspective the next step should have been to set up the long range administration of the empire and to assure a successor as his father, Philip, had done in educating Alexander. But Alexander decided to move east, to secure the northern borders of his empire, and to conquer India. The troops mutined, but with an impassioned speech Alexander won them over. Later a plot against his life was discovered. He had the suspected leader, a close friend, Philotas, tortured and when he confessed, both Philotas and his father, General Parmenio who led the cavalry, were killed as well as many others. At this point, what would you have done next if you were Alexander? It was clear his troops and some of his close friends were unhappy. The empire needed attention. Should Alexander have returned to Susa?

Alexander did not. There was a pretender for the throne in northern Bactria, Bessus. Alexander led his troops after him and killed him brutally. Still he did not turn back. He wanted to pacify the northern border tribes but he may have also wanted to see this far distant part of the world. He must have believed he was close to the northern limit of the earth. He marched north into Sogdiana to Marakanda (modern Samarkand in the Soviet Union). The fighting against the small rebellious tribes in the semi-desert and mountainous area was rugged and Alexander displayed his brilliant military leadership.

At Marakanda two important events occurred that reflect on Alexander's character and which might have changed history. Alexander was drinking heavily. During a brawl he believed Cleitus who had saved his life at the Battle of Granicus insulted him. He hurled a spear at him and killed him. This event has been recorded throughout history to illustrate Alexander's temper and drinking habits.

The second event was Alexander married Roxana, daughter of a Sogdian tribal chief, whom he had defeated. Roxana is reported as one of the most beautiful women in the empire. She was a captive after her father's defeat. The story is told she danced before Alexander and he fell in love. Historians do not mention her again until four years later and so some have suggested it was merely a political marriage to secure the northern borders. Whether it was for love or politics the empire had a Queen and she is reported to have been hot tempered and emotional, perhaps another Olympias?

Marriage did not distract Alexander from conquest and turn him to planning the empire's future. Instead he planned to invade India. In 327 B.C. he moved towards India with all his troops. their wives and baggage and his new Queen. His campaign against King Porus at the borders of modern India was brilliant but his troops finally refused to go further. It is reported Alexander dreamed of pushing on to the Ganges River which, with his view of geography, he thought would be the end of the world, but he finally turned back towards Persepolis in September 325 B.C. since he realized his Macedonian troops would not go further. Still ready to explore, Alexander followed the coast of the Persian Gulf on his return trip to Persepolis rather than retracing his steps or taking an easier more established route. He sent a fleet he built at the mouth of the Indus River along the Persian Gulf under the command of his old friend, Nearchus.

Throughout his campaign, Alexander traveled in places no scholar of Aristotle's had ever been. As reported above, he sent samples back to his teacher. Another aspect of Alexander's character is illustrated in this action. Was he really a naturalist or scientist at heart? Had Aristotle instilled in him a curiosity which led him on his great campaign? Were his military conquests and travels inspired by a desire to know more about the world and not just for military glory?

Alexander arrived back at Susa in the spring of 324 B.C. The empire was in disorder. His conquests had earned him a place in history and the title, the Great. Now, at age 32, he faced the problem of effectively ruling the huge empire.

C. Empire Organization and Death

There is dispute as to what Alexander's goal was. From his actions described above do you have, any concept what his goal could have been? There are several clues as to what it might have been. First, he accepted the local gods. Second, he appointed his enemies to positions of importance within the empire. Third, he founded cities as he went including one named Bucephalus after his famous horse. Many of these cities did not last as the Macedonian troops did not wish to remain on garrison duty so far from home. They were, however, an attempt to control the empire and to establish a new mixed culture where Greek ideas introduced by the Macedonians would combine with local customs. This syncretism or marriage of different ideas was successful in many areas and it provided the basis for the whole Hellenistic culture of the following centuries.

An example of this idea of syncretism was the habit Alexander had of encouraging his troops to establish liasons with captured women. This increased the baggage train but made the troops happier and set the basis for a mixed civilization. More importantly, on his return to Susa, Alexander arranged over ninety marriages between his officers and high ranking Persian women. He took two more wives. He married Statira, daughter of Darius III, and made her his Queen replacing Roxana to whom he remained married. He also married Parysatis, daughter of Artaxerxes III, Darius' predeccesor as Great King, who had been deposed by Darius in a coup d'etat. By these marriages he eliminated any potential rival in the Persian royal family, a wise political move, but he also established that his successor, when and if born, would combine the blood of both Persia and Macedon as his legitimate successor would be the offspring of his Persian Queen. What better expression is there of a marriage of customs than that symbolized by physical union? Alexander's closest friend, Hephaistion, married Statira's younger sister and thus he became a relative by marriage of Alexander and connected with Persian royalty.

Alexander replaced many Persian satraps with Macedonians. At the same time to show impartiality he brought Persian youngsters, who had been carefully trained to fight in his phalanxes, into his army. Alexander was beginning to plan for an expedition into Arabia. It was premature. There were small revolts and he used force, including killings, to enforce order. There were rumors of disaffection in various quarters of the empire. His friend, Harpalus, had been Royal Treasurer at Susa. He wasted funds and then fled to Greece to stir up a revolt. Olympias was plotting against the regent, Antipater, in Macedon. Alexander was dealing with these matters and had decided to send a third of his forces to Macedon when his troops again mutined. There were several complaints. They did not want to be absorbed into Persia. They all wanted to go home and take Alexander home with them. They claimed Alexander referred to himself as the son of Zeus–Amon and this was difficult for them to comprehend. He allowed Persian satraps to kiss him on the cheek and he required visitors to prostrate themselves on the floor before his presence, the Persian royal custom adopted probably to gain the respect of the Persians. The troops felt alienated and abandoned by Alexander. They could not understand his goal and they believed many of them would never see Macedon again.

Alexander's response to the troops was to tell them to go home. It must have been a dramatic moment as he said leave me to those I conquered and go. Alexander then went to his tent and made plans to transfer the military command to Persians. His troops then came to beg forgiveness and a story is told that illustrates what must have been Alexander's goal. A soldier basing his comment on the way Alexander allowed Persians to kiss him and his marriage to Queen Statira said, "You make Persians your kinsmen", Alexander replied that no, he was making everyone his kinsman and he always considered all the Macedonians his kinsmen and they could kiss his cheek if they wished. There was a reconciliation, but the mutiny illustrates how shaky and how personal was Alexander's rule. He had yet to achieve a permanent system of control. It would take at least a generation before his marriage policy could be proven and there was still no heir to the empire but Alexander was only 32. Then personal tragedy struck.

Hephaestion became ill and died. Alexander was distraught. His behavior at this event which one should expect at any moment in a military life has led scholars to wonder what the relationship between Alexander and Hephaestion actually was. Alexander mourned for months. He had a huge monument to Hephaestion built at Babylon. In the spring of 323 B.C. Alexander moved to Babylon to worship at Hephaestion's bier and to prepare the Arabian campaign. He was drinking heavily. In June he caught what seemed to be a cold. He was ill and nothing helped. He may have had malaria, but several accounts suggest he was poisoned. We are not sure. Finally, it was clear he was dying. His army filed passed to say farewell. No successor was named. In keeping with his character, it is reported when just before he died he was asked who his successor would be. He replied, "The best."

Thus ended a twelve year reign of conquest and glory. There are more legends about Alexander than any other man. They are told everywhere but especially throughout the western world and the territory he directly affected—the Near East, Greece, Egypt, India, and the southern Soviet Union. What was he really like? What is your opinion of Alexander on the basis of the above account of the life of one individual in history? Does he honestly deserve the title "The Great"? Did he have any effect on history other than as a conqueror? Historians from his day to ours have argued on the point. Let us end our study of Alexander with a consideration of how several writers have viewed him. It will force us again to realize the importance of understanding a writer's biases before judging his work.

Section IV—*Interpretations of Alexander III of Macedon*

The five ancient historians mentioned earlier, Arrian, Plutarch, Justin, Diodorus, and Curtius varied in their interpretations of Alexander. We will not consider Diodorus and Curtius. Arrian's life is perhaps the best. He used the memoirs, which are now lost, of two contemporaries of Alexander, his old friend, Ptolemy, who became King of Egypt, and Aristobulus, his engineer. Arrian provides us many stories about Alexander which are open to interpretation as to Alexander's motives or character.

Plutarch, a Greek, wrote two accounts of Alexander. The one he wrote while young was full of praise for the young conqueror and organizer. His life of Alexander written when Plutarch was older, is not as complimentary and points out Alexander's drinking and other characteristics which are damning.

Justin, the Roman, writing in the early 4th century B.C., depicted Alexander as a cruel despot. He did not consult any original sources and may have been heavily influenced by the actions and rule of the Roman emperors of his age. His account has been used over and over again by those who wish to discredit Alexander. Justin followed a philosophical tradition which opposed Alexander. The basis of the opposition had nothing to do with Alexander's philosophical position or training. It was based on the fact Alexander had Callisthenes, Aristotle's nephew, executed for his involvement in a murder plot against Alexander. This fact clearly illustrates how important is the role of the historian in creating our image of individuals and of events in history and how we must always be aware of the biases of the writer when reading history. Incidentally, have you considered what my biases are as you have read this account of the Greeks in the Aegean? An example of Justin's interpretation of events is the fact he ascribed the marriage of Persians and Macedonians to Alexander's calculation that if the soldiers had connections with females in the camp, they would be less likely to want to return home. What do you think of that idea?

Throughout history men have speculated about Alexander. Both Julius Caesar and Napolean admired him for obvious reasons. In the medieval era he was considered the finest example of knighthood and the early English poet, Chaucer, referred to him as, "The pride of man."

In this century, the English historian, Sir William Tarn[2] has written on the Hellenistic Age and Alexander. His thesis states Alexander was guided by a concept of world unity and the brotherhood of man and he was the first person in history to apply it internationally. Tarn interprets Alexander's entire career in these terms. Tarn's thesis has had a profound impact on historians, historical thought, and interpretations of Alexander.

Zeno, the later founder of the Stoic school of philosophy, has usually been considered the first to articulate the Greek concept of world unity and brotherhood. It is an idea closely connected with Stoicism. The idea was obviously abroad in the Greek world

[2] See William W. Tarn *Hellenistic Civilization* and *Alexander the Great.*

of the 4th century B.C. It was a logical outgrowth of the political, economic, and philosophical events of that century. Such events as the internationalism of the Persian Empire, the failure of the Greek poleis to unite, the growing cosmopolitanism of the Greek world and the eastern Mediterranean, and the emphasis on the individual as opposed to the society could clearly lead individuals to consider an idea of brotherhood. Alexander, a student of a great philosopher and a Greek at heart, may well have been guided by a dream of world unity and brotherhood. Tarn emphasized in his account of Alexander the mixed marriages between Macedonians and Persians, the worship of local gods by Alexander, and the other events which stress cooperation between the two peoples. He lays great importance on a feast which celebrated the end of the mutiny at Susa. At the feast the preparation of the sacrifice was shared by Greek priests and Zoroastrian Magi or priests. The Tarn thesis has had widespread appeal in this age of the United Nations.

Arnold Toynbee,[3] the great English historian of civilization, presents a slight variation on the Tarn thesis. Toynbee suggests that Alexander learned from experience there was no difference between Greek and Persian and from this realization came his dream of unity. Toynbee goes on to say the dream of world brotherhood or homonia[4] was an essential element of Hellenic civilization and was present long before Zeno. Alexander espoused Hellenic civilization and the idea of homonoia. Toynbee indicates that as long as there is an element of Greek civilization in the world, this dream of homonoia which the great Alexander made his own will continue.

Controversy rages over the Tarn thesis today. Some scholars reject it totally, among them the English historian Ernst Badian. Closely analyzing the sources used by Tarn, Badian shows Tarn is not always accurate. Badian concludes Alexander was not the dreamer Tarn presented. Other historians take positions between these two extremes. How would you interpret the aims, personality, and character of Alexander the Great?

The English historical novelist, Mary Renault, has recently completed a two volume work on Alexander.[5] In it she creates a fascinating portrait of the man using all the sources available. It is well worth reading. The work clearly illustrates two points we

[3] See Arnold Toynbee *A Study of History* Vol. VI.

[4] The Greek word homonoia can be translated concord or harmony.

[5] The first volume, *Fire from Heaven*, deals with Alexander until he becomes king. The second volume, *The Persian Boy*, deals with his twelve year reign.

have made in this chapter about the writing of history; first, how often the novelist can better picture the individual in history, and second, how complex and important a person Alexander the Great was.

The fact controversy still rages among scholars as to Alexander's role in history, his motivation, and his character clearly illustrate he is still considered of significance in history and that it is important to consider Alexander as a person. Although Alexander III of Macedon only reigned twelve years he had a great impact on history. He ended the Persian Empire and paved the way for a new syncretistic civilization that combined elements of the Hellenic or Greek and the Near Eastern or Persian. It was this civilization that affected Rome and ultimately us of the western tradition. He was the greatest conqueror the world had known to that time and few have equalled his feats, certainly no one as young has conquered as much. Although his empire broke into several smaller nations after his death, Macedonians ruled these small empires and a common, civilization, Hellenistic civilization, flourished throughout. Mankind was not united politically but a unity of culture and attitudes did develop which made the establishment of the Roman Empire easier and, from my perspective, greatly affected the development of Christianity. Perhaps it is too much to ascribe all these changes in history to one man, but it must be clear that Alexander's conquests and his attempts at organizing his empire changed history. The Greeks of the Aegean area were now in a position to influence the history of the entire Mediterranean basin and Near East to the borders of India.[6] The ideas and attitudes we've studied in this book were spread throughout this huge region. Life in the Greek poleis would never be the same. The individual, Alexander III of Macedon, called The Great, had changed world history.

In Chapter IV the idea of the polis was presented. At that time it was indicated there would be a great change in how the polis functioned and how important it was to the average Greek between the sixth century and the time of Alexander the Great. What changes can you identify? We have suggested that Alexander's

[6] One direct influence of Alexander's conquests on India is seen in Indian art. Several statues of Alexander done while he was alive showed him with his hair in a knot on the top of his head. After his death, Indian sculptors began carving statues of the Buddha. They modeled many of these after the great conquerer and included the top knot. These features became a standard part of statues of Buddha and statues of Buddha executed today, 2,300 years later, still carry Alexander's top knot.

conquest emphasized the cosmopolitan quality of civilization. What does the word cosmopolis mean do you think?[7] Does this provide a clue as to the changes that had taken place in the Greek world by the death of Alexander? Would you have preferred to live in the age of the polis or in the age of the cosmopolis? What advantages are there in each? Your answers to these questions will help identify the changes that took place in the Aegean area during the time of Hellenic civilization. What happened to Alexander's empire and the Greeks of the Aegean after his death until they were all incorporated in the next great empire, the Roman, will be briefly considered in the last chapter.

Section V–*Chapter Review*

The focus of this chapter is on the role of two individuals in history. A number of projects involving the impact of individuals on history can be developed. For instance, you could pick any individual mentioned in this text or any person who interests you and research what impact that person had on history. You need not confine yourself to political or military figures. Think of any person you've heard about from the past. Why has the name been passed down to you? Some suggestions for individuals to consider are: Copernicus, Galileo, Newton, Darwin, Freud, Madame Curie, Leonardo da Vinci, Cezanne, St. Augustine, Abelard, Petrarch, Chaucer, Addison and Steele, Dickens, Jane Austen and from the more familiar political arena Julius Caesar, Cleopatra, Theodora and Justinian, Eleanor of Aquitane, William the Conqueror, Catherine the Great, Napoleon, Winston Churchill. The list is endless. Who would you like to investigate? Remember, the goal of the research is to determine the influence the individual has on civilization or on the course of events known as history. Can an individual change history? What do you think? Did Alexander the Great change history?

Another topic raised in the chapter is the question of the bias and attitudes of the historian, the writer of history. A good project to illustrate how the historian can affect our understanding of and feeling for the individual in history would be in investigate how different historians portray the same event in Alexander's life. A few of the many biographies of Alexander are listed at the end

---

[7]Cosmopolis combines the word polis which we have discussed at length with the word for world or universe. It might be translated as world city.

of the chapter. Pick an event such as Philip's assassination and read of the event in as many biographies as you can. Then present a paper or a speech on how the accounts vary and the conclusions you have drawn from 'this. For instance, what is the author's view of Alexander as a person? What are the author's biases? What do you think actually happened? How do the different accounts make you feel about Alexander as a person?

An interesting project can be done on the manner in which Alexander has been portrayed by sculptors and artists through the ages. Many biographies include photographs of sculptures and paintings of Alexander created at different periods. Study as many of these as you can and try to decide what Alexander looked like. Perhaps you could draw your own conception of how Alexander looked or prepare a slide presentation comparing various sculptures or paintings.

It was indicated in the chapter that novelists often create a better sense of an individual than do historians. Decide what you consider are Alexander's most important personality traits. Then create an incident that might have involved Alexander. Be certain the circumstances surrounding the incident fit the conditions of the age of Alexander. Write an account of the incident. Try to bring out in the written account of the incident the important personality traits you ascribe to Alexander. This is what the historical novelist does. Share your account with others in your class. You might like to read incidents in historical novels involving famous people as a basis for comparison or for inspiration.

The following questions will help you recall and organize specific information in the chapter. In addition you should be prepared to answer the questions at the end of Section IV. Those questions will provide a review of the entire book.

1. How would you describe Philip II of Macedon
   (a) as a person (b) as a political leader? (c) as a military leader?
2. What were the achievements of Philip II of Macedon's reign?
3. What "wondrous tales" have been told about the birth of Alexander the Great? Do you know any "wondrous tales" about the birth of other famous men?
4. What evidence do we have which would indicate Queen Olympias and perhaps Alexander were involved in the assassination of Philip II? On the basis of what you know of Alexander, do you believe he was involved? Why?

5. Trace the conquests of Alexander either by drawing a map showing his movements or by writing an account of the steps he took to conquer the Persian Empire.
6. What steps did Alexander take to set up a system of government for his empire?
7. What was Alexander's attitude toward
   (a) the city of Athens (b) Aristotle   (c) women
   (d) religion   (e) Persians.
8. How have historians and others interpreted Alexander's motivations and actions? What do you think is the author's interpretation of Alexander? What is your interpretation of Alexander?
9. Would you like to have known Alexander? Why?
10. What impact did Alexander the individual have on the course of history?

After reading the chapter you should be able to identify the following people, places, and events:

People	*Places and Events*
Alexander III	Alexandria, Egypt
Aristotle	Athens
Arrian	Babylon
Bucephalus	Battle of Chaeronea
Cleopatra	Battle of Gaugamela (Arbela)
Cleitus	Battle of Granicus
Darius III	Battle of Issus
Demosthenes	Epirus
Justin	League of Corinth
Olympias	Marakanda
Philip II	Pella
Renault	Persepolis
Roxana	Susa
Statira	Temple of Zeus—Amon
Tarn	Thebes
Toynbee	Tyre

The following books will provide additional information on Alexander the Great. The bibliography at the end of Chapter X includes works dealing with the entire Hellenistic period.

There are innumerable biographies of Alexander and many fictional works. Any of the following are worthy of consideration but you must remember each writer has his own interpretation so you should consult more than one biography if you plan to do further research into the life of this remarkable individual.

Arrianus, Flavius. *Life of Alexander the Great.* Tran. Aubrey de Selincourt Harmondsworth, Middlesex, Penguin Books, 1958.

Cary, George. *The Medieval Alexander.* Cambridge, University Press, 1956.

Green, Peter. *Alexander the Great.* N.Y., Praeger Publishers, 1970.

Plutarch. *Lives of Noble Grecians and Romans,* Trans. John Dryden. N.Y., Modern Library, 1932.

Snyder, J. W. *Alexander the Great.* N.Y., Twayne Publishers, 1966.

Tarn, W.W. *Alexander the Great: Volume I—Narrative; Volume II—Sources and Studies.* Cambridge, England, University Press, 1948.

Wilcken, Ulrich. *Alexander the Great,* Trans. G. C. Richards. N.Y., W. W. Norton, 1967.

The recent carefully researched two volume fictionalized account of Alexander's life is very readable and, as do the more traditional historical accounts, presents a very personal interpretation.

Renault, Mary. *Fire from Heaven.* N.Y., Pantheon Books, 1969.

Renault, Mary. *Persian Boy.* N.Y., Pantheon Books, 1972.

CHAPTER X

AFTERMATH–THE HELLENISTIC KINGDOMS AND THE ROMAN CONQUESTS

Section I–*The Hellenistic Kingdoms*

The years after Alexander's death were years of confusion and bloodshed. A son, apparently Alexander's only offspring and certainly his only legitimate child and thus his potential heir, was born to Roxana after Alexander's death and the baby had no chance of uniting the contending forces. The ever jealous Roxana arranged the murder of Queen Statira. Roxana and her son then turned to Queen Olympias for support and went to Macedon. Queen Olympias led a revolt in Macedon against Antipater. She lost and was murdered as were Roxana, Alexander's son, and Alexander's sister. Athens revolted led by Demosthenes. Antipater, Alexander's regent in Macedon, attacked, won, forced Demosthenes, to take poison, and established his control over Greece and Macedon. The control thus established was never very firm and the Greek cities formed their own petty leagues which attempted to play the growing power of Rome off against that of Macedon. The area, however, remained under Macedonian hegemony under the family of the Antigonids. They were unable to control any other part of the empire conquered by Alexander. Thus was established the weakest of the three major successor states to Alexander's empire.

Alexander's generals fought over the main part of the empire for twenty years. Finally, the region we call the Near East, the Tigris-Euphrates Valleys and the eastern Mediterranean coast, came under control of Seleucus. He established his capital at Antioch which became one of the great cities of the Hellenistic Age. The city was laid out on a grid plan. One of the great developments of the Hellenistic Age which affects us today was the idea of planned cities following carefully laid out grid plans.

Antioch prospered from its location. Antioch controlled the trade between the Mediterranean and the Euphrates as well as the luxury trade with Arabia. The ruling class of Macedonian Greeks prospered as they did in other cities of the Seleucid empire such as Seleucia on the Tigris River. This city was the terminal point of the trade route to Iran and India. In an age of international trade and growing luxury the Seleucid empire enjoyed an excellent location for profiting from this internationalism. The culture of the empire was cosmopolitan, the mixture of Greek and Persian, which was probably Alexander's goal.

The conflicts between later Seleucid kings and the Hebrews of Judea form an important story in Biblical history. Finally, the Seleucid empire was conquered with the western part, modern Lebanon and Syria, falling to Rome in 64 B.C. The Parthians, a new kingdom in the east, and the Romans fought continually for control of the remainder of the Seleucid kingdom.

The third great successor state to Alexander's empire was the Egyptian kingdom established by Alexander's friend and general, Ptolemy. In fact Ptolemy's capital of Alexandria was the most brilliant city and probably the wealthiest in an age of great and wealthy cities. The city had been laid out on a grid plan by Alexander himself. The major thoroughfares of the city were lighted by torches at night. The city boasted three excellent harbors. The population of Alexandria under the Ptolemies is estimated at well over half a million people. People from all over the world mixed in this greatest of the Hellenistic cities.

Ptolemy had secured Alexander's body after his death and he built a great mausoleum for it in Alexandria. Besides Alexander's mausoleum the city boasted a lighthouse on the island of Pharos which was considered one of the Seven Wonders of the Ancient World. It led ships safely to the three harbors where the wealth of Europe, Asia, and Africa was exchanged under the watchful administration of the Macedonian Ptolemies and their Greek advisors.

The Ptolemies were noted as patrons of science and built and subsidized a famous museum and library. Great scholars from all over the known world came to study there and Alexandria replaced Athens as the cultural center of the Greek-speaking world. Only in the study of philosophy did Athens surpass Alexandria. The Ptolemaic Empire lasted with varying periods of greatness until seized by Augustus Caesar in 30 B.C. when he made Egypt the personal possession of the Roman ruler. The last Macedonian ruler of Egypt was the famous Cleopatra, the last of the Ptolemies.

Besides the three major successor kingdoms there were several smaller countries established. Two smaller ones are worthy of note. They shared the common Hellenistic civilization of the age. Pergamum in northwest Asia Minor gained prominence by withstanding an attack of barbarians, the Gauls, about 280 B.C. Several cities on the Aegean coast accepted the rule of the King of Pergamum. Trade flourished. The kings beautified the city so that it rivaled Athens and supported cultural establishments as was the Hellenistic custom. They built a library and since the Ptolemies forbid the export of Egyptian papyrus fearing other libraries might rival that of Alexandria, Pergamum developed its own writing material, parchment. Parchment was stronger and lasted longer than papyrus. It was widely used throughout the Roman and Medieval periods until paper was invented. The most famous building built by the kings of Pergamum was the Great Altar of Zeus which crowned the acropolis. Its sculpture was famous in the ancient world.

A very realistic school of sculpture was developed at Pergamum. The main theme of the sculptors was the victory over the Gauls. These works were later very popular with the Romans. Many copies were made and distributed about the Roman Empire. Pergamum remained an independent state until 133 B.C. when the king willed his kingdom to Rome. This last king saw that the future of the eastern Mediterranean would be determined by Rome. He decided he might as well give in to the inevitable and give his kingdom to Rome and avoid bloodshed. It is a unique event in history.

The second small successor kingdom developed on the island of Rhodes. Her location at the southwestern tip of Anatolia where the Aegean Sea joins the Mediterranean made her potentially very prosperous. Rhodes supported freedom of the seas and developed a code of maritime law that Rome later adopted. Parts of the code are still in use today. Her navy was strong and kept her out of the Antigonid Kingdom of Macedonia. She taxed all ships using her harbor a flat rate for their cargoes which brought in a large income. She also had a flourishing trade in wine which brought in wealth.

Following the Hellenistic pattern her rulers beautified the city. Rhodian sculptors were famous. The most famous Hellenistic statue, *Laocoon,* in which the Trojan priest, Laocoon, and his two sons are shown struggling to free themselves from snakes coiled about them, was created by Rhodian sculptors. It reflects both the emotional and realism liked by the age. There was also a famous school in Rhodes where rhetoric was taught and where both Cicero and Julius Caesar studied. Rhodes flourished until she came into conflict with the growing power of Rome. Rhodes supported Macedon in a fight, they lost, and Rome seized the Rhodian possessions on the mainland of Asia. As with the other successor states, Rhodes thus came under the domination of the Roman Empire.

Statuette of a Standing Woman

Courtesy, Museum of Fine Arts, Boston

With a little thought you should be able to answer the question, "What did these successor kingdoms have in common?" You should be able to state they shared a common culture and common attitudes. All had great and beautiful cities and all were wealthy. The arts were patronized and the ruling class was Macedonian Greek. How would you describe the common Hellenistic culture? We will consider its elements in the next section.

Section II–*Hellenistic Culture*

As indicated before, Hellenistic civilization combined the Hellenic or Greek with the Near Eastern. It was a syncretism of the two great streams of eastern Mediterranean development.

Hellenistic culture flourished as a result of the most extensive and thriving international trade known until that time. Political rivalries did not prevent economic cooperation. Trade between the kingdoms flourished and trade routes went to Arabia, east Africa, and all the areas conquered by Alexander. By the first century B.C. the trade routes to Marakanda (Samarkand) and India were extended to China. The third century B.C. was one of the most prosperous the ancient world knew. Economic prosperity made possible the building of great cities and the patronage of the arts.

The unity of the Hellenistic world called forth a new word, ecumene. It meant the inhabited world and it reflects what Professor Tarn said was Alexander's dream and goal—a united world held together by a sense of a common purpose. Ecumene meant the "inhabited world" and Hellenistic culture was dominant throughout it. Roman senators raged against the Hellenistic influence on the old Roman virtues much as Charles de Gaulle, President of France in the 1960's, spoke against the all pervasive influence on France of post-World War II American culture. But there was no stopping the spread of Hellenistic ideas any more than American jazz or blue-jeans or ideas of government have been kept out of France or other nations. Incidentally, today American worn blue jeans are a hot black market item in the Soviet Union and are popular throughout the "inhabited world." We have no evidence for a similar trade item in the ancient world but the concept of an all pervasive item which blue jeans symbolize today illustrates how items and even ideas can become world wide. Hellenistic culture was as pervasive in the second and third centuries B.C. as

American culture represented by cars, blue jeans, and jazz is today. Hellenistic culture spread to the entire inhabited world known to the ancients.

Supporting the spread of Hellenistic culture, much as the international knowledge of English supports the spread of American culture, was a new Greek dialect, the Koine, which developed throughout the region conquered by Alexander. Basically Koine was Athenian or Ionic Greek with many new words from other Greek dialects and from the oriental languages. Koine Greek provided a common tongue for business and governmental operations as well as for cultural developments. Jews living in Alexandria translated the Bible from Hebrew into Koine Greek, a version of the Bible that has been of great importance in Biblical scholarship. The written masterpieces of Greek civilization, such as the great Athenian plays and philosophical works of Plato and Aristotle, were translated in the Hellenistic schools and made available to all peoples throughout the inhabited world in the new libraries.

Koine Greek permitted scholars working anywhere to exchange knowledge. They passed on to posterity their studies written in the new dialect. Alexandria with its library and museum, in those days a place of study of those arts supported by the seven muses of Greek mythology, led the world in scholarship. The Alexandrian museum was particularly noted for scientific research. The Hellenistic Age was an age of great scientific advances much as our own has been. You may have heard of Euclid, the father of geometry, and Ptolemy, the geographer, whose view of the earth centered universe dominated thought until Copernicus produced his great work on the sun centered universe in 1542 A.D.

Astronomy flourished during the age as Greek thought was combined with Babylonian measurements. Aristarchus of Samos concluded the earth moved about the sun but his ideas were rejected in favor of Ptolemys' which seemed more logical. Eratosthenes was an outstanding geographer whose calculation on the circumference of the globe was correct within 200 miles.

Besides geometry, trigonometry was developed during the age. Later the Arabs built on Hellenistic mathematics and the results have greatly influenced us in the west. Finally, in Syracuse on the island of Sicily, Archimedes worked not only to develop scientific theory as did most scientists of the age but found practical applications for his work. He studied levers and found many uses for them as well as rules of how they worked on their fulcrum. He developed a method of focusing the sun's rays with mirrors which was used to burn Roman ships attacking Syracuse. Archimedes invented the double pulley and a water screw used for irrigation systems. He came close to calculating *pi* in his study of geometry and discovered the law of specific gravity which we all learn in science as Archimedes' principle. Thanks to Koine Greek these ideas, developed in one part of the world, could spread easily to other regions.

Literature flourished in the Koine dialect. The first professional writers appeared in the Hellenistic Age. We know the names of over a thousand Hellenistic writers but few of their works have come down to us intact. The world lost a great source of knowledge when the library at Alexandria burned.

Drama was popular but those plays which have been preserved appear shallow and superficial compared to the great works of the Athenian dramatists. New forms of drama were developed. The New Comedy of manners was most popular especially those comedies written by the polished Athenian playwright, Menander. Mimes, course dramatic pieces with themes from every day life somewhat like our soap operas, were very popular with the common people. Poets experimented with new forms. The idyll, a short poem that paints a picture in words, was developed and proved popular. Ptolemy I of Egypt began a literary form which is very popular today, the eye witness account of history written by a participant. Ptolemy wrote of his campaigns with Alexander the Great using his journals written on the campaigns as sources. As we've said, the work is lost. Many other histories were produced as well as many other forms of literature. A great deal of the Hellenistic writing which exists today appears light and less significant than the literature produced in the Classical age. Perhaps Hellenistic literature was written to appeal to a wider audience. As stated above, we know there were many professional writers whose livlihood depended on what they wrote.

Education became more widespread in the Hellenistic period and in some cities the wealthy citizens even supported public schools. Physical education, reading, writing, and mathematics formed the core of the curriculum. Does it seem familiar? Education usually ended at 14 but some students continued studying music, geometry, and the works of the great Greek writers such as Homer, Plato and Euripides. A few young men continued their studies under the tutelage of the philosophers of the age.

Three schools of philosophy dominated the Hellenistic Age. They all had as their goal to define the "good life" and in each case the "good life" was viewed as the "good life for the individual". There was little concern for the state except as it affected the individual and his actions. The ideal of the Greek polis was far in the distance.

The three schools of philosophy were Cynicism, Epicureanism, and Stoicism. The Cynics held material needs were unimportant for the "good life" and emphasized endurance. It had an appeal for the poorer people in society. Epicureans held that evil was bodily pain. One should attempt to escape this evil, but it should be endured if it made possible the higher pleasures of the mind. Epicureans believed the "good life" was found in the avoidance of bodily pain but not in mere pleasure. Epicureanism is complex and highly intellectual. It had little appeal to the masses.

Stoicism taught that a Divine lawgiver, whose essence was fire, created the universe, and the world followed set natural laws that determined history. Implied in this concept was the idea that all men are equal or brothers in the eyes of the creator — an idea which had great importance for history and which supported philosophically what Alexander the Great was probably striving for. Also, this concept introduced the idea of laws of nature which underlay the universe. Man's lot in the universe was to learn and follow these natural laws. A man who lived by these laws had character and happiness. Zeno, the founder of Stoic philosophy, taught that possessions, wealth, and health were incidental to living the "good life", and that what was important was to live a moral life seeking to follow the laws established by the Divine lawgiver. Stoicism was popular in Syria and Rome. During the years of the Roman domination of the Mediterranean it evolved into a set of moral precepts and teachings which many scholars consider the religion of Rome. Stoicism had a great appeal to the upper class Romans. One emperor, Marcus Aurelius, was a great stoic writer and philosopher. Roman stoicism had a strong influence on the development of Christian thought.

Hellenistic philosophy emphasized the individual. Hellenistic sculpture, as we have mentioned, emphasized the real and the emotional. Our study of Greek sculpture should have prepared us for this growing emphasis on the individual and the emotional in Greek thought. The Hellenistic Age developed it further and stressed this aspect of classical Greek thought. Compare the statue of the archaic Greek with that of *Laocoon* from Rhodes or the *Dying Gaul* from Pergamum. The contrast vividly illustrates the change that had taken place in Greek thought and attitudes as Hellenic culture was replaced with Hellenistic.

Hellenistic culture was rich, varied, complex, and cosmopolitan. It combined many elements from the ancient world. It had strong Greek or Hellenic elements, those elements which formed most of the material of this book. It was Hellenistic culture, absorbed by Rome and adapted slightly by the addition of Roman ideas, that eventually became the base of Western Civilization.

Would you agree there are many ways in which the present age is reminiscient of the Hellenistic Age? In what ways are they alike? Not alike? Can you summarize the main characteristics of Hellenistic culture?

Section III—*Rome, The Hellenistic World and Us.*

We've already indicated how the Hellenistic kingdoms which succeeded Alexander's empire eventually fell to Roman power. During the third century B.C. Rome was involved in the long struggle with Carthage known as the First and Second Punic Wars. It was in this period that Hellenistic culture flourished. Rome was on the edge of the inhabited or civilized world but was under strong Hellenistic influence. In the second and first centuries B.C., after the defeat of Carthage, Rome was pulled into the political affairs of the eastern Mediterranean. Epirus was acquired in 168 B.C. and Macedon in 148 B.C. after a series of three wars the first of which began in 215 B.C. during the Second Punic War. Rome inherited Pergamum in 133 B.C. and with this foothold in Asia, it was only a matter of time before the Hellenistic world would be a Roman world. The Romans destroyed the city of Corinth in 146 B.C. and in 86 B.C. the Roman general, Sulla, conquered Athens. The final end of freedom for the ancient Greeks came in 27 B.C. when the first Roman emperor, Augustus Caesar, turned the Peloponnesus into the Roman province of Achaea. The independent history of the Greeks in the Aegean ended for a long period of time.

Many of the events in the expansion of Roman power can be traced in *Roman Rulers and Rebels*.[1] Although Rome conquered the Greek world of the Aegean and most of the Hellenistic world, the culture and civilization of Rome was greatly affected and Roman culture was unable to keep out Hellenistic ideas although Rome made an attempt to do so. There was no place politically

[1] *Roman Rulers and Rebels* by Gordon Stillman is the next book in the series of texts on ancient history published by the Independent School Press.

for the Hellenes in the Roman world as there had been in the Hellenistic world where Macedonian Greeks and others from the peninsula formed the core of the ruling, wealthy, and learned population in each of the kingdoms. However, the culture of the Hellenes had been fused with that of the east in Hellenistic culture. The Hellenes with their impact on Hellenistic culture changed the inhabited world of the third century B.C. and influenced Rome both directly and indirectly through Hellenistic civilization. Classical Greek influence has thus come down to affect us of the twentieth century in innumerable ways. Hellenic ideas, from democracy to tragedy, from philosophy to music, are a part of each of us. No matter how hard we try to escape, our ancient heritage is a part of our lives and affects what we do and how we do it. The people, events, and ideas presented in this book are ancient history but they prove how alive the past is for everyone.

Section IV—*Chapter Review*

In this chapter the emphasis was on factual information. The following list of items will help you to recall the most important factual information. The list, however, should not be considered a final list. You should look through the chapter and add items which appear important to you. In the case of each of these items you should not only be prepared to identify the item but you should be able to write at least a paragraph on its importance in the Hellenistic Age.

Alexandria, Egypt	Laocoon
Antigonids	Macedon
Antioch	Parchment
Archimedes	Pergamum
Cynicism	Ptolemies
Ecumene	Ptolemy I
Epicureanism	Rhodes
Euclid	Seleucids
Hellenistic	Stoicism
Koine	

The following questions will also help you to recall facts from the chapter and to place them in an ordered form.

1. What were the five most important kingdoms which succeeded Alexander's Empire? Where was each located?

2. What did the five most important successor kingdoms have in common? What differences were there in the five kingdoms?
3. What were the chief elements in Hellenistic culture?
4. How did the three philosophies developed in the Hellenistic Age, Cynicism, Epicureanism, and Stoicism, differ? What did they have in common?
5. What is the relationship between Roman culture and Hellenistic culture?
6. How did the growth of Roman power affect the kingdoms of the Hellenistic Age?

Each of the above questions could be expanded into short essays if you wish. The following are suggested as topics for research projects or papers.

1. In what ways is the present age similar to the Hellenistic Age?
2. Which of the three philosophies developed in the Hellenistic Age has the most appeal to you? Why? What has been the importance of these philosophies through history? Are they of any importance today? Do any people now follow the ideas presented by these philosophies?
3. Compare Hellenistic works of art with several from the Hellenic period. You may pick several pieces of sculpture, a play, or poetry from each period. Decide which period's art is more appealing to you. Compare your opinions with your classmates.
4. Investigate the expansion of Roman power into the eastern Mediterranean. How did Roman power affect the history of the Greek peninsula in the period immediately after the Hellenistic Age? Investigate Emperor Nero's attitude towards Greece and Greek civilization.
5. What impact have ideas developed in the Hellenistic Age had on you? You might start with a consideration of Euclidean geometry. You may develop other topics you would like to research.

The following books will help you in your investigation of the Hellenistic Age.

Farrington, Benjamin. *Greek Science.* Baltimore, Md., Penguin Books.
Grimal, Pierre. *Hellenism and the Rise of Rome.* N.Y., Delacorte Press, 1968.
Hadas, Moses. *Hellenistic Culture.* N.Y., Columbia University Press, 1954.
Hellenistic Age, Selections by J. B. Bury, E. A. Barber, Edwin Barber, W. W. Tarn. Cambridge, England, Cambridge University Press, 1923.

Stocks, J. L. *Aristotelianism.* N.Y., Cooper Square, 1963.

The Stoic and Epicurean Philosophers, ed. W. J. Oates. N.Y., Random House, 1940.

Tarn, W. W. *Hellenistic Civilization.* London, E. Arnold and Co., 1927.

Toynbee, A. J. *Hellenism: The History of a Civilization.* N.Y., Oxford University Press, 1959.

Wenley, R. M. *Stoicism and its Influence.* N.Y., Cooper Square Publishers, 1963.

APPENDIX A

The following chronology lists major events of Greek history mentioned in the text. Within the text are several chronologies to which the reader may also wish to refer. There is a chronology of important events in the Near East in Chapter II; a chronology of art styles in Chapter III; a chronology of colonization in Chapter IV.

Often one will find dates in Greek history presented as two dates with a slash as in 432/31 B.C. The reason for this is that the Greek New Year did not begin at the same time as ours does. Therefore, our dating system does not fit exactly with the Greek system of yearly measurements, and scholars are forced to give two dates to be accurate. For the sake of simplicity and at the expense of accuracy only one year has been given in this text and in this chronology. The result should be easier for students, but when consulting other sources, the reader may find two dates given or a disagreement of a year in the case of certain dates.

All dates are B.C.

c. 1600	Height of Minoan Civilization
c. 1400	Height of Mycenaen Civilization
c. 1288	Battle of Kadesh between Hittites and Egyptians
c. 1200	Invasions of Sea Peoples; Traditional date of Dorian Invasion of Southern Greece
c. 1194-1184	Trojan War
1100	Sub-Mycennaean Pottery (see chronology in Chapter III)
c. 1000	"Dark Ages" in Greece; Hebrew Kingdom of David and Solomon; Greeks from mainland emigrate to Aegean Islands and Anatolian coast (Ionia)
c. 900	Al-Mina in Near East flourishes
c. 800	Homer; Dipylon Vases; Greek writing
c. 830-751	Tyre and Sidon flourish
776	Traditional date of first Olympic Games
754	Rome founded
753	Colony of Cumae founded
c. 750	Poet Hesiod — *Theogony, Works and Days*
c. 750-c. 550	Age of Colonization (See chronology in Chapter II)
740 ff.	Conquests of Tiglath-Pileser, King of Assyria
c. 730	Spartan conquest of Messenia
c. 700	War between Chalchis and Eretria
_ 700	"Orientalizing" Corinthian pottery

c. 700	Reign of Midas, King of Phrygia; Introduction of coinage by Lydians
664	Naval battle between Corcyra and Corinth
c. 650-c. 500	Age of Tyrants
645	Egypt throws out Assyrians
630	Poet Tyrtaeus
621	Draco reforms Athenian law
620	Sparta crushes Messenian revolt
612	Fall of Nineveh to Chaldeans and Medes
c. 600	Sounion Apollo – Archaic Sculpture; Sappho; Black figure Attic pottery; Periander, Tyrant of Corinth; Reforms of Lycurgus at Sparta
c. 600-c. 500	Lyric Age
594	Solon's reforms in Athens
584	Thales of Miletus predicts eclipse
560-527	Peisistratus rules Athens
550	Poet Anacreon
546	Persian conquest of Lydia
c. 540	Red figure Attic pottery; Poet Theognis of Megara
538	Cyrus, Great King of Persia, conquers Babylon
c. 530	Pythagoras; Pre-Socratic Greek Philosophers
510	Hippias, Tyrant of Athens, forced into exile
508	Cleisthenes reforms in Athens
c. 400	Poet Simondes
499	Revolt of Ionian cities
492	Mardonius, Persian general, conquers Thrace
490	Darius invades Greece; conquers Eretria; defeated at Battle of Marathon
480	Xerxes invades Greece; Battles of Thermopylae and Salamis; Leonidas and Themistocles; Carthage defeated in Sicily at Battle of Himera.
479	Battles of Plataea and Mycale
479-404	Classical Sculpture (See Appendix B)
478	Walls of Athenian Acropolis rebuilt
477	Delian League formed
476	Death of Pausanius
c. 470	Historian Herodotus; Poet Pindar
469	Naxos forced to remain in Delian League
462	Spartan Helots revolt
461	Pericles elected strategos in Athens; Cimon ostracized.
458	Aeschylus' *Oresteia*

454	Egyptian expedition fails; Treasury of Delian League moved to Athens
448	Peace treaty with Persia
447	Parthenon begun
445	Thirty Years' Peace between Athens and Sparta
443	Sophocles' *Antigone*
435	Democrats of Epidamnus attacked by barbarians and Epidamnian nobles
433	Demands of Athens on Potidaea
432	Meeting of members of Peloponnesian League before Spartan assembly to discuss issues of war or peace
431	Outbreak of Peloponnesian War; Euripides' *Medea;* Socrates teaching in Athens
429	Plague in Athens; Death of Pericles
428	Revolt of Mytilene crushed by Athens
421	Peace of Nicias; Historian Thucydides
415-413	Sicilian Expedition
404	End of Peloponnesian War
404-331	Late Classical sculpture
399	Death of Socrates
387	Peace of the Great King
371	Sparta defeated by Epaminondas of Thebes
c. 370	Philosopher Plato
362	Battle of Mantinea – death of Epaminondas
359	Philip II, King of Macedon; Demosthenes at Athens
338	Battle of Chaeronea – Philip II conquers Greece; League of Corinth
336	Assassination of Philip II; Alexander III, King of Macedon; Aristotle
334	Battle of Granicus
333	Battle of Issus – Darius III defeated
332	Siege of Tyre; Conquests of Egypt
331	Battle of ~~Issus~~ Gaugamela – Persian Empire conquered by Alexander the Great
330	Death of Darius III
327	Alexander marries Roxane and prepares to invade India
323	Death of Alexander the Great
333-30	Hellenistic Age
312	Seleucia founded; Seleucid Empire controls Near East
c. 306	Philosopher Epicurus, founder of Epicureanism

304-30	Ptolemaic Empire rules Egypt
c. 300	Antioch founded as Seleucid capital; Philosopher Zeno, founder of Stoicism; Euclid
264-241	First Punic War between Carthage and Rome
c. 250	Archimedes at Syracuse
c. 230-133	Kindom of Pergamum at peak
218-201	Second Punic War
215-205	Rome's first Macedonian War
168	Rome conquers Epirus
149-146	Third Punic War
148	Rome conquers Macedon
146	Rome conquers and destroys Corinth
133	Attalus III, King of Pergamum, wills Kingdom to Rome
86	Sulla captures Athens
64	Western part of Seleucid Empire conquered by Rome
30	Octavian (Augustus Caesar) conquers Egypt — death of Cleopatra
27	Roman Empire established; Peloponnesus becomes Roman province of Achaea

APPENDIX B

In this appendix the reader will find additional information on Greek sculpture. The section should *NOT* be read until the exercise on sculpture described in Chapter III, Section II is completed.

When one analyzes Greek sculpture of young men carved during the 7th through 4th centuries B.C., what one usually notices first is the stiffness and unnaturalness of some statues and the natural or realistic appearance of others. Upon further study the latter can be placed in two groups, those that present beautifully sculptured, idealized, somewhat too perfect male bodies and those that present more momentary and somewhat emotional aspects of the human being. This rough delineation summarizes the three major trends of Greek sculpture of these centuries.

Students often have difficulty deciding if the more momentary and emotional came before or after the idealized sculptures. So often we believe the more accurate or realistic a work is, the later it must be. This is not true as any look at modern art will indicate. Therefore, it shouldn't be difficult to accept the fact that the latest works are not the most realistic. Instead the general pattern of Greek development is from the stiff or Archaic to the idealized or Early Classical (which includes the so-called Transitional sculpture) to the more particularized, momentary presentation of Late Classical sculpture. The Late Classical style was followed by the highly emotional sculptural style of the Hellenistic period discussed in Chapter 10.

Students are often confused by the inclusion of a bronze statue in the six statues for analysis. They assume bronze is a more difficult medium to handle and so it must be late. This is not true. We have excellent bronze statues from all periods, and one should not date sculpture by the medium alone.

What are some of the items one can focus on in analyzing these free standing statues of young men or Kouroi? Miss Richter, the great authority on the subject, has written detailed analyses of all parts of the anatomy to help one trace the evolution of style. The pose of the earliest work is stiff and Egyptian influence is strong. The early works are heavily geometric and patterned with little desire, apparently, to be realistic. The geometric patterns are probably derived from Near Eastern influences and are reflected in the pottery of the Archaic Period. The patterns can be seen especially in the facial area, the chest, the pubic region, and in the knees and calves. The geometric patterning of the ears, hair, eyes, and mouth is clearly seen in the earliest statue of those presented for study. This is the Sounion Kouros or Apollo and it is number three in the series. Number one is a close-up of the face. The face is modeled in flat planes as are the knees and calves. Notice the lines drawn on the chest to indicate the thorax and the geometric navel. If one notices the change in the portrayal of these parts of the body, one should be able to trace the evolution to greater realism with ease. Changes take place slowly. For instance, as ears and eyes are portrayed more naturally or "realistic," hair styles remain rather stiff and geometric. So does the frontal pose. The gradual move from a stiff, geometric presentation to a more natural look should be obvious when the second statue in order of creation, number six, is compared with the Sounion Kouros.

The third statue in chronological order, the bronze sculpture of Poseidon or Zeus,[1] identified as number nine, shows mastery of the details of the human body — arm and leg muscles, face, chest and thorax, and the pubic region. But notice the balance and symmetry of the pose. In spite of the appearance of motion, the weight is clearly distributed on each side of a vertical drawn from the top of the head down between the two legs. Also, note the geometric patterning of the hair.

The same characteristics are seen in the fourth statue in chronological order, the Early Classical statue of Apollo from the west pediment of the Temple of Zeus at Olympia. The piece of cloth seen in number five, close-up number two, often confuses students who decide this is the latest statue done since it is so "perfect" and so real and includes cloth. Actually, the hair and stiff pose again identify this as Early Classical, as is the Zeus. I often ask myself what the artist was trying to indicate this young god was thinking. I find the question leads in many directions, and I've often asked it of students. The resulting discussions have been very rewarding.

The fifth statue presented for analysis is a century later than the Apollo. The Hermes, number four, probably sculpted by the great fourth century sculptor, Praxiteles, was created c. 340 B.C. and was also found at Olympia. The pose, the finely sculpted face, the total mastery of muscles and joints and the differing texture of body, cloth, and hair, now realistically curly, indicate the greatness of the sculptor. They also clearly indicate the artist wishes to portray something more than an ideal form. The out-

---

[1] Controversy rages over who this statue represents. Personally, I think of this as Zeus, although I appear in a minority today.

stretched arm of the baby, believed to be the god Dionysus, reaching for a grape (?) held by Hermes gives a sense of emotion and momentariness to the scene. The total impact of the statue is very different from the Sounion Kouros and, although I like the Hermes greatly, I keep returning to the Sounion Kouros as a favorite for the strength and vitality and uniqueness it presents. Each student will have reasons for picking one of the six statues as his or her favorite. Each statue has a beauty and quality of its own. Each reflects both the sculptor and the age. If one can realize this and come to appreciate both the changes of style and mood reflected and the effectiveness of each individual work presented in this exercise, then one will have a fine appreciation, both of Greek sculpture and of its development.

The final work, a statue of the boxer and wrestler Agias who won many contests in the various Greek games, is number eight with number seven being a close-up. Agias is an individual and not a god — the only *person* portrayed. This fact, unknown to the student when writing the exercise, sums up many of the changes that the student hopefully noted. The natural relaxed pose, the curly hair, the deep-sunk eyes, all focus to indicate we now have a new idea the artist wants to portray. Can you tell what this moody, thoughtful individual is thinking at this particular moment? We have here more of a portrait than an idealized presentation of a young man. The anatomy is good but does he appear just a little flabby? The head is a little too small for the body. The pose is based on movement — a counterpose between the supporting leg and the moving leg — and one wants to walk around the statue in viewing it, as there is no one way to look at it. Contrast Agias with the Sounion Apollo. The individual, captured in a moment of time and fully revealed both physically and mentally, has become the goal of the fourth century sculptor. As Greek history from the 7th to the 4th centuries is studied, keep in mind this development in sculpture and see if there are parallels to it in political, social, and economic activities.

The marble statue of Agias is thought to be a copy of a bronze work by Lysippos (c. 330 B.C.). Lysippos, Praxiteles (c. 340 B.C.), and Scopas (c. 370 B.C.) were the greatest sculptors of the 4th century. Praxiteles was particularly noted for his naturalism in flesh and surface texture (note the Hermes); Lysippos for an emphasis on realism and for attempts to portray men as they appeared to the eye (as opposed to earlier sculptors who he believed portrayed men as they were, note Agias); and Scopas for an intensity of individual expression. All three emphasized the immediate, the individual, and the emotional. They paved the way for the Hellenistic style which followed the conquests of Alexander the Great (See Chapters 9 and 10). In fact, Lysippos was Alexander's favorite sculptor.

In the previous century the most famous sculptors were Phidias (c. 440 B.C.) and Polycleitos (c. 430 B.C.). Phidias was in charge of the Parthenon sculptures. In his early years he may have influenced the carving of the Apollo at Olympia. He was noted for self-contained works in which the ideal of the age, a detached, perfectly proportioned individual, was captured. Polycleitos wrote a treatiese in which he set forth the rules for sculpting the perfect figure. He gave sets of ideal proportions for the sculptor to follow so that statues would reflect the ideal or perfect individual with set relationships between the size of the head, the length of the torso, the length of the arms, etc.

During the Golden Age he and Phidias broke entirely with the Archaic ideal. They abandoned the stiff pose and introduced a curved or S-pose in which the weight was on one foot. They sculpted hairs individually and they demonstrated a total mastery of male anatomy. However, their naturalism was restricted by their desire to portray the perfect or idealized figure.

These five great sculptors each contributed to the evolution of Greek art which in turn heavily influenced the art of western civilization at the time of the Renaissance and up to the present. Statues of the type presented in this assignment would probably not be produced in America today but many of the ideas the artists wished to present – power, the ideal, the immediate emotion – are portrayed today and the forms in which to present them have been strongly influenced by our Greek roots.

If you now look back at the questions in Chapter 3, or the paper you wrote in answer to them, you should be able to add several insights you did not have before. An analysis of the portrayal of the anatomy, especially the face, thorax, pubic region, and legs reveals a great deal about the changing ability of the artists but such an analysis also reveals the changing ideals of the artists. The pose and hair patterns are particularly important to note. If you look at faces and ask what each person was thinking you will gain valuable insights into Greek ideals and values. The influence of Egypt and the Near East is obvious in the earlier works, but apparently fades away. The final result is a distinctly Greek art that has influenced us greatly.

Three final comments are in order. First, in the book we have made no comments on Greek painting. The ancient Greeks admired their painters and thought many were greater than the sculptors, but no paintings have survived for us to judge. Second, the Greeks normally painted their statues in bright colors. The color has worn off and we see only the plain marble. What a different impression these painted marble statues must have made on the ancient Greeks. Third, I indicated in the exercise sculptors did carve females, but that it was harder for the amateur to trace the evolution of sculptured style because until the 4th century, females were portrayed clothed. Therefore, in order to do this exercise with female statues or Kouras, one had to be able to analyze the changes in clothing styles as well as sculptural techniques.

Included in the book is a photograph of a fourth century statue of a standing woman. It shows many of the characteristics of the male statues of that century — the momentariness, the relaxed pose, the control of anatomy — but it also illustrates the need to know about clothing styles. The woman is wearing the typical peplos of the 4th century. The artist uses what is often called the wet sheet style of drapery allowing the anatomy to show through the clothing, but we still can't analyze the statue only on the basis of anatomy. The statue does, however, provide you a glimpse of how beautifully sculptors were able to portray Greek women.

APPENDIX C

The analysis of society according to basic functions introduced in Chapter VII, is a very helpful tool contributed to the historian by the sociologists. The five basic functions — replacement, economic activity, political organization, education, and cohesion — approach mentioned in the text is just one of several similar approaches. Students may insist that communication (a common language, etc.) is also essential and thus a basic function and a case can be made for this viewpoint. The five terms suggested here may be phrased differently and after thorough discussion other basic functions, communication and recreation for instance, may be added to the class list. Although there appears to be general agreement as to what is necessary for survival of a society, even very small ones, sociologists do not generally agree on the terminology used or the number of functions under which to list the essential activities.

Bennett and Tumin suggest six functions as they suggest one is to maintain the biologic functioning of the group and a second is to replace members. Both of these necessary activities of a society are incorporated in the replacement function suggested here. Likewise, communication and recreation are incorporated in my mind under the cohesion or unifying function. It is possible, therefore, to disagree with and/or to decide on more than the five basic functions presented here, but it is helpful to try to keep the number of functions low.

What societal activities are included within the area represented by these five words? A great many different functions and institutions created to meet the functions fall under each heading. Replacement would include not only the maintenance of the biological functioning of the group but the maintenance of a steady supply of new leaders. Most societies use the institution of the family to supply biologically the necessary replacement, but this is not the only institution nor the only way to replace members. Illegitimate children, concubinage, war captives, and immigrants all supply replacements for a society. If the society under consideration is a small subdivision, such as a boarding school, of a larger society, then the replacement function is filled by new students picked by the Admissions Office. As you can see, there are many interpretations of replacement.

Likewise the economic function incorporates many areas where goods and services necessary to life are produced and distributed. Food, clothing, and shelter are considered the basic economic needs of human societies and they are supplied in a variety of ways. Our more complex society may find the automobile and television necessary to life; whereas more primitive societies are less complicated. Again, the boarding school reference can illustrate how this function is essential to all societies — can you imagine a boarding school without dorms, a kitchen and dining room, and school athletic uniforms?

The political function is complicated and everyone will have ideas to offer. Essentially a society must have internal order and a method of defense against outside threats "to maintain the biological functioning of the group" — an illustration of how the functions interrelate. Laws, police, army, leaders are all necessary politically, even in the smallest society where rules are not written down and the police do not wear badges. Consider how these four roles are filled in that microcosm of society — the family.

The educational function should not be confused with the institution of school. Education takes place in many other institutions within each society — home, church, office, peer group, Boy Scouts, baseball teams, T.V., etc. Each of these have an important function in educating the future member of a society as to what is expected. This function or purpose is often called socializing the individual. It means teaching the new member of the society what the society expects in the way of behavior and attitudes. Members of Women's Lib organizations have made many observations recently as to how boys and girls are socialized into American society. School education is certainly important but the broader implications of each of the five basic functions must be considered if they are to be of benefit in understanding societies.

Perhaps the most complicated and at the same time most important function is the cohesive function. This function is sometimes referred to as the goals of a society and again as the religious function. When the latter term is used, students often focus much too narrowly on this function and talk only in terms of religion. Bennett and Tumin refer to the need in a society "to define the 'meaning of life' and maintain the motivation to survive."[1] This is a very helpful summary of the unifying function. It includes such items as the moral and ethical teachings, the aspirations and dreams as well as the concerns and fears, and the history and myths of the

[1] John W. Bennett and Melvin M. Tumin, "Some Cultural Imperatives," in *Cultural and Social Anthropology*, p. 9.

society. In different ways the 4th of July, the Constitution, the "Myth of the West," the Puritan work ethic, the Hebraic-Christian and Graeco-Roman traditions, the "American Dream," and the idea of equality all help to provide the United States with unity. The list could be expanded greatly but it illustrates what is meant by the unifying function. Language and communication also provide a unifying force for a society. Again to illustrate from the boarding school the idea of school spirit incorporates or suggests the cohesive function.

With this clarification of the five basic functions it is hoped they will become a useful tool in your study of history. Further information on this type of analysis can be found in many sociology and anthropology texts. As mentioned in footnote 3, page 164, *Family Form and Social Setting* prepared by SRSS and published by Allyn and Bacon, Inc. uses basic functions to analyze the Israeli Kibbutz and the ancient Hebrew family. It provides a very helpful introduction to this method of analysis.

APPENDIX D

The simulation, based on *Simulex* developed at UNH, suggested in the text is a form of gaming. If you have participated in role playing or simulation exercises, the process described will probably seem familiar. If you have not been involved, the first experience may seem somewhat confusing, but the benefits are great and worth the confusion.

In the introduction to *Simulex 1968,* James Egan has this to say about gaming.

> Gaming has many purposes. Each group that engages in it has, perhaps, its own specific motives. Generally, games may be used as a means of testing the abilities of the participants (actors) to find a solution to a difficult problem or to act more rationally in a crisis situation. They may be employed as a method of imparting knowledge to the players. Games may be used as a method of studying how individuals react under certain conditions. Or games can be employed simply to find some solutions to the problem presented.
>
> Inter-National Simulation (Simulex) is a method of teaching the intricacy and complexity of relations between and among nation-states (poleis in this exercise) while stimulating the student's interest in the subject. It is hoped that he will come to have a greater understanding of . . . the decision-making process. It is also hoped that by taking part in Inter-National Simulation, the student will realize that the decision making process must often take place with imperfect information, within a limited time period and within a framework dictated by the ideology, politics, institutions, and constitution of the nation-state. The success of gaming is judged by its effect on the student. If it gives him a clearer understanding of these concepts, stimulates his interest and gives him a clearer understanding of a complex situation, then it is a success.
>
> The problems of Inter-Nation Simulation are caused by the simple fact that it is but a game, an attempt to duplicate a real life situation. How good the duplication is, and will continue to be, depends to a very large extent upon what the participant does. It is important that he thoroughly research his role and his nation-state. This information is essential if he is to act in a realistic manner. It is also vital that the actor strive for objectivity while participating in the game. By this it is meant, he should attempt to only consider the interests of his role and his nation, while disregarding his natural inclinations as an American. . .

In the simulation of the outbreak of the Peloponnesian War as developed at St. Paul's the basic framework is as follows: the class is divided into teams; a crisis situation developed by the teacher and the control team is presented to the teams; the teams react to the crisis by making moves; information (messages) on the moves is exchanged and in turn reacted to with moves (messages); as the pace of the activity increases, more moves are made; the situation becomes very hectic, very emotional, and very revealing of how decisions are made. A major part of the simulation is the debriefing of the participants at which time the actions, reactions, values, and decision-making processes used can all be analyzed. In order to act realistically as an Athenian, Spartan or Persian, the student must learn a great deal about these societies. In addition, by means of the simulation, they learn a great deal more about many issues.

This simulation can be played with either of two basic assumptions. Simulation was introduced in Chapter VIII to explore the possibility of avoiding war through compromise while not sacrificing a society's basic values and this idea is based on the assumption the Greeks wanted to avoid war. This may not have been true, but you *can* operate the game with that goal or assumption. The alternative assumption under which you can operate the game is that all societies pursue their own national interest. The simulation can be run based on each team seeking what it views as its own national interest. This might lead to war and no compromise and might involve moves of troops and ships. There are gaming techniques which provide results of military confrontations based on random numbers and the computerized version of the game used at St. Paul's includes this feature. A student knowledgeable with computers could develop such a program.

The following outline presents the steps to follow in setting up the simulation.
1. Plan at least two hours for the simulation. The time can be spread over several days or periods.
2. Divide the students into teams: Athens, Sparta, Persia form the three basic teams; a fourth team, city-states (Corinth, Potidaea, Epidamnus) may also be formed. Choose several students to run the game as Control. To make the game run well, at least three students should be on each team. More than eight on a team leaves some students with little to do.
3. Have students do research on the history and values of the country they are to represent. The research should be on the time *before* 431 B.C.
   a. Suggest the Basic Functions approach to guide the research.
   b. Position papers on various functions or attitudes of the society may be written and can provide helpful background.
   c. Students may be assigned particular people or groups to represent: for instance, on the Athenian team a student may be assigned to play Pericles, another to be the Assembly, another the Navy, another the Slaves, etc.

    d. Each team needs time to work as a group sharing the information each has collected.

    e. Each team may present to the class before the simulation begins information on the society represented. These may be in the form of a speech, a skit, a booklet, etc. This allows for sharing of research and gives each team a chance to learn about the opposition.

4. The members of the Control Team should do research on the general history of Greece 479-431 B.C. and on the outbreak of the war. The Control Team should prepare a scenario – a brief summary of the situation from 445 to a date between 435 and 431 at which time the simulation will begin. All participants should read the scenario just before the start of the simulation. The teacher should be designated as the final arbiter of actions or "Zeus." Other members of Control are assigned as messengers, a referee, a recorder of message times, and perhaps the military expert but each control team will want to divide their functions as is most agreeable to them.

5. The simulation begins with an event fabricated by Control. It should be a secret until the start of the game. It should be a realistic event that requires a response or move on the part of all participants. For example, a revolt of the Spartan Helots or a failure of the Athenian grape harvest could be used as opening events.

6. During the simulation each team is placed in a separate room or different corners of a classroom and all contacts between teams must be in the form of written messages sent *through* Control for clearance. Control can be requested to arrange conferences between teams (see below).

7. Teams act and react through moves. A move is defined in Simulex as, "An act, not necessarily involving physical action, which establishes or changes a nation's position towards (vis a vis) a particular situation; moves may initiate, modify, nullify or continue a particular course of action." The basis for moves is described as follows, "Moves should follow on one another and be designed to follow a logical sequence of events with the aim of developing a favorable position regarding the situation in question. Rational decisions must be based on personality role (both of individuals leading the society represented and the general personality of the people in the society), national policy and interests, and realistic assessments of the society's resources." The ability to achieve the end sought and an appraisal of the moves and abilities of other societies must also be considered.

8. Moves are conveyed to Control as written messages which are the key to the simulation. Control after approving moves sends the messages to the participating teams. The written messages should be clear, concise statements of what the team is doing and/or how it reacts to other teams' moves. These messages correspond to the press releases, announcements, white papers, troop movements, information collected from spying, etc. used in international relations today.

9. Conferences may be requested by participating teams. Control must approve the conference, set a time and place for it, and limit the number of participants (usually no more than two from a team). A time limit (10 minutes) should be set on conferences and a message summarizing the results of the conference should be released.

10. Messages should be neatly written on message slips with enough carbons so that each team can receive a copy (special message forms can be ordered from UNH or you can make your own with carbon paper and thin paper). All copies go to Control. Message slips should include the following:

Example:

From Team_____   Type of Move
To Team(s)_____   Secret_____   Open_____

    For Control only
    Time Received_____
    Message Number_____

11. Secret moves will go only to Control and the Team addressed but will be released to all teams after a period of time (10-15 minutes). It is assumed few moves in international affairs can be kept secret for long with international spy networks. Secret moves should be kept at a minimum.

12. Control should keep a copy of all moves and record the time at which each move is received. This record becomes an important part of the debriefing exercise at the end of the game.

13. "Zeus" must keep abreast of the overall operation of the game and direct the debriefing. Brief visits to the participating teams will help in the latter. When "Zeus" is away from Control, the referee should be in charge of approving all moves. "Zeus" can call brief halts in the simulation if Control becomes overloaded with messages. "Zeus" has the ultimate control in determining the rationality of all messages, has the power to end the simulation, and has the right to introduce "acts of god" which may be arbitrary actions needed to force more careful analysis of issues by the participants.

14. Throughout the simulation students are asked to make decisions. How these decisions are made — what factors are considered, what goals appear worthwhile — provides an important element in the simulation. Some teachers may find this an important introduction to the entire subject of decision-making. In any case comments should be made during the debriefing on the steps used to reach decisions.

Further information on gaming can be had by writing to the Political Science Department at the University of New Hampsire, Durham, N.H., or to the author. There are many books now available on gaming and articles are continually appearing in educational journals.

Index